Longman Self-help guides

How to Complain

Brigid Avison

Longman

Longman Group Limited,
Longman House, Burnt Mill, Harlow,
Essex CM20 2JE, England
and Associated Companies throughout the world.

First published 1986

British Library Cataloguing in Publication Data

Avison, Brigid
How to complain—(Longman self-help guides)
1. Consumer complaints—Great Britain—
Handbooks, manuals, etc.   2. Consumer protection
—Great Britain—Handbooks, manuals, etc.
I. Title
640.73   HC260.C63

ISBN-0-582-89269 4

Set in 11/12 Linotron Plantin
Printed in Great Britain
by Richard Clay Ltd, Bungay, Suffolk

Contents

Contents

Part 2 Goods

Contents

Contents

Contents

Introduction

Most of us are already dab hands at complaining, if all it means is
having a moan to our family or friends about the niggling little
annoyances of daily life: late buses, supermarket queues and the
like. Sometimes, there is little else we can do than vent our
frustrations and then try to forget about them. In many cases,
though, complaining can actually do something to put matters right
– if the complaint is made to the right person, in the right way, at
the right time. But it's at this point that many of us feel unwilling or
unable to follow up our moans and groans with positive action.

Being able to make a complaint effectively is not a natural gift,
although your character may make a difference (and when it comes
to complaining, having a short temper is as great a disadvantage as
being naturally shy). It is a skill that can be learned – and
fortunately you don't require frequent practice to become good at
it! So what do you need?

The four basic requirements for effective complaining

■ First and foremost, you need to know whether your complaint is
justified – and that means knowing enough about your rights to
assess whether you have been unfairly treated or whether you've
only yourself to blame. For example, if you buy a shirt and it
shrinks the first time you wash it, even though you've carefully
followed the laundering instructions on the label, you have a right
to return the shirt to the shop where you bought it and claim a full
refund. If, however, you want to return a new shirt simply because
you decide when you get it home that it's the wrong colour, you
have no right to take back – though, if you are lucky, the shop may
have a policy to allow customers to return goods in such
circumstances.

■ Second, you need to know whom to complain to – otherwise you can waste a lot of time and energy. This means knowing who, in law, is responsible for putting matters right, and who, in practice, will have the authority to deal with your complaint. In the case of the shrinking shirt, even though there is obviously a manufacturing fault, the responsibility lies with the shop from which you bought it, and they must refund you; it's then up to them to try to recover the money they have lost from the manufacturer or wholesaler who sold them the shirt in the first place.

But, though you know who is responsible, to which individual should you complain? In the case of a clothes shop, any of the assistants should be able to tell you; you'll probably be able to see the right person there and then. So far, so simple – but what if you don't get a satisfactory response to your complaint and want to take it further? Or what if the complaint concerns a large organisation like the Gas Board or a government department, and you don't know where to start?

■ Third, you need to know how to make your complaint. Should you make it in person or in writing? What proof will be needed that your complaint is justified?

■ Fourth, you need to know whether there is any time limit involved, so that you don't forfeit your rights just because you left it too long before taking any action.

The purpose of this book is to provide you with this essential information. It looks at the various areas in which you may encounter unfair treatment, and gives practical advice about what you can do. Since prevention is always preferable to cure, it also suggests ways in which, with a little forethought, you can limit the chances of something going wrong.

The personal factor

Although this book can help you to decide whether you've got a justified complaint and, if so, to whom, how and when you should make it, only you know how much energy and determination you can summon up to see your complaint through if obstacles arise. Although right may be on your side, pressing your case can be time-consuming and even expensive. There is no doubt that persistence pays – but you can also pay for persisting. It is therefore always worth asking yourself what you hope to get out of making a complaint. Frequently it's a sum of money – you've been sold short in some way, whether by a shop, a tradesman or a professional adviser – and your main concern is to obtain recompense. In other cases, such as being victimised at work or threatened with the closure of the local school, wider issues of individual rights and community welfare are at stake.

If it becomes clear that you may have to spend more money in pursuing your claim than you can hope to obtain if successful, or that the time involved is out of all proportion to the inconvenience or loss you have suffered, you may be wiser to give up. On the other hand, your persistence may well be to the benefit of others if it exposes malpractice to public scrutiny. If your sense of natural justice has been sufficiently outraged, you may be determined to carry on regardless – but do be aware of the possible consequences.

Might versus right

For many people, though, the mere idea of taking on a business or organisation, particularly a large one, can be intimidating, so it is worth emphasising that you need not fight your battles on your own. The individual has considerable legal muscle as a result of a number of significant laws relating to consumers' rights, and in Part One you'll find details of the various ways in which you can get help and support to use that muscle effectively.

Readers in Scotland and Northern Ireland

Scotland and Northern Ireland each has its own body of law, which in some respects, particularly in Scotland, differs from the law of England and Wales on which this book is based. It has been impossible in a book of this length to refer to all the variations, though attention is drawn to major differences. If you live in Scotland or Northern Ireland, your local consumer advice centre or solicitor will be able to explain how the law affects your complaint.

Background briefing

Complaints, like people, come in all shapes and sizes, and in Parts Two to Five you'll find specific advice about your legal rights and the complaints procedures to follow in a wide range of circumstances. This more general section looks at the common framework of legal principles and practical measures which can help you, whatever your complaint.

The legal background

As knowing enough about your rights to assess whether you have a justified complaint is the most important requirement for effective complaining, it is inevitable that much of this book is concerned with the law. Laws are established in two ways: by Acts of Parliament and also orders and regulations which government is authorised to make (known as statutory law) and by the decisions of judges over the centuries (known as common law). The difference between the law of England and Wales and the laws of Scotland and Northern Ireland has already been mentioned in the Introduction; however, certain principles are common throughout the United Kingdom.

Two kinds of law

One such principle is the distinction between criminal law and civil law. Criminal law is concerned with banning certain types of behaviour which society as a whole finds unacceptable. Those who are accused of breaking such laws are prosecuted by the state, in the form of the police or another arm of government such as a local authority. If found guilty, they are punished, usually by imprisonment or a fine. Civil law, on the other hand, is intended to protect the individual's rights, in relation to other people and also to the state; if it is broken, it is up to the wronged person (known as the *plaintiff*) to sue the responsible person or organisation (known as the *defendant*) for compensation.

If you have been harmed by someone breaking a criminal law, you must pass on your complaint to the relevant official body and hope that it will decide to prosecute. However, you may also be able to bring a civil case and so claim compensation, because criminal and civil laws often cover the same area, even though they view it from different standpoints. For example, a jeweller who sells you a ring labelled '24-carat gold' when it is only 18-carat gold is guilty of a criminal offence, under the Trade Descriptions Act, and so could be prosecuted by the local authority's Trading Standards Department; but this doesn't stop you from suing him/her for a civil wrong, that of breach of contract.

The law of contract

At the heart of many complaints lies the civil law of contract – a common law that has existed for centuries. Put simply, the law of contract says that if two people reach an agreement about something, they must honour that agreement. Of course, life is never that straightforward, and so it has been necessary to qualify and add to this basic rule.

For an agreement to be enforceable in law, it has to have five features:

- an offer by one party

- an acceptance of that offer by the other party

- a 'consideration' – that is, payment in some form, usually money (in Scotland, however, this is not an essential feature; if someone agrees to do something for nothing, Scottish law says they must honour that agreement)

- the intention of both parties to make a legal contract (this is assumed unless the agreement is between friends)

- the legal capacity to enter into a contract (for example, a contract made with someone under eighteen years old cannot be enforced unless it was for the purchase of 'necessary items' such as food and clothes, although Scottish law allows some exceptions).

Most contracts do not have to be in writing to be enforceable (exceptions include hire purchase and other consumer credit agreements, and contracts for the sale of land). The majority of the contracts we enter into every day are unwritten, and many do not even involve speech. For example, by picking up a newspaper from a stall and handing over the money, you have made a contract. If you then change your mind, you have no right to return the paper and demand repayment. This principle also applies even if the money has not changed hands, as long as the offer has been made and accepted; if you order goods and agree a price, you can't then cancel your order (unless the seller has broken the contract in some way, for example by failing to deliver the goods by an agreed date). Nor does the precise amount of the payment have to have been agreed; if you leave your car with a garage for repair, without agreeing a price in advance, you are liable to pay the bill as long as it is reasonable (hence the importance of getting estimates and quotations – see p 97).

IMPLIED TERMS

When entering a contract, each party accepts certain obligations which are the terms of the contract. Even an unspoken contract has terms; for example, when you bought that newspaper, you had the right to expect that none of its pages would be missing. This is because the law recognises that some types of contract, whether they are silent, spoken or written, require certain terms to be implied. Implied terms are particularly important in a *consumer contract* – that is, an agreement between a trader (an individual or private or public organisation making the contract in the course of a business) and a consumer (someone not making or claiming to make the contract in the course of a business), for goods or a service ordinarily supplied to private individuals. These implied terms are spelt out in two important consumer laws, the Sale of Goods Act 1979 (see p 50) and the Supply of Goods and Services Act 1982 (see p 93).

EXPRESS TERMS

There may be a need or wish to add extra terms to those implied in law, and these are called express terms. Express terms can be agreed in conversation but it is generally advisable to put them in writing (see 'Evidence of a contract', p 5). It is often unnecessary to draw up a special document to record an express term; for example, if you agree a definite delivery date for some goods, this can be noted on the order (see 'Complaints about late delivery', p 65).

Written contract terms proposed by a trader can take several forms. They may appear as a notice displayed in a shop or as 'small print' on the back of an invoice or in a guarantee or formal contract document. To have any legal significance, they must be brought to your attention before you make the contract. This does not mean that they should be pointed out or explained to you, simply that you must have been given the opportunity to read them. Unfortunately, many contracts are written in legal jargon that seems intended to obscure their meaning and implications. Generally, you will be held to have agreed to the terms of any contract you make, even if you didn't understand them (though see 'Exclusion clauses', below), so don't feel embarrassed about taking time to read order forms and other documents thoroughly before making your decision. If necessary, ask the trader to give you a copy which you can take away and consider at your leisure; if it still defeats you, seek help from one of the local consumer advisory services discussed later in this section (see p 13).

EXCLUSION CLAUSES

Exclusion clauses are express terms in a written contract that seek to take away one party's legal rights. Fortunately, the law (set out in the Unfair Contract Terms Act 1977) has made it much more difficult for traders to shirk their responsibilities in this way. In particular, no clause that limits or excludes liability for negligence resulting in death or injury is legally valid (see 'The duty of care', p 6). It is positively illegal for consumer contracts to exclude the implied terms set out in the Sale of Goods Act (see p 50) or even to mislead customers into thinking that they do not have these rights (for example, by displaying notices such as 'no refunds on sale goods' or 'sold as seen'); this is why contractual documents such as manufacturers' guarantees often include a statement that the terms are in addition to, and do not affect or reduce, the customer's statutory and other legal rights. Note, though, that this applies only to consumer contracts; if you are buying goods in the course of a business, or at an auction, your Sale of Goods Act rights can be excluded (see p 86).

Whatever kind of contract is involved, the law also says that any exclusion clause must be fair and reasonable. This means that, even if you have signed or accepted a contract which excludes some of your rights, you may be able to contest its terms in the event of a dispute; and it will be up to the trader to prove that any exclusion clause was reasonable, not for you to prove that it was unreasonable.

EVIDENCE OF A CONTRACT

Your legal rights to claim compensation for faulty goods or inadequate service do not depend on whether you can produce any evidence of the original contract; but, in practice, having some proof of the transaction, such as a receipt or credit card slip showing the date and amount of the payment and the name and address of the trader, will greatly improve your chances of getting a swift and satisfactory response to your complaint. If you've lost the receipt, a clearly filled-in cheque stub may reassure the trader that your claim is genuine.

The more complicated the contract's terms, the more important evidence becomes in the event of a dispute. Disagreements about express terms agreed in conversation will be more easily settled if you can call on a witness to corroborate your version of what was said; if possible, get the witness to make notes of the conversation and keep these with any other proof, such as a receipt or order. You should also record what is said in any relevant telephone conversation. Better still, have a written contract of some kind which sets out all the express terms you have agreed; this reduces the risk of misunderstanding and innocent forgetfulness as well as strengthening your case if the trader lets you down.

Any correspondence about a contract, for example estimates and quotations, or responses to your complaint, must be kept safely, ready to be referred to quickly or produced in a clean and legible state. Your own letters should be typed, unless your handwriting is easy to read, and you should always keep a copy for your own records by using carbon paper or a photocopier.

For more advice about making complaints in person, by telephone or in writing, see pp 9–13.

STORING THE EVIDENCE

So that you can produce any helpful evidence easily, consider creating your own home filing system instead of shoving receipts in the nearest drawer or leaving them to disintegrate in your handbag. You can use the same system for storing instruction manuals and guarantees, bank and credit card statements, copies of insurance policies and so on. A concertina file with separate pockets for letters of the alphabet should be roomy enough for this. Decide for yourself how you want to organise it; you may want anything to do with electrical appliances under 'E', or prefer to file them separately, so that the receipt and guarantee for your iron go under 'I', those for your washing machine under 'W'. As you'll probably forget what you filed things under, make up your own index on sheets of paper or in a booklet, divided alphabetically, with plenty of space after each letter so that you can note new items as you buy them. Then you need only refer to the index instead of laboriously going through all the papers in each pocket of the file. Check periodically to discard any out-of-date records.

The duty of care

In addition to the law of contract, which imposes specific obligations on anyone entering into a legally enforceable agreement, common law imposes a general obligation on all of us to take reasonable care not to injure anyone or damage their property. Failure to exercise this care is called negligence. You may be able to sue someone for negligence even if you've never met them, for example if you are injured by a careless motorist. However, a person cannot be sued if they could not reasonably be expected to have foreseen that their behaviour would cause injury or loss to another.

If someone acts on the basis that they have a particular skill, then their duty of care includes the responsibility to use that skill. Moreover, the level of skill must be that which could reasonably be expected; an incompetent garage mechanic, solicitor or chef cannot defend a claim for negligence on the grounds that they 'did their best'.

Although a duty of care is assumed in all contracts, whether for goods or services, it is possible for a trader to reduce his/her liability by inserting an exclusion clause (see p 4). However, such a clause is never valid if it attempts to exclude or limit liability for death or personal injury caused by negligence; and liability for loss or damage to property can be excluded only if the trader can prove that the clause is 'fair and reasonable'.

Negligence claims must be made within six years of the event (three if claiming for personal injury) except in some cases when the period runs from the date when you became aware that you had a claim.

Making a complaint

If you find yourself in a situation where your rights have been ignored and you have a claim under civil law, for example for breach of contract, then your ultimate means of obtaining compensation is to sue the responsible party in the civil courts. But taking someone to court should be undertaken only as a last resort; there are other methods you should use first.

■ Give the person, company or organisation a chance to admit responsibility and offer you compensation. Find out who is responsible for handling complaints, explain your case to them clearly and politely, in person, by telephone or in writing as appropriate (see pp 9–13 for details of how to do this), and allow them a reasonable time to respond.

■ If your initial complaint is rejected, or you are in any way dissatisfied with the response, keep calm but make it clear to the person dealing with your complaint that you intend to take matters further. If you have any doubts about your rights, you can arrange to discuss your complaint with a local consumer adviser (see 'Where to go for help and advice', p 13). The next step may be to write to a more senior person in the company or organisation. Your letter will be taken more seriously if you address it to the individual by name rather than just their title; to find it out, ask the person to whom you first made the complaint, or telephone and ask the organisation's switchboard operator. If it's a fairly small company, your best bet may be to write to the managing director (whose name should appear on the firm's stationery); in larger organisations, there is often a separate department responsible for handling customers' complaints, run by a senior manager. If this proves ineffective, a personal letter to the chairman can get results.

■ If letters from you or your consumer adviser do not lead to a satisfactory settlement, you will have to look for support elsewhere. A trader may belong to a trade association to which you can complain, and which may act as conciliator, if necessary using sanctions such as the threat of expulsion to pressurise the trader into meeting his/her obligations. Some associations, and other bodies such as British Telecom and the Post Office, have codes of practice which may help you (see p 9). If you are dealing with a professional person or organisation – a doctor or solicitor, for example – then you may be able to complain to their professional body, depending on the nature of the complaint.

■ You may be able to opt for arbitration as an alternative to going to court. This means that an independent person, appointed by both parties in the dispute, considers the facts of the case and reaches a legally binding decision (see pp 25–28).

Codes of practice

Partly as a consequence of the strengthening of the consumer's legal position, many trades, businesses and industries have been encouraged to monitor their own conduct more closely, and to devise ways of avoiding and settling disputes outside the courts. In particular, a number of trade associations and national organisations have drawn up codes of practice, several in consultation with the Office of Fair Trading. Each code sets certain standards of conduct and service for members, in addition to those required by law. Although these codes have no legal status, they do give you several advantages:

- by giving your custom to a member of an organisation which has a code of practice, you have greater reason to feel confident that the trader will be aware of your rights, and so will be able to deal with any straightforward complaint correctly

- if a dispute with a trade association member ends in deadlock, the organisation can act as a conciliator between you. If you wish to use this free service, get in touch with the organisation's headquarters; they will probably ask you to present your complaint in writing, and may provide a special form

- many codes of practice offer a low-cost, independent arbitration scheme as an alternative to going to court (see p 25)

- even if the trader you are dealing with does not belong to a relevant association, the code of practice for that type of business can be of use in the event of a dispute in defining what are 'reasonable' standards.

How to complain in person

Complaining in person is usually most appropriate when you have a complaint about faulty goods. The most important evidence is the goods themselves; you can insist that the seller collects them, but it is often easier and quicker to take them back yourself, together with the receipt or other proof of purchase. Here are the guidelines to follow.

■ Satisfy yourself before you start that you have a justified complaint by reading the relevant sections of this book.

■ Make your complaint as soon as possible; if faulty goods are involved, stop using them as soon as you spot the defect.

■ Be clear in your own mind what you hope to achieve by complaining – an apology, an offer of free repair, a replacement, a refund, a deduction from the bill, a change of decision or policy.

■ Take any helpful evidence with you, such as receipts and, where relevant, the faulty goods. If a friend or member of your family was a witness to any conversation in which express terms were agreed, ask them to accompany you to lend their support. Take writing materials with you so that, if necessary, you can make notes of what is said and the name and position of the person you speak to.

■ Ask to see whoever is responsible for dealing with customers' complaints. If possible, avoid making your visit around lunchtime or shortly before the end of the working day to have the best chance of getting the attention of the right person. If they are not available, arrange an appointment for another time, or write to them.

■ Keep calm and stay polite. Start out with the assumption that the person to whom you complain will be as anxious as you are to put matters right.

■ Make your complaint as specific and brief as you can.

■ If you have to leave faulty goods with the supplier – for example, if you have accepted an offer of free repair – then get a receipt for them. If you have agreed to leave them for inspection only, then have this written on the receipt. Never hand over your original receipt.

■ Don't be fobbed off with second best; if you have a right to your

money back and that's what you want, don't be intimidated into
accepting a credit note or replacement.

■ If your complaint is rejected or you aren't satisfied with the
response, don't lose your temper. Do not threaten to report the
person concerned – this can be blackmail – but make it clear that
you intend to take matters further. Ask if the company has its own
complaints procedure, and if possible get the name and address to
write to.

■ If, on the other hand, your complaint is dealt with courteously
and efficiently, show that you appreciate this.

COMPLAINING BY TELEPHONE

Generally speaking, it is better to make complaints in person or in
writing. However, if an initial telephone call is necessary, or if you
are telephoned in response to your complaint, make sure that you
have all the relevant documents, such as receipts, easily to hand,
and keep a note of the date and time of the conversation, the name
of the person you speak to, and the substance of what is said on
both sides.

How to complain in writing

Complaining in writing is often the next step to take if a personal
complaint has been rejected; it is also more appropriate for serious
complaints and for disputes over services, particularly where a
written contract is involved. Here are the guidelines to follow.

■ Satisfy yourself before you start that you have a justified
complaint by reading the relevant sections of this book.

■ Make your complaint as soon as possible; if faulty goods are
involved, stop using them as soon as you spot the defect.

■ Be clear in your own mind what you hope to achieve by
complaining – an apology, an offer of free repair, a replacement, a

refund, a deduction from the bill, a change of decision or policy.

■ Address your letter to an individual rather than just the name of the company or organisation: the managing director, the head of customer relations or whoever is appropriate. Telephone to find out his/her name – a letter addressed personally is more likely to get the relevant person's attention, and says something about your seriousness and competence.

■ Make sure your letter is legible – type it if possible – and always keep a clean copy.

■ Check that the letter contains all the relevant facts: your name and address, of course; the date; the name and address of the person to whom you are writing; the circumstances and details of the original contract – for example, if you are complaining about faulty goods, the item's name (with model number if one exists), when you bought it, how much it cost, the invoice or receipt number; the reasons for your complaint (set these out as clearly and briefly as you can – in a list, if you wish); and what action you wish them to take.

■ Adopt a polite and formal style – no threats, no insults, no personal remarks. If the case ever comes to court, you will need to show that you have acted reasonably.

■ Evidence that the letter has been posted and received is often helpful, particularly if any previous correspondence has been ignored. Take your letter to a post office and ask for it to be sent by recorded delivery service (there's a small charge in addition to the normal postage cost); you will be given a certificate of posting, and the letter will be signed for on delivery. If you intend to do this, write 'by recorded delivery' at the top of your letter. You can also, for a further small charge, request an advice of delivery to be sent to you (you can request this after you've posted a letter, but it costs more).

■ Although it is the seller's responsibility to collect faulty goods, you may agree to post them back; if so, make it clear in writing that you expect to be refunded for the cost of postage and, if the goods are of any value, insurance (you can arrange cover at the post office at the time of posting for an extra charge). A free certificate of posting will prove that you have sent the parcel.

Where to go for help and advice

Making a complaint does not have to be a solitary pursuit. There are various sources of information and advice, some local, others national. Specialist advice agencies are mentioned when relevant throughout the book; the following organisations and individuals can help with a broad range of problems.

Public library

Public libraries, particularly those with reference as well as lending sections, are a valuable source of information in various ways:

- the books and journals they stock provide free and ready access to facts and opinions about many subjects, including the law and your rights, and many libraries will obtain a book for you from another library in the area if they don't have it in stock. However, there's an important point to bear in mind when consulting any book that deals with the law: how up-to-date is it? Look for the year of publication, usually printed on the page following the main title page, and use the most recent edition available

- most librarians are very helpful if you are not sure where to start looking for information on a particular subject, and will give you the benefit of their knowledge of the area in which you live

- major libraries usually possess a lot of detailed local information, such as the names and addresses of advice centres, local government departments, local councillors and MPs

- many libraries hold stocks of useful free leaflets, such as those published by the Office of Fair Trading.

Citizens' Advice Bureau (CAB)

This is a free advice service, mainly funded by local government grants. Bureaux staff – the majority of whom are unpaid volunteers – have been trained to deal with problems in a wide range of areas; they get around $6\frac{1}{2}$ million enquiries every year. There are some 750 CABx throughout the United Kingdom, so there should be one near you; look in your local telephone directory or ask at your local library. Telephone the Bureau before visiting to check its opening times; if they are very busy, they may suggest you make an appointment.

The CAB staff can offer various kinds of help:

- if you are unsure whether you have cause for complaint, they can advise you; they can explain how the law applies in your case; they can help you to decide whether you have anything to gain by complaining, and what your chances of success are

- they can provide copies of various free publications, for example those issued by the Office of Fair Trading

- they can write letters of complaint on your behalf

- they can help to see your complaint through, as far as the courts if necessary, and may be able to accompany you as an adviser to a court hearing or represent you at a tribunal

- they can provide copies of certain standard forms, for example for legal aid applications and complaints to the commissions for racial and sex discrimination (see p 228); and they can help you to complete them correctly

- they can usually provide you with a certain amount of free advice from a qualified solicitor. A few CABx employ a 'community lawyer', whose main job is to train and advise staff but who may be able to take up individual cases. More commonly, there will be an 'honorary legal adviser', a local solicitor who works for the CAB on a voluntary, occasional basis and who can give you some basic legal advice but can't see your case through; and many CABx run a rota system of solicitors who visit the Bureau and give free advice and who can, if you both wish, take up your case on a professional

fee-paying basis (you may be eligible for legal aid towards the
fee – see 'How to get help with legal expenses', p 20)

● alternatively or additionally, they can help you to find and
choose a solicitor who specialises in the kind of complaint you
have.

The amount and type of help you can get from a CAB depends on
how stretched it is by lack of resources, but it is a good place to
start. If the staff feel they can't handle your case as well as a more
specialist agency, they will tell you and give you details of what to
do next.

Trading Standards/Consumer Services/Consumer Protection Department

These are different names for the same thing: the local government
department responsible for enforcing a range of criminal laws
relating to goods and services. In England and Wales, it is part of
the district council (in London, the borough council); in Scotland,
it is part of the regional authority; and in Northern Ireland, it is
known as the Trading Standards Branch of the Department of
Economic Development for Northern Ireland. To contact the
department, look up the relevant authority's name in the telephone
directory.

The department uses various means to enforce the law in its area:
by monitoring local businesses – for example, buying items to check
that traders are giving the correct weight or measure; by taking up
relevant complaints brought to its attention by members of the
public; by giving warnings to anyone infringing the law; and, if
necessary, by prosecuting offenders in the criminal courts.

The main kinds of complaint that concern them are: dangerous
goods; food or drink that is unfit for human consumption; short
weights and measures; unsolicited goods; false descriptions or
statements about goods or services; and misleading price
information. If your complaint falls into one of these categories, you
should contact the department as the matter is likely to be one of
public concern. If the offender is prosecuted and found guilty, you

may be awarded compensation by the court (this is discretionary); and you are still free to sue the other party if there has also been an offence in civil law.

As well as looking into a specific complaint, the department may be able to answer general queries about consumer law, and provide copies of useful leaflets such as the Office of Fair Trading's series.

Consumer/neighbourhood/housing advice centre

A number of local authorities have set up advice centres to give free advice and information on areas outside the scope of their Trading Standards Departments. To find out whether there is one near you, telephone your Town Hall (listed in the telephone directory under the name of the local authority).

Legal advice centre

There are around 100 centres, although most of them are in London. Some are run on a full-time basis, others open for only a few hours a week. They deal with all types of legal problem, but particularly those that concern welfare rights, immigration and housing. A solicitor may hold a 'clinic' at the centre once or twice a week, on a voluntary basis. The advice is usually free, though some advice centres are allowed to use the legal advice and assistance scheme (see p 21). As well as giving legal advice, they can help with letter-writing and form-filling.

Law centre

These are managed by representatives of the local community, and are staffed by community workers and full-time solicitors. There are relatively few law centres – just over fifty in England, of which half are in London, and one each in Cardiff, Belfast and Glasgow – and they will only help people who live or work in their catchment areas; to find out if there is one near you, ask at your local library or Citizens' Advice Bureau or telephone the Town Hall. The centres are selective about the work they take on, and each has its own priorities, depending on the problems of its area – commonly, housing, employment, welfare rights and immigration. If they take on your case, they will provide free legal representation.

Consumers' Association

Consumers' Association is an independent organisation concerned with protecting and advancing the interests of consumers. It does this in several ways:

- by publishing unbiased information about goods and services to help you buy wisely and so reduce the likelihood of something going wrong. Much of this is contained in the Association's three magazines – the best-known, *Which?*, also *Holiday Which?* and *Gardening from Which?*; to buy them, you have to become a subscriber, but your local reference library should stock current and back issues if you want to look up a particular article. The Association also publishes a range of books; these are sold in bookshops and are also available direct from the publisher by mail order; or you may find your library has copies

- by offering a personal legal advice service to deal with consumers' complaints. To use this, you will have to become a member of the Association, and you must pay an additional annual subscription; but there are no further charges and so this may well work out cheaper than employing a solicitor yourself. Hundreds of cases are handled each year by the Personal Service lawyers, and *Which?* frequently publishes descriptions to show how they are settled

- by acting as a watchdog and pressure group, to influence manufacturers and others to improve their standards, and to campaign for changes in law and government policy.

For further information, write to Consumers' Association (see 'Addresses', p 231).

Your local councillor

Many of the areas of everyday life in which problems can arise – education, housing, social services, refuse collection, the local environment – are in the care and control of local government. Your first step when you have a complaint about the quality of a local government service is to raise the matter with the relevant department (to find out the name and address to write to, telephone the Town Hall, listed in the telephone directory under the name of the local authority; or ask at your local library). If you are dissatisfied with the response, you can seek support from your councillor, who is your elected representative in local government (again, your Town Hall or local library should have his/her name, address and phone number). The councillor may hold a regular 'surgery' – a consultation session which gives you the opportunity to explain your problem in person. If your community has a parish council (also known as a community or town council), try one of its members first if your complaint concerns local facilities such as public lavatories or street lighting.

If your complaint concerns maladministration of some kind, and your councillor can't or won't get the local authority to sort out your complaint, you can ask him/her to forward your complaint to the Commissioner for Local Administration (see p 154).

Your Member of Parliament

If you have a major complaint, particularly one that concerns a general principle, policy or point of law that affects other people as well, you may find your MP sympathetic and willing to give you support. Some MPs spend a considerable amount of time and effort looking after their constituents' interests and using their influence to speed up the resolution of long disputes. Most MPs hold 'surgeries'; to make an appointment, get the surgery's address and phone number from the MP's local party headquarters or your library. You can also write to your MP at the House of Commons, London SW1A 0AA. If your MP is unsympathetic and you know of another whose particular interests are relevant to your complaint, you can write to him/her instead.

A solicitor

If your complaint is serious or complicated, and particularly if you suspect that you will have to take legal action to enforce your rights, you may wish to go straight to a solicitor. You may also be recommended to see one by any of the organisations or people already mentioned. A solicitor can help you with a complaint in several ways:

- by advising you whether your legal rights have indeed been infringed

- by suggesting courses of action

- by writing letters on your behalf (and a solicitor's letter often proves effective in settling a long-running dispute)

- by helping you to fill in various forms

- by advising you whether you are eligible for legal aid (see pp 20–24)

- by representing you in court or, if you decide to conduct your own proceedings, by advising you how to do so

- by arranging for the services of a barrister, most commonly to advise on a difficult point of law or on the conduct of a case, or to represent you if your case goes to one of the higher courts in which a solicitor is not allowed to appear on your behalf.

If you think you need a solicitor, your main concerns will probably be: how do I choose one and how much will I have to pay?

HOW TO CHOOSE A SOLICITOR

- ask your local Citizens' Advice Bureau or other advice agency for their suggestions

- ask your friends or professional acquaintances, such as your bank manager, for their personal recommendations (but bear in mind that solicitors specialise in different kinds of work, and a solicitor that proved ideal for one type of case may not be the best choice for another)

- if your complaint concerns your job, and you belong to a trade union, ask the union if it can recommend solicitors' firms that specialise in employment law

- shop around before you decide: telephone or call in, and ask a few questions. Do they have experience in handling the kind of complaint you have? Do they do legal aid work (see pp 20–25)? Do they operate the fixed fee interview scheme (see p 22)? If not, what will be the charge for, say, one hour's initial advice? Who would deal with your case, and what would the average hourly cost be? How soon could you be seen?

HOW A SOLICITOR'S CHARGES ARE CALCULATED

The basis of a solicitor's charges is the time spent on your case, calculated on an hourly rate that varies enormously depending on, for example, the location of the firm and the seniority of the person handling the work. The complexity of the case will also affect the final bill, as well as the number of documents that have to be prepared or considered.

In addition to the solicitor's own fee, the bill may also include amounts paid to third parties (for example, a barrister's fee or a court fee for issuing a writ); these are called 'disbursements'.

Solicitors' charges do not depend on whether they are successful in sorting out your complaint (though there is a procedure for querying a solicitor's bill – see p 160). Moreover, if you go to court and lose your case, you may find yourself liable for at least some of the winner's legal costs as well; and, if you win, you may still find yourself out of pocket if, for example, the loser is unable to pay the compensation awarded to you (see 'What will legal action cost?', p 29).

How to get help with legal expenses

The main way to get financial help is to apply for legal aid. This is a system whereby solicitors' bills are paid, wholly or in part, out of the public purse. Solicitors who accept legal aid work are listed in the Legal Aid List, available for inspection at your local library or Citizens' Advice Bureau; they usually display the Legal Aid symbol in their window.

There are two legal aid schemes that could help you in pursuing a complaint: legal advice and assistance, commonly referred to as the green form scheme (in Scotland, the equivalent is called the pink form scheme); and civil legal aid. Both schemes are means-tested, and you may have to pay a contribution even though you are eligible for some aid. A leaflet setting out the financial qualifications (which are periodically revised) can be obtained from your local Citizens' Advice Bureau or legal centre as well as from a solicitor operating the schemes.

Legal advice and assistance

This scheme covers a range of services provided by a solicitor, from giving general advice about your case to drafting letters and negotiating agreements. With few exceptions, however, it does not cover court work. There is an upper limit on the cost that will be met under the scheme, currently £50 (a higher limit applies in certain divorce cases); but if this proves insufficient, the solicitor can apply for an extension.

If you decide to apply for aid under this scheme, your solicitor will complete the necessary form, which you must sign. The means test amounts to answering some basic questions about your financial circumstances and commitments. To qualify, your financial means must be shown to be within certain limits. These are based on what is called your 'disposable capital' and your 'disposable income' (and, unless you are separated, your husband's or wife's capital and income will be included in the calculations).

DISPOSABLE CAPITAL

This is the value of your capital assets – your savings, any valuable possessions, but excluding the value of your home, its furniture and fittings, your clothes, the tools of your trade, and any item that is the subject of the dispute – less specified allowances for each dependant, be they husband or wife, child or other relative.

DISPOSABLE INCOME

This is your total weekly gross income, for example your pay, pension, child benefit, less deductions for income tax, National

Insurance contributions and specified allowances for husband or wife and dependants.

You will be eligible for *free* legal advice and assistance if

- you are receiving supplementary benefit or family income supplement

    or

- your weekly disposable income is less than the specified lower limit

    and

- your disposable capital is below the specified limit.

You will be eligible for legal advice and assistance but will have to pay a contribution if

- your disposable capital is below the specified limit

    and

- your weekly disposable income is above the specified lower limit but below the upper limit. How much you will have to contribute is calculated on a sliding scale. You will usually have to pay before the solicitor starts work on your case.

If you find that you are not eligible for legal advice and assistance, you could either seek free advice from one of the advice agencies mentioned earlier in this section and elsewhere in the book, or make use of the fixed fee interview scheme operated by many solicitors, whereby you get half-an-hour's consultation for £5. In either case, you could at least get an idea of whether you should continue with legal action, either at your own expense or, if you qualify, using civil legal aid if the case goes to court.

Civil legal aid

This scheme covers the cost of suing and being sued in court. There is usually no upper limit on the cost; however, if the solicitor feels at any stage that it would be a waste of public money to continue the case, the aid may be stopped.

As with the legal aid and assistance scheme, your eligibility depends on your disposable capital and disposable income, but your disposable income is calculated in a slightly different way.

DISPOSABLE INCOME

For civil legal aid purposes, this is your estimated gross annual income for the twelve months following your application, less deductions for income tax, National Insurance contributions and specified allowances for dependants, but also less rent, rates, mortgage repayments, the cost of travel to work and any other outgoings deemed 'necessary' by the Department of Health and Social Security. The DHSS is sent the part of the legal aid form which sets out your financial circumstances; it must satisfy itself that you are financially eligible, and decide whether you should pay a contribution. You may be interviewed and asked to produce documentary evidence such as bank statements.

You will be financially eligible for *free* legal aid if

- your annual disposable income is below the specified lower limit

    and

- your disposable capital is also below the lower limit.

You will be financially eligible for legal aid but will have to pay a contribution if

- your annual disposable income is above the lower limit but below the upper limit: in this case your maximum contribution will be one quarter of the amount by which your disposable income exceeds the lower limit; you will usually be able to pay your contribution in monthly instalments over a year

    or

- your disposable capital is above the lower limit but below the upper limit: in this case, your contribution will be the amount you have over the lower limit, and you will normally have to pay it in a lump sum in advance; however, if the estimated

costs of the work are less than your contribution, you will
initially be asked to pay the lower amount.

In practice, the lowness of the lower limits for both capital and
income means that most people applying for civil legal aid are asked
to make contributions, and the sums involved can be large –
particularly if you have to make contributions from both your
income and your capital.

Financial eligibility is one factor that will affect the consideration of
your application for civil legal aid – a process that usually takes six
to eight weeks – but there is another: the merits of your case. This
means not only that your case has to be reasonably strong, but also
that it is reasonable to grant you legal aid because the claim is
serious, and one where court action is an appropriate method of
settling the dispute. The application form has to set out the facts of
the case for consideration by the Legal Aid Office (and, if there's
some doubt, by a committee of barristers and solicitors). Although
you can fill it in yourself (copies of the form are available from most
Citizens' Advice Bureaux and solicitors' offices), it is advisable to
involve a solicitor because he/she can ensure that your case is
presented as fully and convincingly as possible. Unfortunately, the
cost of a solicitor's work in completing a civil legal aid form is not
covered by the scheme; you will have to either pay the firm's rate
for the time this takes or choose a solicitor who operates the fixed
fee interview scheme (see p 22) or apply for legal aid and assistance
(but note that the financial means limits of that scheme are stricter
than for civil legal aid, so you won't necessarily be eligible for
both).

When you have to repay legal aid

If you are successful in settling your claim, and as a result you
recover or preserve any money or property, you may have to pay at
least part of the legal costs. This can happen when the loser is not
ordered to pay your costs; or pays only a contribution towards
them; or goes bust or disappears.

The limit on the amount you may be asked to pay is the total
amount of the damages (or the value of the goods) you receive, plus
your original contribution, if any. In this sense, legal aid is rather

like a loan dependent on results. It puts the legally aided winner in much the same position as the privately funded winner who would also be responsible for making up any shortfall between costs awarded and his/her solicitor's bill (see 'What will legal action cost?', p 29). The legally aided winner has the advantage that the amount to be repaid cannot exceed the damages plus the original contribution; if the costs of the case are higher, the balance is made up by the Legal Aid Fund. Also, the costs that a solicitor can claim for legal aid work are more strictly defined than those allowed when calculating a private client's bill.

If you are ineligible for legal aid

If you are unable to get legal aid, and you cannot pay the costs of taking your case to court out of your own pocket, or if you are judged eligible but are asked to make a contribution which you feel you cannot afford, you have four options:

- make sure you have exhausted all the other ways of pursuing your complaint, for example through a trade association or other organisation with a code of practice arbitration scheme (see below), your MP or local councillor

- consider using the small claims procedure (see p 36), even if it means having to accept less compensation

- find out whether, if your case involves a general principle that affects many others, some organisation or pressure group might be willing to support you

- give up.

Arbitration schemes

Arbitration is a method of settling a dispute by reaching a legally binding decision that does not involve formal court proceedings. Both sides put their case to an independent person known as the arbitrator (arbiter in Scotland), who considers the facts impartially and, taking the law into account, decides who is in the right and what form any compensation should take. The small claims procedure (see p 36) is a form of arbitration, but the schemes under consideration here are those set up by a number of trade associations and other organisations, often as part of a code of practice.

Code of practice arbitration schemes

Many codes of practice (see p 9) offer the dissatisfied customer the chance to go to arbitration rather than to court. The Office of Fair Trading, which helped to draw up some of the codes, has published a useful pamphlet describing these schemes, *I'm going to take it further* (for how to obtain a copy, see p 241). A number of goods and services are covered, including the supply and repair of cars, motorcycles and household electrical appliances, and the sale of holidays, furniture and postal services; details are given in the relevant sections of this book. Remember, though, that trade association membership is optional; if your dispute is with a non-member, the association cannot help.

The key features of these arbitration schemes are as follows:

- as claimant, you have the right to insist on arbitration

- if you opt for arbitration, you cannot then take your case to court if you are dissatisfied with the arbitrator's decision. For this reason, it is important to weigh up the pros and cons in your particular case before you apply; your local Citizens' Advice Bureau or other consumer adviser can help

- the arbitrator will decide who is in the right on the basis of written evidence sent in by both sides (this is known as a 'documents only' system); with few exceptions, you will not have to attend a hearing. This is fine if you feel you can express yourself clearly and fully on paper, otherwise you may consider this feature a disadvantage; however, you can get help from a Citizens' Advice Bureau or other adviser in drafting the necessary documents

- the decision should be reached quite quickly, usually within three months of your request for arbitration

- in most cases, there is no upper limit on the amount you can claim, so arbitration may be a less risky way of settling a case than court action if your claim exceeds the small claims procedure limit (see p 37)

- both parties have to pay a registration fee in order to go to arbitration. The amount will depend on the size of your claim, and the sliding scale operating under the code of practice concerned. For most of the schemes, the minimum fee, covering claims up to £2,500, is currently £17.25; this makes arbitration more expensive than court action for smaller claims, but cheaper for larger ones

- the loser may be ordered to pay the winner's registration fee, but no other costs can be claimed, for example those incurred in the collection or preparation of evidence

- if you win your case, the arbitrator can order compensation to be paid to you; payment must be paid within twenty-one days of the announcement of the award

- the trade association can bring pressure to bear on a member who is slow to pay up; but if this fails, you will have to go to court to enforce the award (see 'Getting your money', p 37).

Other arbitration schemes

Arbitration may also be offered as an alternative to court action without being linked to a code of practice – examples include schemes offered by some companies in the insurance and house building industries (see the relevant sections of this book).

It is legal for a contract to contain a compulsory arbitration clause which says that, in the event of a dispute, you have to submit your claim to the arbitrator appointed under the terms of the contract. If you lose, you may find that you have to pay the full cost of the arbitration. If you spot such a clause in the small print of a contract, you can ask for it to be deleted before you accept, but the trader may well refuse. If a dispute does arise, and you don't want to go to arbitration under the terms of the contract, you can still start court proceedings; if the other party lodges a defence, the right to insist on arbitration is then considered to have been waived (this manoeuvre is not allowed in Scotland, however, where the law says you must go to arbitration if you have signed a contract which makes it compulsory).

Taking a case to court

Seeking redress through the courts is not as drastic or complicated a process as you might suppose. However, it is always best to use this method of settling a dispute as a last resort.

Before you decide to sue

■ Seek advice from a solicitor, Citizens' Advice Bureau or other legal adviser about the merits of your case, your chances of success, the likely costs and whether you are eligible for legal aid.

■ Consider what you hope to gain by suing. In many cases where a complaint is concerned, you are seeking financial compensation, known as 'damages'; there may be a specific amount involved, for example if you are owed wages by your ex-employer, or it may be up to the court to name a figure, for example if the complaint is about poor service. In either case, the amount in question is significant because, if it is less than £500 (£300 in Northern Ireland), the case will usually be dealt with under the small claims procedure, also known as arbitration (see p 36 for details, including the difference in Scotland). Arbitration is not available, however, if you are seeking something other than damages, for example the return of goods.

■ If you are seeking damages, assess how likely you are to get your money if you win. The court may reach a judgement that damages are owed; but if you don't receive the money, it is up to you to go back to court to arrange enforcement, and you will have to pay for this (see 'Getting your money', p 37). If your complaint is against a trader who does a moonlight flit, or is declared bankrupt, or against a company that goes into liquidation, your chances of ever getting compensation will be slight, and you could end up worse off than if you hadn't taken legal action (see 'What will legal action cost?', below).

■ However good your case may seem, check that you can afford to lose.

What will legal action cost?

If you are thinking of suing someone, you should be aware of the potential cost of such action so that you can calculate whether it is worth it in purely financial terms. Even if you are quite convinced of the justice of your claim, consider whether you can afford to lose; and there are circumstances in which you may end up out of pocket even if you win.

IF YOU WIN YOUR CASE

The general rule is that the loser will pay your costs. However, there are some important provisos:

- if the case is heard under the small claims procedure, only limited costs can be awarded (see p 36)

- if the case is heard is court, and you have employed a solicitor, the judge will usually decide that the loser is liable for any legal costs you *necessarily* incurred (known as the party-and-party basis of assessment), whereas (unless you are on legal aid) your solicitor will charge you for all costs that were *not unreasonably* incurred. You will have to pay any shortfall between the two out of your own pocket

- if the other party is on legal aid, the judge will order him/her to pay a 'reasonable amount' towards your legal costs, and in calculating this amount will take into account the loser's financial means; so you can end up paying a high proportion of your own costs

- if you decide to handle the case yourself, you will be able to claim some of the costs you incur but there are limitations. You can claim for your time, but only for the number of hours it would have taken a solicitor to handle the case – and as an amateur you will almost certainly have taken longer. Your hourly rate cannot exceed your wage loss (so, if you would otherwise be earning £5 for each hour you spend on your case, you can't calculate your costs on the basis of £6 an hour); and, however much income you have lost, you can't charge more than two-thirds of the amount that a solicitor would have charged for handling the case.

IF YOU LOSE YOUR CASE

The main ways to limit your liability for legal costs are:

- by using the small claims procedure, if your claim is for damages only and the financial limit is appropriate to your case

- by applying for legal aid if your case is to be heard by trial and you decide to employ a solicitor

- by considering whether you could handle your own case, particularly if the defendant is not employing a solicitor; you can employ a solicitor to advise you (you may be eligible for legal advice and assistance – see p 21).

The civil court system

England, Wales and Northern Ireland have the same hierarchy of courts, as follows:

MAGISTRATES' COURT

Few cases of the kind covered by this book are likely to be heard in a magistrates' court; exceptions include complaints about noise.

COUNTY COURT

The court in which most civil claims are heard. Judgement may be given by a judge or a registrar (a junior judge), depending on the nature of the case; claims heard under the small claims procedure (see p 36) are nearly always conducted by a registrar. Members of the public are entitled to attend county court hearings, but arbitration is conducted in private.

HIGH COURT

Claims for debts and damages over £5,000 and claims for defamation (libel or slander) go straight to the High Court. It also handles appeals against decisions in the magistrates' courts and, in some cases, the county courts.

COURT OF APPEAL

This court hears appeals against judges' decisions in the county courts or High Court.

HOUSE OF LORDS

With few exceptions, this is the supreme court. It hears appeals against decisions in the Court of Appeal (and, very rarely, the High Court), but only at its own discretion or if permission has been granted by the court against whose decision you are appealing. In cases concerning the law of the European Economic Community (EEC), the House of Lords can be overruled by the European Court of Justice (not to be confused with the European Court of Human Rights – see p 222).

SCOTTISH COURTS

In Scotland, most claims are heard in the Sheriff Court. Appeals are heard in the Sheriff Principal Court, then in the Inner House of the Court of Session in Edinburgh, thereafter in the House of Lords and, when relevant, the European Court of Justice.

How to start civil proceedings in the county court

Assuming your complaint is one that involves an infringement of a civil law, and you have given the other party plenty of opportunity to put matters right, you can start civil proceedings. This involves the following stages.

1 Send a letter to the other party, by recorded delivery, telling them that if you do not receive a satisfactory response to your

complaint within the next seven days, you will start legal proceedings against them. You can ask your solicitor or consumer adviser to draft the letter for you.

2 Obtain a copy of the free booklet, *Small claims in the county court*, from your local Citizens' Advice Bureau or county court (its address is listed under 'courts' in the telephone directory); this sets out the small claims procedure in helpful detail, and also gives general information about the workings of a county court.

3 If you have had no satisfactory response to your warning letter, you should now compile the 'Particulars of Claim'. This document is intended to give the defendant enough information to understand the substance of your claim; it is not meant to be a complete statement of your case. Many county courts provide a simple form; or you can use plain sheets of paper. Type it (or handwrite it, if the result is legible), and make at least three copies: one for yourself, one for the court, and one for each of the named defendants (which the court will pass on for you). The following facts should be included.

■ In the top left-hand corner, type the name of the court where the case will be heard. You may have a choice, because this can be either the court for the area where the defendant's business is located (if it is a registered company, this will be the location of its registered office, which should be shown on its stationery; if a firm or partnership, it can simply be the location of the branch you dealt with); or the court for the area in which the events leading to your complaint took place. Choose the one most convenient for you to attend; if you are not sure of its official name, ask at your local court.

■ In the top right-hand corner, type 'Case no.' with a space for the court to fill in the reference number.

■ Beside the heading 'Plaintiff', give your full name and address; beside the heading 'Defendant', give the other party's name and address. It is vital that the defendant's name and address are correct, and there are various ways of checking them. If he/she is a private individual, try the latest edition of the appropriate telephone directory or inspect the electoral register or rate books kept at the

Town Hall. If you are suing a registered company (does it have 'Ltd', 'Limited' or 'PLC' as part of its full name?), you must give its registered office address, which should be printed on its stationery; otherwise, ask the company directly or enquire in writing to the Registrar of Companies in Cardiff, Belfast or Edinburgh, who will charge a small fee (see Addresses, p 231). If your claim is against a partner in a firm, you must give either the firm's name or the names of all the partners. If you are suing a business which operates under a name other than that of its owner or partners, you must give the registered business name and address.

■ Under the heading 'Particulars of Claim', set out the facts of the case in numbered paragraphs as clearly and simply as you can. References to yourself and the other party should be made in the third person: 'the Plaintiff has suffered this', 'the Defendant did that', not 'I' or 'he/she/they'. The facts to include are:

- the circumstances and terms of the original contract (for example, if claiming for faulty goods, give the type of item, its model number if any, where and when it was bought and for how much; if for inadequate service, describe where, when and how the arrangements for the service were made, what was involved, and the cost that was agreed)

- the grounds for your complaint (keep this short – you'll have ample opportunity to explain the history of your complaint in person to the judge or registrar if the defendant disputes your claim)

- the law on which you are basing your claim, if appropriate (for example, the Sale of Goods Act 1979)

- the remedy you are seeking: if claiming damages, distinguish between the different aspects of your claim and quote a precise amount where possible (for example, the cost of repair; the expenses you have incurred); and state that the plaintiff is claiming damages plus costs (meaning the legal costs), also whether you wish the case to be heard by arbitration if the defendant disputes your claim.

■ Insert the date.

4 Obtain a 'request for summons' form from your local county court; to get the right form, tell them whether the court you have chosen to hear the case is in the area where the defendant lives or works; and whether you are claiming only money – in which case, you require a 'default summons' – or something else – in which case, you require a 'fixed date summons' (see below for an explanation of the difference). Also check with the court the fee you must pay them to issue a summons; the amount will depend on the size of your claim (if you win, you may get it back from the loser).

5 Take or send to the court where the case is to be heard:

- at least two copies of the Particulars of Claim (one for the court, one for each defendant)

- one copy of the completed request for summons form (keep a copy for yourself)

- the court fee.

The court will serve the summons on the defendant(s) by post. If this proves a problem – for example, the summons is returned to sender – the court bailiff can serve it in person (there is a fee for this of £5 – again, claimable from the loser). In either case, you will be informed by the court of the date on which the summons was served.

After the summons is served

What happens next depends on the type of summons served.

Default summons

The defendant has fourteen days in which to respond, in one of four ways.

■ By admitting liability and agreeing to pay your claim in full. He/ she may propose to pay you the money in instalments rather than as a lump sum; you can dispute this but it will be up to the court, having considered the matter at a special hearing attended by both parties, to specify how quickly the money is paid.

■ By defending the claim, setting out the grounds for the defence; or, more unusually, by making a counterclaim against you. In either case, the court will send you a copy of the defendant's reply and will set a date for both parties to attend the court, usually for a preliminary hearing.

■ By contacting you (or your solicitor, if you are using one) with a proposal to settle out of court. The defendant will usually offer less than you are claiming, and you'll have to weigh up the pros and cons; by all means try to negotiate a higher figure and remember to include in your calculations the costs you have incurred in starting proceedings, such as the court fee. Perchance the case still comes to court, cover yourself against the defendant's use of any negotiating letters you write by heading them 'without prejudice'. If you reach a settlement out of court, the money must still be paid into the court rather than direct to you; check that this has happened before you write to the court to tell them that you wish to drop the proceedings.

■ By ignoring the summons, in which case you have automatically won and you should ask the court to 'enter judgement'. To do this, you complete and return a simple form, obtainable by post from the court if you send a stamped addressed envelope. If part or all of the damages you are claiming have to be assessed by the court, you must apply for an appointment with the registrar.

Fixed date summons

If a fixed date summons was served (because you are claiming something other than, or in addition to, money), then it will have specified a date, usually about six weeks ahead, for a court hearing which both parties must attend. This is what is commonly known as a pre-trial review, and it is conducted by the registrar. If the defendant does not attend, you may be able to obtain judgement if you can prove your case to the registrar's satisfaction – so make sure you take along all your evidence. If both parties attend, the registrar will discuss the case with you and see whether an agreement can be reached without trial. If it cannot, the registrar will be concerned to see that both parties understand the procedures they must follow and will discuss plans for the trial. You can ask to see copies of any relevant documents held by the other party, or for further details about their case (the defendant can ask the same of you).

The small claims procedure

Also known as arbitration (but not to be confused with voluntary or compulsory arbitration schemes run by trade associations and other organisations – see p 25), the small claims procedure was set up in England, Wales and Northern Ireland to provide a simpler and cheaper way of settling a dispute than embarking on a formal court case.

The main advantages of arbitration

■ It is simpler, because it is less formal than a trial. Arbitration is conducted in private, and the parties usually sit round a table. Unless both sides have agreed on the appointment of an outside arbitrator, because they feel that the case requires specialist knowledge, the court registrar conducts the hearing. Witnesses may or may not be asked to take the oath, and the strict rules of evidence which apply in a trial are relaxed so that, for example, documents and descriptions of conversations can be more freely referred to. The arbitrator also has greater freedom than a judge presiding over a trial in deciding how the hearing should be conducted; it may even be held in your home, if this is necessary in order to inspect crucial evidence (for example, damage caused by faulty workmanship).

■ It is cheaper because, with few exceptions, you will not be liable to pay extensive costs if you lose. As plaintiff in a claim for less than £500, the costs for which you are liable are:

●   the costs listed on the summons (the court fees)

●   any costs which the arbitrator certifies have been incurred as a result of unreasonable conduct on your side in relation to the proceedings or the claim.

The main disadvantages of arbitration

■ If you are unhappy with the arbitrator's decision, you have little chance of getting it reversed. You would have to show that the arbitrator conducted the hearing improperly or that the decision involved an error such as an inconsistency with the proven facts. Before lodging an appeal, you should take legal advice.

■ You must limit your claim to £500 (£300 in Northern Ireland), excluding court costs. However, if the other party agrees, you can apply for arbitration in cases involving a higher amount; then solicitors' costs can be claimed by the winner unless both parties have agreed to exclude them.

In Scotland

At the time of writing, Scotland has no equivalent to the small claims procedure, though government proposals to introduce such a scheme are likely to come into effect in 1986. Currently, all claims of up to £1,000 are heard in the sheriff court under the summary cause procedure, which can also be used for non-damages claims. The main drawback of the summary cause procedure is that legal costs are allowed; this means that, if you lose, you will be liable to pay all the expenses of the case – the winner's as well as your own – and these can be high if solicitors have been employed. A free booklet explaining and describing the summary cause procedure is available from sheriff courts (see under 'courts' in the telephone directory), Citizens' Advice Bureaux and other consumer advice centres.

Getting your money

If you are successful and obtain an award for damages, you should normally receive the money from the court within three weeks or so, unless the court has ordered that it be paid in instalments. If, however, the loser fails to pay up, you will have to go back to court to get the judgement enforced. This will cost a fee that varies with the method of enforcement you select; you have a choice of five:

- a warrant of execution against goods: in other words, sending in the bailiff to seize the debtor's possessions, which are then sold by public auction. In practice, most debtors pay up before their goods are collected

- attachment of earnings: this method can be used if the debtor is an employee (this includes directors of companies); the court orders the employer to make deductions from the debtor's pay and pass the money to the court

- garnishee proceedings: if someone else owes the debtor money, they can be ordered to pay it to the court instead (or as much of the debt as it needed to pay you). In practice, this is usually used to obtain money held in the debtor's bank account

- charging orders: if the debtor has an interest in any land or securities, for example he/she owns a house or flat, the court can order that the debt is paid from the proceeds of any sale or disposal of such property, otherwise that the buyer becomes responsible for the debt

- appointment of a receiver: if the debtor owns a business or property from which he/she derives an income, a receiver can be appointed to collect the income in order to pay your debt.

Of the five methods available, the first three are quite straightforward, but the last two require specialist knowledge and you should consult a solicitor before using them. If one method fails, you can try another; but this can be costly.

Details of how to apply for enforcement are given in a free booklet, *Enforcing money judgements in the county court*, which you can obtain from your local county court, Citizens' Advice Bureau or other consumer advice centre.

When group action is appropriate

So far in this opening section, the emphasis has been on how you, as an individual, can make a justified complaint and seek to have matters put right. In certain circumstances, though, you may stand a better chance of success if, instead of going it alone, you join with others in some form of group action.

For group action to be appropriate, your complaint must be about something that directly affects a number of other identifiable people. It may be about the poor standard of teaching at your child's school, or the local authority's proposal to re-route heavy traffic down the residential road in which you live, or the Post Office's announcement that it intends to close your local branch. The more private the circumstances in which your complaint arises, the less likely it is that group action will be possible or effective. For this reason, group action tends to be most useful in disputes with public bodies or large organisations rather than with individual traders, and in bringing about changes in existing or planned policy rather than seeking damages or other forms of personal compensation.

The pros and cons of group action

■ A group of people voicing a complaint together usually has a greater chance of being heard and listened to than a few isolated individuals. This is particularly true when the person or body in a position to put matters right is accountable or vulnerable to public opinion, for example a local councillor or MP, or a well-known company with an image to protect.

■ A group of people can draw on a range of skills and useful contacts. One or two members may be particularly good at presenting the group's case and at dealing with counter-arguments; another may know a reporter on the local paper willing to publicise the issue in an article. People with more specialist skills – in financial management, for example, or able to design publicity material such as pamphlets – may be persuaded to give their services on a voluntary basis.

■ An individual is more likely to be demoralised, even defeated, by repeated setbacks; whereas members of a group can encourage and support each other, as well as sharing in the work. This makes them more resilient and better able to fight bureaucracy's favourite and perhaps most powerful weapon, delay.

■ To be effective, a group must be well-organised and efficient. This will require considerable work and commitment from its members – so don't make the mistake of thinking that group action is a way of getting others to do all the work while you sit back and wait for results.

■ In working as part of a group, you may find that some of your views, for example about the methods it should use or the way it should react to offers of settlement, are ignored or outvoted. Accepting the need for a certain amount of compromise, however frustrating, may be necessary if the group is to present the strong and united front on which its power depends.

Canvassing initial support

How do you find out how many other people share your grievance and how far they'd be prepared to join you in taking positive action about it? In many cases, you'll have some idea from conversations with neighbours, friends or, if it concerns employment, your colleagues at work. There may be an opportunity, for example at a parent–teacher, tenants' or union branch meeting, to raise the issue formally or sound people out casually. If no such ready-made channel of communication exists, one of the cheapest ways of inviting support is to have a letter published in an appropriate publication's letters page – most local newspapers have one – in which you can briefly describe the reasons for your complaint, explain how the issue affects other people, and ask them to contact you direct to discuss possible action.

Once you've established that a number of other people also feel strongly about the issue, you can start to discuss how best to work together towards achieving your common goal. Many of the methods you can use and the rules and guidelines you should follow are generally applicable, even though the scale of the operation will vary with the nature of the complaint and the number of people willing to become involved.

General guidelines for organisers

■ Hold a preliminary meeting to be attended by people who have responded to the suggestion of group action and indicated a willingness to get involved. Give everyone an opportunity to express his/her views. Consider electing a committee which would be responsible for the day-to-day organisation of effort needed to carry out the wishes of the group.

■ Prepare a statement that briefly sets out your group's aim, the reasons for the complaint and, if possible, the time in which you reasonably expect something to be done about it. This is a good way of discovering any basic differences of opinion or uncertainty about the issues involved that should be tackled at this early stage; and you'll also end up with a useful summary of your group's intentions.

■ Take steps to find out who is *really* responsible for putting matters right and consider how best to approach them. If a complaints procedure exists, try that method first, unless the problem necessitates a more urgent response.

■ Before taking any action, find out whether there are any legal restrictions you should observe so that you don't unwittingly lay yourselves open to being sued or prosecuted.

■ If you need to raise money to support your campaign, get sound financial and legal advice before you start (preferably from professional people willing to give their services free or at discount in aid of your good cause!).

■ Remember that publicity can be one of your most effective weapons, both in drumming up wider support or raising funds and in forcing the responsible person or authorities to react.

■ Seek support from people who can influence public opinion and whose social standing or relevant qualifications command respect. This makes it much more difficult for the other side to dismiss your group as a bunch of politically-motivated extremists.

■ A petition is likely to have real impact only if you can get either

100 per cent support from those affected (for example, all the parents of children attending a school threatened with closure) or a really impressive number of signatures; otherwise, the time it takes would be better spent on other campaign work. If you do organise a petition, it should carry a simple statement of your request at the top, preceded by the words, 'We, the undersigned, ask [the title of the person being petitioned]'. People should give their addresses and occupations as well as their signatures. You can collect signatures in the street, but take care: you may risk being had up for obstructing the highway. When you present the petition, turn it into a publicity event by inviting the local press and getting someone well-known to deliver or accept it (for example, a petition to the Secretary of State for Education could be accepted at the House of Commons by your MP).

■ In many cases where group action is appropriate, part of your case may be that the other side is abusing its power or ignoring society's notions of common justice and fair play. In order not to lose your moral advantage, make sure the group's behaviour is always decent, honest and, other than in exceptional circumstances, legal.

■ There are two sides to any argument. You'll have a better chance of winning it if you find out what the other side is likely to say, both in its own support and to undermine your case. You can then prepare yourselves with relevant evidence to support a counter-argument.

Publicising your cause

The purpose of publicity is to present your case clearly and convincingly to the people whose support can help you to win. It is *not* true that all publicity is good publicity; careful thought and meticulous planning are needed when selecting which methods to use. Whenever possible, you should avoid causing inconvenience other than to those responsible for provoking your complaint, or you risk alienating potential supporters.

PUBLIC MEETINGS

Public meetings have a number of uses. First, they suggest the level of support for your cause in that particular community. This is useful if the complaint concerns the absence or threatened withdrawal of a local service or amenity, the quality of the neighbourhood's environment or any issue that could involve a locally elected representative such as a councillor or MP. Second, they provide an opportunity to convert the undecided by explaining your case more fully than is possible in a leaflet or newspaper article. Third, they can encourage and inform existing supporters. Fourth, they can provide an opportunity for raising funds.

A number of factors affect the success of a public meeting.

■ The venue: find somewhere pleasant, convenient to reach, just large enough for the number of people you expect, with adequate seating and any other facilities you require. If it is hired, let the owner know in writing the reason for the meeting and the expected attendance level so that ignorance of these facts can't later be used as an excuse for withdrawing permission.

■ The agenda: the meeting may attract more people if, in addition to the two key components of speeches and the answering of questions, it offers a degree of entertainment – a film or slide show, for example, or a drinks party afterwards.

■ The speakers: choose effective speakers and, if possible, get someone well-known to address the meeting in support of your cause – your MP, perhaps, or a local celebrity. Speeches should be kept brief, and the audience given every opportunity to ask questions and so get involved. Make sure that the speakers are comfortable – provide a glass of water and a lectern on which they can rest any notes – and audible (by microphone, if necessary, in which case check *before* the meeting starts that it works).

■ The audience: for a public meeting to be a success, it must be well attended by the people at whom it is aimed. This means advertising it in advance, for example in the local press and on leaflets and posters (see p 46); it also means fixing the meeting for a day and time that will be most convenient for the intended audience, and even taking into consideration rival attractions such as television programmes. When they arrive at the meeting, members of the audience must feel welcome; stewards and other officials should be friendly and helpful, seating arrangements for the speakers and audience should avoid a 'them and us' impression (have the speakers on the same level as the audience, not 'talking down' from a platform or barricaded behind a table) and there must be a reassuring sense of organisation and purpose.

■ The publicity: invite the local press (from radio and television as well as newspapers). If they don't attend, write your own report of the meeting in the form of a brief article and get it round to the editors the next day; newspapers may be able to use an illustration, for example a photograph of the main speaker.

As far as the law is concerned, you don't have to get permission from the police to hold a public meeting, though it is advisable to consult them in advance. You should also check with your local authority in case there are any bye-laws regulating public meetings in your area. You can charge for admission if you wish (make this clear in any advertisements or advance publicity); and you can also refuse admission (as long as you do not do so on racial or sexual grounds).

MEDIA COVERAGE

Getting your cause covered in a newspaper or radio or television programme is a very cost-effective way of reaching the general public. Few of us would deny that our opinions are considerably affected by what we do – and don't – hear or read in the media, and most of us are more inclined to believe what we judge to be an objective report in the 'free press' than we would a statement produced by an interested party. A newspaper article can therefore give your case extra weight and significance – even if it simply reproduces, almost verbatim, a cleverly written account that you have supplied.

Getting national media coverage is very difficult, because there is so much competition. Causes where such coverage would be appropriate and possible are unlikely to fall within the scope of this book, however, so the tips that follow relate to getting local media coverage.

■ Establish good contacts with the reporters covering local news or the subject to which your complaint relates. Invite them to come and talk to you personally about your cause. If possible, engage their sympathies, but also make it clear why your case is newsworthy: an article that will interest only a handful of readers or listeners won't get past the editor, however strongly the reporter may support you.

■ Be accessible to the media at all times: let them know who in your group they should contact for statements or reactions to events (if possible, give two names and telephone numbers). Needless to say, your spokespeople should be well briefed, articulate and confident.

■ Local newspapers in particular are often short of news and so are receptive to ideas for one story or a series of articles. They may also be short-staffed and be happy to get purpose-made copy, written in that paper's style and to an appropriate length, rather than assigning a reporter to cover the case. Make sure you know what deadlines are involved.

■ A photograph with a brief caption may be of more help to an editor than another article (though not, of course, to the editor of a radio programme!). If no-one in your group is willing and able to act as an unpaid photographer at the events you arrange, consider hiring a professional. Aim for a lively, interesting picture that has immediate impact and which also makes a clear statement about your cause.

■ If you are able to enlist the support of any well-known people, find out if they are willing to get involved in publicity work such as appearing on a local radio or television programme, as well as attending any public events you organise.

■ Without losing sight of your objectives, find new angles to your story. This is particularly important if your campaign lasts months or even years, and you want to keep the media interested in your cause.

■ Real-life examples of how the circumstances of your group's complaint are affecting people's lives are more likely to attract the media's attention and the public's sympathy than just an abstract discussion of the principles and policies involved.

PAMPHLETS AND POSTERS

Although the media constitute a useful publicity tool, you cannot control their coverage of your case in either quality or quantity, and so you may consider producing your own printed material, in the form of leaflets, news sheets or posters. Such material requires careful thought, particularly about its design. Whether you distribute it in the streets or through people's letter boxes or display it on notice boards or hoardings, it will be jostling for attention with all the other printed matter around. A powerful photograph can help, as well as a clever use of typefaces and layout. Don't try to cram in too much information; it is better to be brief and simple, making it clear how the reader can find out more or join your campaign.

As far as the law is concerned, you can distribute or sell printed material such as leaflets in the street as long as you don't cause an obstruction. Posters can be stuck up in public places if they are an advertisement for a political, social, educational or religious meeting (which should cover any public meeting in the context of this book), if they are no larger than six feet square, and if they don't obstruct the highway (check with your Town Hall that they don't have any additional bye-laws you should observe). You are not allowed to stick up posters on private property without the owner's permission (by doing so, you risk a hefty fine).

DEMONSTRATIONS

Holding a demonstration may seem like a good way of getting into the headlines, but there are a number of disadvantages. It will require considerable, detailed planning and careful control if you are to avoid laying yourselves open to police prosecution. You run the risk, particularly if the demonstration includes a procession through the streets, of alienating members of the public who suffer delay and inconvenience as a result of your action. If attendance is poor – perhaps because of bad weather – you weaken your demand to be heard. These drawbacks are sufficient to make demonstrating a last-resort method of publicising your cause.

As far as the law is concerned, you do not need permission to hold a demonstration or march in the streets, although there may be bye-laws in your area that require you to notify the police – check with your Town Hall. The police have powers to regulate the route you take, and may, if there are grounds for believing that the demonstration could lead to serious public disorder, impose other restrictions, for example on banners and placards. You must also give the police forty-eight hours' notice if you intend to use a loudspeaker; even if you have done this, you could be charged with creating a public nuisance. If the demonstration takes place on private property without the owner's permission, the owner can use 'reasonable force' to eject the trespassers, and sue them in the civil court.

Many of the laws which you and your supporters might infringe in the course of a peaceful procession or meeting are enforced at the discretion of the police, whose powers in this area are both wide and loosely defined. It is therefore sensible to consult the police beforehand and, wherever possible, comply with their requirements and suggestions. The organisers of a demonstration are not themselves liable for any criminal or civil offence that takes place during the march or meeting, unless they are personally responsible; however, if only to avoid bad publicity, every attempt should be made to maintain close discipline and encourage a reasonable, good-humoured atmosphere.

When planning a demonstration, work out how to exploit its publicity potential to the full:

- invite the press along, and employ your own photographer as well

- make sure that any placards or banners are legible from a distance and instantly understandable

- have plenty of leaflets to distribute which clearly explain the reason for your demonstration

- consider featuring some sort of eye-catching, relevant and possibly humorous 'gimmick' that will grab people's attention and make a good photograph (don't be afraid to show a sense of humour even when your cause is serious – some light relief can be a welcome break for all concerned, and shows that you are reasonable people, not single-minded fanatics)

- ask well-known people who support you to attend, and make sure the press can take photographs of them.

Goods

Every year, hundreds of thousands of complaints about goods are reported to Citizens' Advice Bureaux and local authorities, and many more go unreported because they are settled privately or the customer drops the claim when the seller proves uncooperative. This section looks at the various causes of dissatisfaction with goods, the ways in which you can make an effective complaint and the compensation you can expect; and it also considers special circumstances which can affect your rights and the procedure you should follow.

The basis of your rights when buying anything from a bar of chocolate to a new car is the law of contract, discussed in Part One. There are also a number of other laws which set out to protect the consumer when buying goods, of which the most important is the civil law set out in the Sale of Goods Act 1979. It is worth familiarising yourself with the principles of this Act, because the knowledge will help you in three ways:

- you'll be able to assess whether you have the right to make a complaint (there are circumstances in which you do not, even if the goods are faulty)

- you'll be better equipped to tackle any attempts to duck responsibility or fob you off with inadequate compensation

- you'll be forewarned about the factors that could affect the strength of your case, should a dispute arise, so that you can take steps to put yourself in a strong legal position.

Your rights under the Sale of Goods Act

This law states that, when you enter into a contract with a trader (that is, someone selling the goods in the course of a business), certain terms are implied in the transaction and do not have to be mentioned by either party, in speech or in writing. The four key terms are:

- the trader has the right to transfer the goods to you (for example, they aren't stolen)

- the goods correspond with the description

- the goods are of merchantable quality

- the goods are fit for their purpose.

Accurate description

A description can take several forms: a label, words printed on packing material, a display sign, a shop assistant's statement about the goods. It might refer to the colour, size, quantity, place or year of manufacture or composition of the goods. A sweater labelled '100 per cent wool' must not contain any other kind of fibre; 'pine-scented bath salts' must not smell of lily-of-the-valley; a toy marked 'made in Great Britain' must not have been made in Taiwan.

Merchantable quality

This means that the goods are in a suitable condition to be sold, and match the standard that could be reasonably expected, given the price being charged, the description that is applied to them and any other relevant circumstances. You can therefore demand a higher standard from an expensive item than you can from a cheaper version bought in a sale or second-hand. For example, if you order a new washing machine, having seen a sample model in a shop, and discover on unpacking yours that it is scuffed and scratched, then you can reject it. If, on the other hand, you buy a machine marked 'shop-soiled' and offered at a discount, you have implicitly accepted a lower standard of finish. It is assumed, though, that the machine will still carry out its proper function; even a heavily discounted washing machine bought from a trader must be able to wash clothes.

The price and other circumstances, such as whether the goods are new or second-hand, will also affect the standard of performance and the length of useful life you can reasonably expect of your purchase; an eight-year-old car that has done 45,000 miles can't be expected to perform as well or last as long as a brand-new car, though you could expect it to be in better condition than an identical model of the same age which has clocked up 120,000 miles.

Fitness for purpose

Although the rules about description and merchantable quality might seem to cover fitness for purpose, this implied term relates to circumstances when you let the seller know, either expressly or by implication, that the goods are being bought for a particular purpose, even if they are not normally put to that use. For example, if you tell an assistant in a do-it-yourself shop that you wish to use the paint you have selected for decorating the inside walls of a fireplace, you are implying that you need a paint able to withstand higher-than-usual temperatures. If the assistant says nothing, or remarks that it should be all right, and you go ahead only to find that the paint blisters in the heat, you can claim damages (see p 57). However, if the assistant warns you that the paint may not be suitable, or simply admits ignorance on the matter, you take the risk and have no claim against the shop if it doesn't work.

When the Sale of Goods Act may not protect you

The terms laid down in the Sale of Goods Act do not apply to all types of transaction, and there are also circumstances in which you could lose your right to reject faulty goods.

■ Goods bought from a private seller (see pp 84–86) rather than from a trader do not have to be of merchantable quality or fit for the purpose, though they must correspond with the description.

■ If you buy goods in the course of a business (see p 86), or pretend to be doing so in order to get a better deal, the trader may be able to limit your rights by putting exclusion clauses (see pp 4–5) in the contract that overrule the implied terms (such clauses are invalid and illegal in consumer deals). However, in the event of a dispute, a court will subject any exclusion clause to a test of fairness.

■ Exclusion clauses are also allowed when goods are sold by auction, and usually seek to limit your right to complain about faults (see p 86).

■ Any specific defects in the goods which the trader points out to you, in speech or in writing, before the sale is made cannot then constitute grounds for rejecting the goods, regardless of the price you paid.

■ Similarly, if you examine the goods before buying them, you cannot later reject them because of any defect which you should have noticed during the examination. To avoid forfeiting your rights in this way, you should either decline to examine the goods or make a thorough inspection; in some cases, you might agree to look at those parts which you feel you'd be able to recognise as being of merchantable quality (take care to make the extent of a limited examination clear to the trader – preferably in front of a witness, otherwise you should note the basis of your acceptance on the invoice).

■ Only the person who bought the goods can claim if the trader fails to fulfil the implied terms of the contract; for example, if a woman buys her husband a camera, and pays by cash or a cheque from her own personal bank account, she will have to make the complaint if the camera turns out to be faulty. (In Northern Ireland, however, the husband, wife or child of the buyer can claim, if the goods were bought expressly for them.) For more about gifts, see p 89.

■ The goods must not have been damaged in any way after you bought them, even accidentally – so don't tinker with faulty goods in the hope of mending them yourself, thinking that you can still take them back if your attempt proves unsuccessful.

■ The claim must be made within six years (five in Scotland) of your having bought the goods, even if the length of useful life you can reasonably expect of them is longer.

Adding to your rights

Most purchases we make are adequately covered by the implied contractual terms already discussed, but in some instances it is necessary to specify or agree to additional 'express' terms. For example, the law assumes that it is the buyer's responsibility to collect the goods; if you want them to be delivered, you will have to arrange this with the trader, and check whether an extra charge will be made. The law does not say how quickly goods should be supplied, just that it should be within a 'reasonable' time; if you want them by a particular date, you must make this part of the contract (see 'Complaints about late delivery', p 65).

Before buying goods, always consider whether there are any ways in which you can add to the rights already given you in law; the trader may be happy to accept them in order to get your custom, as long as your demands are reasonable. For example, if you are buying a new pair of curtains but you need to check that they match your sitting-room carpet, ask if you can buy the curtains 'on approval', on the basis that you can return them within three days, say, if they prove unsuitable, and get a refund. To safeguard yourself in the event of a dispute over express terms, put them in writing on the order form or invoice. Make sure that you observe any conditions such as time limits, or you will lose the additional right you have negotiated.

Manufacturers' guarantees

Many manufactured goods are offered with a guarantee or warranty of some kind, giving you additional rights to those set out in the Sale of Goods Act and other consumer laws (there is some doubt as to whether guarantees are enforceable in law, but in practice most manufacturers observe the promises they make in such documents). Guarantees usually cover faulty parts or faulty workmanship, and the manufacturer may offer to repair or replace defective goods if notified of the complaint within a certain period after the date of purchase (a guarantee can last for any length of time, though twelve months is common). You may be asked to complete and return a card within, say, fourteen days of buying the goods, giving details such as the date and place of purchase, and your name and address; in practice, many manufacturers will honour a guarantee even if you have failed to do this, if you can provide some other evidence of the original transaction, such as a copy of the receipt.

Whether you should make use of a guarantee if goods prove faulty depends on a number of considerations.

■ If you bought the goods from a trader, you will probably have a claim under the Sale of Goods Act, in which case it is up to the trader to deal with your complaint regardless of whether the goods are under guarantee. This is usually your best bet but, if you decide to make use of a guarantee, the trader's responsibility is not diminished and you can always go back to him/her if the manufacturer doesn't offer you adequate redress.

■ A guarantee can be as generous or as limited as the manufacturer wishes (except that it cannot limit the manufacturer's liability for negligence – see p 7), and may be expressed in impenetrably legalistic 'small print'. It may not cover certain types of fault (second-hand car warranties often exclude clutches from an offer to replace defective parts), or it may make you responsible for the costs involved in returning the goods for repair, or the labour costs of fitting a replacement part. If you have a claim against a trader but decide to make use of a guarantee, perhaps at the trader's suggestion or because you think that this will be a quicker or more reliable way of sorting out the problem, then you could claim from the trader any costs such as postage and packing, or compensation for inconvenience, loss of use or damage to property, that are not covered by the manufacturer's guarantee.

■ In some cases, a guarantee may be more generous than a trader is legally obliged to be. For example, if you buy a clock which, given the type and price, might be expected to last for four years, you wouldn't be able to claim against the trader for a breach of the implied term of merchantable quality if it went wrong after five years; but you could claim against the manufacturer if the clock carried a guarantee for a six-year period.

■ If you have been given the goods as a present, you have no right against the trader who sold them (except in Northern Ireland, if the buyer was your husband, wife or parent, and the goods were bought specifically for you); however, you can make use of any guarantee supplied with the goods if they prove faulty and you don't wish to bother the present-giver.

■ Similarly, if you buy the goods from a private seller, you have little hope of redress if they prove faulty (see p 84), so it's a good idea to ask the seller at the time of purchase whether there is a guarantee, and when the goods were originally bought so that you know whether they are still within the guarantee period. However, a guarantee can specifically exclude second-hand goods.

■ If the trader from whom you bought faulty goods goes out of business or cannot be traced, a guarantee may be the only way of getting some form of redress.

■ If you bought the goods in another part of the country, on holiday perhaps or before you last moved home, it may be more convenient to deal with the manufacturer than with the trader.

Complaints about unsatisfactory goods

These are goods that do not live up to the customer's reasonable expectations, in most cases because the trader's obligations as laid down in the Sale of Goods Act have not been fulfilled. Remember that you cannot reject an item simply because you have changed your mind about buying it; you must stand by your side of the contract unless the goods are faulty in some way.

The quickest way to settle a complaint about goods is usually to take them back to where you bought them and complain in person, but if this is inconvenient you can telephone or, better still, write (see pp 9–13 for advice about making complaints). What you can claim from the trader for the breach of contract will depend on whether you have accepted the goods in the eyes of the law. Acceptance is indicated by any of the following:

- after discovering the fault, you have continued to use the goods or done anything else with them inconsistent with an intention to reject them and repudiate the contract

- you have failed to reject the goods within a reasonable time of receiving them, during which time you might be expected to have detected the fault (what constitutes a 'reasonable' time will depend on the nature of the goods and other circumstances, and can often be a matter of dispute)

- you have indicated to the trader in speech or writing that you have accepted the goods (for this reason, it is advisable when signing a receipt for delivery to add a note that the goods are 'received but not yet inspected').

Once you've made your complaint, what you do next depends on the response you get from the trader.

If your complaint is accepted

You have got over the first hurdle, and you now have to agree with the trader how you are to be compensated.

A FULL REFUND

If you made the complaint before you could be said to have accepted the goods, you are entitled to reject them and claim a full refund of the price you paid (the exception to this is in Scotland where, if the defect is a trivial one, you may only be able to claim damages). You can also claim for any extra costs you have reasonably incurred or losses you have suffered as a direct result of the breach of contract. For example, if your new cooker ruins a batch of cakes you have baked for your child's birthday party, you could claim for the price of the ingredients and the cost of buying

replacement cakes from a shop as well as the price you paid for the
cooker. However, you must not attempt to make a profit when
claiming damages, and you should take reasonable steps to limit
your losses. If your new medium-sized family saloon car breaks
down just before you set off for a holiday in Cornwall, don't hire a
Rolls Royce or decide to fly off to the Seychelles instead, in the
belief that you'll be able to claim it all back from the dealer.

DAMAGES

If you have accepted the goods, you have a right to claim damages
from the trader for the losses you have directly and reasonably
incurred as a result of the breach of contract. Your calculation could
include the following costs:

- for repairs needed to mend the faulty goods (the trader may
  offer you a free repair – see below)

- for any replacement hired while the goods are out of action

- for repairs or replacements required because of damage caused
  to property; however, this must be damage which could be
  foreseen as a natural consequence – for example, if your new
  bicycle's brakes fail and as a result you crash into someone
  carrying a box of expensive china which is smashed into
  smithereens, you cannot add the cost of compensating the
  china's owner to your claim for damages from the bicycle seller

- for extra outlay required to deal with the complaint, such as
  fares or postage

- for inconvenience and frustration suffered.

In cases where repair is inappropriate, for example if you have
bought a jacket which starts to wear out at the collar and elbows
sooner than it should, the damages will amount to the difference
between the value of the faulty item and what it would be worth
without the defect but allowing for a normal amount of wear and
tear – *not* what it would cost you to replace it with a new one.

FREE REPAIR

If you are entitled to a full refund, it is generally unwise to accept
an offer of free repair; but if you do, you should make it clear to the

trader in writing that you reserve your right to reject the goods if you are not completely satisfied with the repair or if it is not carried out within a reasonable time (you can give a deadline). A problem may arise later if another defect appears, because you will probably have lost your right to reject the goods by then.

If you are not entitled to a full refund because you have accepted the goods, you could either accept the trader's offer to put the fault right or, if you prefer, arrange for someone else to carry out the repair and send the bill to the trader. You must make sure that the bill is reasonable, so get several estimates which could be used as evidence if the bill is disputed.

A REPLACEMENT

You have no right to insist on a replacement, nor do you have to accept one, but in many instances this may suit both you and the trader best, particularly if you feel confident that the problems of the original were not basic design or manufacturing method faults. If the replacement also turns out to be faulty, your rights are the same as for an original purchase.

A CREDIT NOTE

This is a common response to complaints, because it is to the trader's advantage; you are unwise to accept it, particularly if you have the right to claim a full refund. If you are persuaded to accept a credit note, you won't be able to ask for a refund later if you can't find anything you want to buy at that price, and the likelihood is that you'll buy something you don't really need or want, just to use the note up.

If your complaint is rejected

A trader may refuse to accept your complaint in several ways:

- by telling you that the responsibility for the fault lies with the manufacturer

- by denying that there is a fault

- by saying that you caused the fault.

Do not be fobbed off with a suggestion that you should get in touch with the manufacturer; your contract is with the seller, even if he/she was ignorant of the fault. Sometimes confusion arises because the goods are under a manufacturer's guarantee, but any such guarantee can only give you additional rights over those you already possess in relation to the seller (see 'Manufacturers' guarantees', p 53).

If the trader attempts to deny that there is a fault, you may need to seek a second opinion, if necessary by having the goods examined by an independent expert. Some traders belong to a trade association that offers testing facilities as part of their conciliation service (see 'Getting help from a trade association', p 89).

Similarly, if the trader says that you caused the fault, an expert might be able to disprove this by examining the goods; alternatively, you might be able to call on a witness for support, for example a relative who was present when you discovered the fault.

Taking your complaint further

If you fail to get a satisfactory reponse to your initial complaint, either because the trader denies responsibility or because you are offered inadequate redress, don't be put off. Make your complaint in writing to someone more senior in the company, for example the chairman or managing director (see p 8). If you can't go up – for example, the uncooperative trader is the owner of the business – then you'll have to go out: to a trade association, if the trader is a member of one, or to a consumer adviser or solicitor, in the hope that they will be able to break the deadlock and help to arrange a settlement of the dispute out of court. If this fails, then you will have to consider suing the trader (see Part One for details).

Complaints about dangerous goods

There is no general law that all goods made or sold must be safe. However, if you buy or hire goods that prove unsafe – an electrical appliance that gives you a shock, or a toy which, when broken, contains dangerously sharp wires, or a bicycle with faulty brakes – then you should make a complaint and you may be able to claim damages for any injury or other loss caused. Who is responsible, and how you should make your complaint, will depend on a number of circumstances.

When the trader is responsible

The trader is obliged, under the Sale of Goods Act, to supply you with goods that are fit for the purpose and of merchantable quality; unsafe goods are likely to be inadequate on both counts, making the trader liable for breach of contract. If you buy goods that turn out to be unsafe, you can either reject them and claim a full refund, plus compensation for any costs or losses you have incurred; or, if you have accepted the goods (see p 56), you can claim damages. If you have been injured by the faulty goods, then you can claim appropriate compensation (you will need to get expert advice on this). However, anyone else who has been injured will not be able to make a claim against the trader under the Sale of Goods Act because they were not a party to the contract (except in Northern Ireland, if the injured person is the husband, wife or child of the buyer, and the goods were bought specifically for him/her); but they might have a claim against the trader for negligence (see 'The duty of care', below). Alternatively, they might have a claim against the manufacturer.

When the manufacturer is responsible

Under common law, manufacturers have a 'duty of care' (see below) towards anyone using their products, and may be liable to pay damages for any injury or loss caused by their failure to take reasonable care. However, the law requires the person claiming damages to prove that the manufacturer was negligent, and this can be difficult. The buyer who is injured or suffers a loss may have an alternative claim if the goods are under guarantee, as the manufacturer may then be in breach of contract; unfortunately, in such cases a guarantee does not protect anyone other than the buyer.

The duty of care

This law demands that anyone involved in putting goods into circulation – manufacturer, sub-contractor, importer, wholesaler, retailer – must take reasonable care to ensure that the goods will not cause injury or damage to people or property, assuming that they are used with reasonable care. In order to make a successful claim, you would have to show that

- the goods were defective

- the defect had caused injury to you or damage to your property

- the defect existed at the time the goods left the possession of the defendant

- you took reasonable care in using the goods

- the defect was not one that you, or a third party (for example, the retailer, if you are suing the manufacturer), could reasonably be expected to have noticed

- the defect was caused by the defendant's failure to exercise reasonable care.

If you think you have a claim for negligence, you should get legal advice (see 'Where to go for help and advice', p 13).

Legal safety requirements

Although there is no general law on safety, certain types of goods are covered by strict regulations (unless bought from a private seller or at a jumble sale, bring-and-buy or coffee morning sale). Products covered include a range of children's goods, from toys, anoraks and nightdresses to children's furniture and carry-cots; goods where there is a particular risk of fire or electric shock, such as electric blankets, gas, electric and oil heaters, inflammable upholstered furniture and domestic electrical appliances; and goods where poisonous substances may be involved, such as pencils and crayons, cosmetics, ceramic and enamel cooking utensils and medicines.

If you see or buy goods that you suspect fall below the standard of safety required by such regulations, then you should contact your local Trading Standards Department. If it finds that the regulations have been broken, it may decide to prosecute the trader in the criminal courts. If the prosecution is successful, you may be awarded compensation by the courts as a victim of the offence; and the conviction will give added weight to any claim you are making under civil law.

FOOD

The law is particularly strict about the standards of care and hygiene required in the production, preparation, storage and handling of food. Anyone who stocks or sells food (or drink) unfit for human consumption is guilty of a criminal offence, and should be reported as soon as possible to the local Environmental Health Department (listed in the telephone directory under the name of the local authority), which may decide to prosecute. If you have suffered food poisoning, evidence in the form of some of the food, or its after-effects, will help the department's analysts in their investigation.

You can also exercise your rights under civil law to reject the goods (unless you've already eaten them!) and claim a full refund plus costs, or to claim damages; and anyone else who suffers injury may have a claim for negligence. For example, if you host a wedding reception at a hotel and, as a result of eating contaminated prawn cocktails, you and several of your guests get stomach upsets, you can sue the hotel for breach of contract under the Sale of Goods Act and your guests might be able to sue the hotel, or anyone else involved in the supply of the faulty food, for negligence.

How to complain about dangerous goods

How you make a complaint about dangerous goods will depend on two factors: whether anyone has actually suffered injury or damage to property, and whether that person bought the goods. In any case involving dangerous goods, it is advisable to contact the appropriate department of your local authority (Trading Standards or, if the complaint relates to food, Environmental Health) as soon as possible, in case its inspectors wish to investigate the matter as one of public concern. Then:

- if you bought the goods, and you fortunately discovered the defect before any injury or damage was caused, you can make your complaint to the trader in person or in writing (see pp 9–13 for advice about making complaints) and either reject the goods, claiming a full refund plus costs or, if you have accepted the goods in the eyes of the law (see p 56), you can claim damages

- if the goods have caused injury, seek medical advice – not only to get any necessary treatment but also to provide evidence – and consult a legal expert about the amount to claim

- if you are making a claim for negligence, always consult a solicitor before you get involved in any correspondence or negotiations with the defendant.

Complaints about food and drink

These fall into a number of categories.

■ Complaints about food or drink that has gone off or is contaminated in some way: the law is very strict about food safety, and you should report such cases to your local Environmental Health Department, which may decide to prosecute the trader. Note, though, that a trader is allowed to sell goods past any 'Sell by' date marked on them, unless they have gone bad. (See also 'Food', p 62.)

■ Complaints about short weight or measure: complain first to the trader – a refund of the amount you were overcharged may be sufficient compensation. You can also report the case to the local authority's Weights and Measures Department (often part of the Trading Standards Department) which can prosecute the trader. Whether you decide to do this may depend on how accidental you think the mistake was.

■ Complaints about labelling: there are strict regulations about the labelling of food and drink, and about the accuracy of advertisements and promotional packaging material such as cartons which show a picture of the item. If you feel that food or drink has been misleadingly described in any way, or that the label information is inadequate, complain to your local Trading Standards Department.

■ Complaints about poor quality: if you are disappointed with food or drink you have bought in a shop or from a market stall, you can try taking it back if you can do this quickly. However, if it has not actually gone bad, and you did not make any contrary demand regarding its quality, nature or substance that the seller accepted, and there was no label or description which has not been observed, you may have little choice but to take your custom elsewhere in future or avoid that particular brand or variety.

If you are served disappointing food or drink in a pub, restaurant or similar establishment, you should make a complaint on the spot. Obviously, to have your complaint taken seriously, you should not wait until you've cleared your plate before calling the waiter over to say that the fish was grossly overcooked or the soup was too salty. In most cases, a polite but firm complaint will be accepted, and you can choose whether to accept a substitute dish. However, if you do not receive a satisfactory response, you may have a right to deduct a certain amount from the bill, as compensation. This is because the seller may be in breach of contract for failing to observe the implied term of merchantable quality (remember that this depends on certain factors, including the price charged, so that you can expect a higher standard from some types of establishment than others). Calculate what would be a fair deduction and explain, as calmly as you can, why you are refusing to pay the whole bill. If asked, give your name and address, preferably showing some proof of identity; it is also a good idea to show that you had the means to pay, had the quality been acceptable. It is then up to the trader to sue you to recover the money you have not paid. Don't be dissuaded by threats to call the police, who have no right to intervene in a civil dispute (though, if a breach of the peace is likely, they can get involved, so make sure you behave reasonably and non-violently).

Complaints about late delivery

If you have to order goods from a trader, it is advisable to agree a date by which they must be delivered at the time you place the order, and to note this on the invoice or order form. This makes the delivery date part of the contract; then, if the goods do not turn up by that date, you can cancel the contract and claim a refund of any money already paid.

If you don't specify a delivery date, the Sale of Goods Act merely says that the goods should be delivered within a 'reasonable' time; it is then up to you to decide when the delay has become unreasonable, and to notify the trader, in writing, that you are not prepared to wait much longer. You can, in effect, alter the terms of your original contract by stating that 'time is now of the essence' and giving notice that if the goods are not delivered within a specific period – fourteen days will usually be reasonable – then you will consider the contract broken. If the trader fails to meet this deadline, write again saying that you are withdrawing from the contract and claim a refund of any money you have paid.

Late delivery can also be infuriating if it involves broken appointments or wasted journeys. In theory, if late delivery forces you to cancel the order because of breach of contract, in addition to any refund due you can claim for wages lost (for example, if you take a morning off work to take delivery) or for costs such as telephone bills or fares incurred because of the delay. In practice, however, you may feel that the extra bother of claiming these damages is not worth it.

Complaints about prices

If you buy an item in one shop and then see an identical item at a lower price in another shop, all you can usually do is to kick yourself for not having shopped around; the only time you have a right to claim the difference is if the first trader displayed a notice offering to match any other trader's price for the goods you bought.

More surprisingly, a trader does not even have to sell you goods at the price at which they are displayed. This is because, in law, the display of goods and prices is merely an 'invitation to treat', rather than a definite offer. In practice, the price you are asked to pay is almost always the price displayed; but if the trader has displayed the wrong price – for example, a sales assistant has mistakenly written '£35' instead of '£55' on a price tag – you cannot insist on paying the lower price if the mistake is noticed before the sale is completed. However, if you suspect that the trader is deliberately trying to mislead potential customers about the prices they will have to pay, you should notify your local Trading Standards Department because the trader may be guilty of a criminal offence under the Trade Descriptions Act. Illegal practices include displaying prices to which special conditions apply (for example, that payment must be in cash) without clearly displaying these conditions beside the price.

Bargain offers

In an attempt to attract your custom, a trader may suggest that the price of an item is exceptionally low in comparison with the price usually charged. In order to protect customers from being misled about the value of goods, the law imposes restrictions on the wording of such claims so that the basis of the comparison between the stated price and any other price is made clear. Vague statements such as 'worth £50, only £35' or 'up to £5 off usual price' or 'reduced price £16' are illegal. The price labelling of sale goods is also regulated; in order for a price reduction to be shown, for example '£29.50, reduced to £15', the goods must have been on offer at the higher price, in that shop or another in the same chain, for a 28-day period during the previous six months. Unfortunately, enforcement of this law is difficult because it is up to the prosecution to prove that this regulation was not observed.

A trader is generally allowed to draw a comparison between the quoted price and the recommended retail price (RRP) or manufacturer's recommended price (MRP) of an item, for example 'RRP £340, our price £295'; however, such a comparison is not allowed in the case of beds and mattresses, furniture, carpets and domestic electrical or gas appliances such as washing machines, televisions and cookers. When an RRP or MRP is quoted, bear in mind that this is the value set on the goods by the manufacturer, not by an impartial assessor; and in some cases, manufacturers pitch the value high in order to give retailers an ample margin within which to fix their 'bargain' price and still make a good profit.

If you see a bargain offer which you feel is misleading, you should contact your local Trading Standards Department. If it decides to prosecute, and the trader is found guilty, you may be awarded compensation for any loss you have suffered, but this is at the court's discretion. You may also be able to sue the trader for breach of contract, on the grounds that the description of the goods was inaccurate; or for a breach of the Misrepresentation Act, a civil law which says that anyone selling goods must not mis-describe them in speech (see p 84).

Price increases

Once you agree a fixed price with a trader and you both enter into a contract on that basis, the trader cannot normally decide to increase the price, except to take account of a change in the rate of VAT (and payment made before the change, for example a deposit, is subject to the old rate). However, it is perfectly legal for a trader to include in a contract the proviso that prices are subject to increase without notice (for example, to allow for any increases in the manufacturer's price); in such a case, you are committing yourself to pay whatever increase is reasonable.

On the subject of VAT, it is assumed that any price quoted, whether given verbally or on price tags or in advertisements, includes VAT at the rate then current; a trader cannot increase a given price to take account of the tax unless the original quote specifically said that the price was exclusive of VAT (for example, 'all prices subject to VAT'). The prices displayed for food and drink on which VAT is payable (for example, in restaurants, cafés, pubs and take-aways) must include VAT, though the menu given to you inside the establishment can be VAT-exclusive if it makes this clear.

Complaints about lost deposits

If you order goods from a trader, particularly something custom-made or not normally stocked, or you ask a trader to reserve some goods to give you more time to make a decision, or you borrow goods for a short while – for example, a fabric sample book from an interior design shop – you may well be asked to pay a deposit. If you then decide not to go ahead with the purchase, or you do not return borrowed goods intact, the trader will usually have the right to keep all or part of the money, unless you agreed circumstances in which it would be returnable.

Suppose that you see a second-hand car for sale at what looks like a good price, and you ask the dealer to withdraw it from sale for three days so that you can arrange for a mechanically-minded friend to inspect it before you commit yourself. The dealer agrees to do this, if you leave a deposit. On inspection, however, the car turns out to be less of a bargain than it seemed, and so you decline to buy it. Whether you can then demand the return of your deposit in such circumstances depends on several factors:

- if you had agreed that the deposit was a prepayment, returnable in the event of no sale taking place, and you got the trader to write a receipt for the deposit making this condition clear, you can claim your money back as long as you returned within the agreed period

- if you had merely agreed to leave a deposit, without specifying circumstances in which it would be returnable, the trader could justifiably keep all or part of the money as damages against the loss suffered. In this instance, a nominal sum to represent lost selling time would probably be appropriate and the balance should be returned to you, but in other cases the trader might be able to claim not only the deposit but an additional sum.

It is advisable, therefore, always to get a receipt for a deposit, setting out how much you have paid, what it is for, any time limit you've agreed, and whether it is returnable. If you are leaving a deposit against an order for goods, you can specify a final delivery

date; if this is not met, you can claim your deposit back and cancel
the contract (see 'Complaints about late delivery', p 65).

Finally, a word of warning: recent figures published by the Office of
Fair Trading suggest that over 200,000 people a year are losing a
total of at least £18 million in advance payments to traders for goods
and services, in many cases because the trader goes bust. If this
happens, you are unlikely to be able to get your money back, so
only agree to leave a deposit if it is really necessary or you have
reason to feel confident about the trader's solvency. (For
prepayments on mail-order goods, see 'Goods bought by post',
pp 74–80.)

Goods bought on credit

Credit comes in many different forms, of which the most common
are credit cards such as Access or Barclaycard, charge cards such as
Diners and American Express, budget accounts operated by
individual firms or stores, hire purchase, conditional sale and credit
sale agreements, check trading schemes, bank loans and finance
company loans. The Office of Fair Trading has published a free
pamphlet, *Shop around for credit*, which contains useful advice about
how to choose the right form of credit and warns you about the
pitfalls (for how to obtain a copy, see p 241).

Generally speaking, your rights if you buy faulty goods on credit are
the same as when you pay the full price in cash or by cheque at the
time of purchase. In certain circumstances, and with certain types
of credit, they are actually strengthened. This is because, under the
Consumer Credit Act 1974, a credit company is equally liable, with
any trader with whom it has 'arrangements', for breach of contract
or misrepresentation, as long as the item cost more than £100 and
less than £30,000 and the credit or hire agreement was for no more
than £15,000. You will therefore have an alternative means of
getting redress if the trader is uncooperative or has disappeared

or gone bust. The only types of credit to which this bonus does not apply are

- personal loans, such as a bank overdraft, which were not supplied to finance a particular purchase (but if you have negotiated a bank loan specifically to buy a new car, say, then the bank is liable)

- hire purchase, conditional sale or credit sale agreements, where your claim is against the finance company involved, not the trader (see p 71)

- budget accounts operated by the trader concerned (because a third party is not involved)

- charge cards, where you have to pay off the whole debt every month (however, if you fail to do this and the card company decides to charge you interest rather than cancel the card, then it will become liable for defective goods bought after the interest charge is imposed).

Cooling-off period

The other main advantage of buying goods on credit is that it may give you an opportunity to change your mind about the purchase. This is because the law allows you a 'cooling-off period' during which you can cancel the deal, as long as the credit agreement was signed in your home or any premises not considered 'appropriate' (so avoid signing an agreement on the finance company's or salesman's premises) and as long as oral statements were made in your presence (this means you do not have a cooling-off period if you sign the agreement only on the basis of something you have read, or a telephone conversation). Any such cancellable agreement must contain a notice, printed in red, of your right to cancel, an explanation of when you may exercise it, and how to do so (including the name and address to whom your cancellation letter must be sent). If the agreement you are offered has no such notice, take care as you may be signing some other form of contract that does not allow a cooling-off period.

The cooling-off period runs for five days after you have received the second copy of the agreement (which must be sent to you by post), excluding the day of delivery. You must notify the appropriate person of your intention to cancel in writing; send the letter by recorded delivery if possible, and always keep a copy. The notification is considered to have been made when you post the letter, not when it is received – so if you receive the agreement on a Wednesday, you have until the last collection on the following Monday (or until midnight, if you have a witness that you posted the letter by then) to post your cancellation.

Hire purchase, conditional sale and credit sale agreements

In a hire-purchase agreement, you hire goods for an agreed period and pay regular instalments to the owner of the goods who then gives you the option to purchase the goods at the end of the period, or earlier if you pay off all the outstanding instalments. A conditional sale agreement is similar, except that you commit yourself to buying the goods. In a credit sale agreement, you also arrange to pay for the goods over a period but they become yours as soon as the agreement is made.

Some traders operate their own hire-purchase, conditional sale or credit sale schemes, but many simply act as intermediaries, putting you in touch with a finance company to which you pay the instalments. Technically, the finance company has itself bought the goods from the trader in order to be able to hire or sell them to you. This is an important point because, if the goods prove faulty, your claim will be against the finance company and not against the trader (unless you have a claim against the trader for negligence – see p 7). Although, if you have hired the goods, the Sale of Goods Act cannot apply, you have similar rights under another law, the Supply of Goods (Implied Terms) Act 1973. You can either reject the faulty goods and claim a full refund of any instalments already paid; or you can keep the goods and accept compensation, for example by opting to have the goods repaired at the hirer's expense. Make it clear in writing to the hirer that you are agreeing to the repair only on the basis that you reserve your right to reject the goods if you are not satisfied with the result.

Making a complaint about goods bought on credit

● in all cases where the trader is liable, you should make your complaint in the usual way, in person or in writing as appropriate

- if your complaint is not accepted or you cannot get a satisfactory response, or if the trader has gone bust or disappeared, check whether you have a claim against the credit company (see p 70 for the exceptions)

- if you do, write to the company setting out the details of your complaint, the steps you have already taken to claim against the trader, and the redress you are seeking

- if you stop paying any instalments due on the goods before your claim is settled, you may be in breach of your contract with the credit company, so it is usually best to keep up with the payments until your claim is settled

- if the credit company rejects your claim, or you are not happy with its offer, you should consult a consumer adviser (see 'Where to get help and advice', p 13).

If you are refused credit

Traders are not obliged to offer credit facilities, or even to accept cheques; but if they indicate that they accept certain credit or charge cards, for example by displaying the relevant stickers, they must allow you to pay in that way if you wish. However, a trader or finance company operating a budget account, hire purchase, conditional sale or credit sale scheme can turn down your application if they consider you uncreditworthy. They don't have to explain their decision but you can ask whether they have consulted any credit reference agency about you and, if they have, you have the right to check that the information held on you by the agency is correct (see p 225 for further details).

Goods bought in a sale

Your rights as a buyer to complain about, and if necessary reject, faulty goods apply to sale goods, but consider the following points before you make your complaint:

- you cannot complain about defects which were specifically brought to your attention before you bought the goods, or which you could have been expected to notice if you chose to inspect them (see p 52)

- 'merchantable quality' is linked to the description and price of goods; you cannot expect the same quality from sale goods marked 'seconds' or 'shop-soiled', or from a 'special purchase' item, as you could from a standard item reduced for stock clearance purposes

- if you reject the goods, the refund you can claim is the price you paid, not the non-sale price

- if you want a replacement, the trader, if agreeing to this, can insist that you pay the difference if the sale price you paid no longer applies.

The same basic principles apply to second-hand goods, except for those bought from a private seller (see p 84).

Goods bought as part of a service

If you employ a trader to do something for you, the work may well include the supply of materials; for example, a plumber hired to fit a shower in your bathroom may buy the shower fitment, and pass the cost on to you in the final bill for the job. If the fitment then turns out to be faulty, you have no claim under the Sale of Goods Act against the trader who sold it to the plumber. Instead, you must claim against the plumber and, under the Supply of Goods and Services Act 1982, you have the same rights in such circumstances as those set out in the Sale of Goods Act. (The Supply of Goods and Services Act does not apply in Scotland, where you'll need to get legal advice for complaints of this sort.)

If you instruct someone supplying a service to obtain a specific item – for example, a particular make or size – which then turns out to be unsuitable for the purpose, rather than faulty, you must take full responsibility for your mistake. For this reason, unless you are quite sure that your specification is correct, it is wiser to explain clearly to the supplier the purpose of the goods and any special requirements you have, but leave them to recommend a choice.

Goods bought in part-exchange

For certain types of goods, such as cars and cookers, it is common for traders to agree to part-exchange, knocking off some of the purchase price in return for the item you are replacing. It is up to you and the trader to agree on the value of the traded-in goods, and the amount should be noted in writing, for example on the order. As a private seller, you are not liable for the quality of the traded-in goods except insofar as you describe them, in which case you would be liable for any mis-description under the Misrepresentation Act (see p 84).

Should the goods you buy in any part-exchange deal with a trader prove faulty, then you have your usual rights against the trader (or, in some cases, against a credit company – see 'Goods bought on credit', p 69) to reject them or claim damages. The goods you traded in must be returned in substantially the same condition as when you handed them over, or you must be paid the cash value they represented – hence the importance of noting this in writing. (The Sale of Goods Act implied terms do not apply to part-exchange contracts in Scotland, where you'll need to get legal advice if you have a complaint about goods bought in this way.)

Goods bought by post

Open any magazine, newspaper or colour supplement and you are likely to find a wide selection of more or less glossy advertisements for goods which you can order by post. Traders who sell goods in this way or via mail-order catalogues have the same obligations to buyers as those selling goods through shops or showrooms. With the exception of advertisements in catalogues, they also have to observe the British Code of Advertising Practice, which says that all advertisements (other than free leaflets posted or given to you) must be legal, decent, honest and truthful. The Code, which is enforced by the Advertising Standards Authority (see p 212), sets out additional regulations if you pay money in advance in response to an advertisement:

- if the ad promises to refund your money if you are not satisfied, this must be done; and in any case you can claim a refund if you return the goods undamaged within seven days of receiving them

- with a few exceptions, such as plants and made-to-measure goods, your order should be delivered within twenty-eight days of the trader receiving it; if this deadline cannot be met, the trader must at least acknowledge your order and give you a despatch date, and you can insist instead on cancelling your order and claiming a refund

- if you have to return goods because they are not 'as described', you can claim the carriage cost (post, packing, insurance).

Any refund should be made as soon as the supplier receives the returned goods or your legitimate request for payment, and cannot be in the form of credit notes or vouchers unless you ask for them.

If you have a complaint about an advertiser who infringes the Code, write to the Advertising Standards Authority. Complaints about radio and television advertisements should be sent to the Independent Broadcasting Authority, which administers a similar code. (See 'Addresses', p 231.)

In addition, you may have a further means of redress if you buy from a mail-order trader who belongs to a trade association with a code of practice, and in some cases the newspaper or magazine in which the advertisement appeared can come to your aid.

Buying from a catalogue

Many of the firms that produce illustrated catalogues belong to the Mail Order Traders Association (MOTA), and are committed to following its code of practice. This code, which is referred to in their catalogues, sets out certain standards covering accuracy of information, delivery, the return of faulty or unwanted goods and after-sales service.

If you have a complaint about the goods or service you have received from a MOTA member, you should start by writing to the company itself (if you have been dealing with one of its agents, ask him/her to write); the Association's code instructs its members to deal with complaints speedily and sympathetically. Identify the catalogue in which you saw the goods, and state the date on which you sent your order, and whether it included any payment. If you do not receive a satisfactory reply, you may find that a local consumer adviser can help, for example by writing to the firm. You can also ask the Association to investigate your claim (see 'Addresses', p 231); and, if court action appears necessary, you can decide whether to opt instead for the Association's arbitration scheme (see 'Code of practice arbitration schemes', p 26).

Buying books and records through the post

Traders who offer to supply books or records through the post often advertise their goods in newspapers, magazines or brochures. Many of them belong to the Association of Mail Order Publishers, which has a code of practice setting out certain standards covering

- advertising: any advertisement must make the main terms of the offer clear

- information: details such as quantity, quality, price and payment terms must be clear and accurate

- prices: any additional charges, such as postage and packing, must be given clearly

- unwanted goods: if goods are sent to you 'on free approval', the trader must meet the cost of return postage; goods must not be sent unless an order has been received

- cancellation: if you commit yourself to buying a number of items over a long fixed period – for example, one book every month, for at least eighteen months – then you have the right to cancel after twelve months, or at any time if prices rise unexpectedly

- delivery: if you are asked to pay in advance, a despatch date must be given, and any undue delay explained.

If you have a complaint about the goods or service you have received from a member of the Association of Mail Order Publishers, you should start by writing to the company itself. Include details of where you saw the advertisement, the date on which you sent your order, and whether you have made any payment. If you do not receive a satisfactory reply, you can seek help from a local consumer adviser. You can also contact the Association (see 'Addresses', p 231); it may be able to act as conciliator, though it does not offer an arbitration scheme.

If the company has gone out of business, you may be able to claim back any money you have lost from the newspaper or magazine in which you saw the advertisement (see below).

Buying through newspaper and magazine advertisements

Most established magazines and newspapers take part in schemes which protect readers' money in certain circumstances if a mail-order supplier who has advertised goods in their pages goes out of business and fails to fulfil the orders. These schemes only cover what are called 'display' advertisements; they do not cover small ads that appear under headings in the classified columns. The ad must have asked for money in advance, and must have advertised the goods themselves, not a catalogue from which you then order the goods.

If the goods do not arrive within twenty-eight days of the trader's likely receipt of your order, or you have not received a satisfactory explanation of the delay, you should write to the newspaper's or magazine's advertisement manager. Do this as soon as possible, because there is a time limit on claims:

- if the ad appeared in a daily or weekly newspaper, you must claim within three months of the date of publication

- if it appeared in another publication, such as a magazine, you must claim within two months of the date you sent the order.

Your letter should include details of when the advertisement appeared, the advertiser's name and address (even better, enclose a copy of the ad – see 'Sensible precautions when buying by post', below), the date you sent your order, the amount you paid, a copy of any receipt you received, details of the goods ordered, and the name and address to which they were to be sent (plus your own name and address, if this is different). The newspaper or magazine will then check whether the trader has gone out of business and, if this is the case, will ask you to submit a formal claim, together with some proof of the payment you have lost.

Premiums

Premiums are goods that are offered to buyers at a low or no price, if they place an order for other goods. For example, a book club may offer you a hardback book, with a published price of several pounds, for 95p, if you enrol as a member. This form of sales promotion is covered by a code of practice, which lays down certain rules:

- premium goods should be supplied by a date stated in the advertisement, and certainly within twenty-eight days; otherwise, you must be given the opportunity to cancel your order

- if the supplier sends the goods but you tell them they have not arrived, they will normally be considered lost in transit and replaced free of charge

- if you pay anything for the goods, and they prove faulty, your rights are the same as if you had paid the full price

- if the goods are free, and they prove faulty, you have no legal right to make a claim but the code of practice says that they should be replaced.

In some cases, premium goods are supplied by a company other than the one making the offer; however, unless the supplier's full name and address is given, your claim will be against the mail-order company. Write, giving details of your order and any payment sent. If the response is unsatisfactory, it will seldom be worth taking legal action; but you can complain to the Advertising Standards

Authority (see 'Addresses', p 231) who may be able to put pressure on the trader.

Sensible precautions when buying by post

- read advertisements for mail-order goods carefully, and check that the newspaper, magazine or catalogue was published recently – otherwise the details may be out of date

- check whether the newspaper or magazine carrying the ad has a readers' protection scheme

- be wary of classified advertisements, particularly those placed by private sellers (see p 84)

- consider whether the goods might be just as easily available from a local trader, at much the same price – buying them in person may be quicker and less risky, particularly if the mail-order supplier requests your money in advance

- if you order goods by post, keep a copy of the advertisement and make a note of when and where it appeared. If you have to send off part of the ad itself, keep a separate note of any important details it carries, such as the advertiser's name and address

- keep a note of the date on which you send the order

- always include your name and address in any correspondence with the supplier and keep copies of all your letters

- if you have to send payment in advance, do not post cash; send a cheque (crossed and endorsed 'Account payee only') or a postal order. Fill in the details on the cheque stub or counterfoil – this could be valuable evidence of payment in the event of a dispute

- if you buy mail-order goods on credit, you may have a right to claim against the credit company if something goes wrong (see 'Goods bought on credit', p 69)

- if you return goods, send them by recorded delivery and, if appropriate, take out insurance (see p 12)

- if you have second thoughts, you can avoid entering into a binding contract if you can contact the supplier by post or telephone before the goods are despatched or a letter accepting your order is posted.

Unsolicited goods

Sending people goods which they have not ordered, in the hope that they will decide to buy them (or will be misled into thinking that they are legally obliged to pay for them) is now a rarely used sales method. If you receive unsolicited goods, the law (which is set out in the Unsolicited Goods and Services Act 1971) allows you to keep them, without payment, if

- you did not receive them in a professional capacity; and

- you do not agree to accept or return them; and

- the supplier does not collect the goods within six months (but you must not unreasonably refuse to allow the collection); or

- you write to the supplier, stating that the goods are unsolicited, and giving your name and address; the supplier then has thirty days in which to collect them, after which they become yours.

Until the goods become legally yours, you will be liable if you use or deliberately damage them, but not if you lose or accidentally damage them.

Any document you receive which gives the price of the goods or in any way attempts to elicit payment must state, in red, 'This is not a demand for payment; there is no obligation to pay' and, diagonally across the document, 'This is not a bill'; otherwise, the supplier is committing a criminal offence. It is also illegal to threaten legal or other action, such as debt collection. In either case, you should complain to your local Trading Standards Department which may decide to prosecute.

Goods bought in your home

Your rights when you buy goods from a trader who sells them to you in your home are the same as when you buy them from a shop. The main problem you are likely to encounter if the goods prove faulty is tracing the trader to make your complaint. Whenever you buy goods in this way, make sure you take a note of the seller's name, and the name and address of the company he/she is representing.

It is wise to be cautious before agreeing to buy goods over the doorstep, or you can end up paying for something you don't really want, or getting a worse bargain than you could find elsewhere. This is because the seller can put pressure on you in a number of ways, without doing anything illegal.

■ Clever sales patter may mislead you about the real purpose of the seller's call – a claim to be conducting some kind of research or survey is a common disguise. This indirect approach is more likely to persuade you to listen instead of immediately saying 'No, thank you' and shutting the door; and the longer the seller can engage you in conversation, the greater his or her chances of making a sale.

■ Seeing you in your home gives the seller useful information about you, so that the sales talk can be carefully tailored to your suggested 'needs'. If you haven't already considered buying goods of the kind being offered, it's probably because you don't need them. If you've any doubts, don't commit yourself: think it over, get advice, shop around. If you think the goods being offered to you may be the best available, you can always telephone the seller's head office and arrange a return visit.

■ If you allow the seller past your door, you can find it much more difficult to end the conversation because you feel you are being rude to a guest in your home. The seller may try to exploit your natural good manners by being particularly friendly and sympathetic; calling you by name, drinking a cup of your coffee, sitting in your chair are all ways of setting the relationship on a more personal footing, making it more embarrassing to ask them to go. Always

remember: they are there to sell you something, and you should
have no more qualms about asking them to leave than you would in
leaving a shop if you couldn't find what you wanted.

■ If you allow a seller to talk to you for some time, don't feel guilty
about 'wasting' his/her time if you finally want to say no; if
anything, you are the one whose time has been wasted.

■ If you are asked to sign anything, the seller may tell you it's just a
formality, in the hope that you won't read the document
thoroughly. Never sign anything you haven't read or don't
completely understand; say that you need time to discuss it, for
example with your husband or wife, and if necessary show it to your
local consumer adviser. Never sign an uncompleted form, or a slip
that says you are satisfied with the goods unless you have received
and inspected them.

Party plan selling

Party plan selling is a method of selling goods direct through an
agent who holds a private party at which goods are displayed and, if
relevant, demonstrated to potential customers who attend as invited
guests. Goods bought in this way are covered by the same laws that
apply to goods sold in shops.

Around thirty companies who sell goods on a party plan basis or
through doorstep sales representatives belong to the Direct Selling
Association. The range of items they offer includes cosmetics,
jewellery, cookware, books, clothes and porcelain ornaments. The
Association has drawn up a code of practice, in consultation with
the Office of Fair Trading, which contains guidelines for the
education and training of sales personnel, advertising, insurance
and indemnity arrangements, the provision of written guarantees
and customers' cancellation rights (you must be given a minimum
of fourteen days in which to cancel your order, and any deposit
you've paid will be refunded). There is also a complaints procedure
which guarantees to resolve any complaints within a maximum of
eleven weeks after the Association has received your complaint, in
writing; this service is free. Details about the code and the
complaints procedure, and a list of the Association's members, are

given in a free leaflet, *Shopping at home*, available from most consumer advice centres and public libraries, or direct from the Association (see 'Addresses', p 231).

Finally, a general warning: although many doorstep salesmen are genuinely trying to sell you goods, some have more sinister motives. Always ask to see identification and check it carefully (a visiting card can be passed to you through the letter box or, if you have a door latch, a gap in the door). If you have any doubts, either say you are not interested or ask them to wait while you telephone their head office. If you are really suspicious, ask them to leave and telephone the police.

Goods bought by telephone

This form of selling is more commonly used by suppliers of services, such as insurance or home improvement work, but, if you buy goods as a result of receiving an unsolicited telephone call, you enjoy the same rights as when you buy from a shop. Never agree to buy anything over the phone; if you are genuinely interested, ask the seller to send you details in the post or, if you prefer, make an appointment for a personal visit – particularly important if you wish to buy the goods on credit (see 'Cooling-off period', p 70).

At the time of writing, telephone selling is not subject to any specific legal restrictions but the Office of Fair Trading has drawn up some voluntary guidelines which you can expect a reputable trader to follow. They include

● no calls at your place of work

● no calls after 9 pm

● no calls to ex-directory numbers

● all calls to start with the caller explaining who he/she is and the purpose of the call

● a 'cooling-off period' to be allowed of seven days after the date when you receive any papers relating to goods you have agreed to buy over the phone.

The guidelines are being included by British Telecom in all new directories.

Goods bought from a private seller

Your rights when buying goods from a private seller are significantly fewer than when you buy from a trader. In particular, two of the four implied terms mentioned in the Sale of Goods Act, that the goods are of merchantable quality and fit for the purpose, do not apply to goods sold privately. For this reason, unscrupulous traders may try to pass themselves off as private sellers, for example by placing ads in the classified columns of local newspapers and specialist magazines which do not declare or make it obvious that they are selling in the course of a business – a practice made illegal in 1977 but which is still fairly common.

However, a private seller must have a right to transfer the goods to you, and the goods must correspond with the description. In addition, a private seller can be sued for misrepresentation.

Misrepresentation

A misrepresentation is a false statement of fact which influences your decision to enter into a contract of some kind. There are three kinds of misrepresentation:

- deliberate or fraudulent, when the person making the statement knows it to be untrue

- negligent, when the person making the statement has no good reason to think it true

- innocent, when the person making the statement has reasonable cause to think it true.

In any case involving misrepresentation, you will have the right to cancel the contract and get your money back if you act quickly, but be careful not to do anything with the goods which means that they can't be returned in the condition in which you bought them. In the case of fraudulent misrepresentation, not only you but anyone else who has suffered loss as a direct result of the fraud can claim compensation. Whether, if it's too late to cancel the contract, you can claim compensation in a case of negligent misrepresentation depends on whether the seller can prove the statement was innocent (except in Scotland, where it is up to the buyer to show it was negligent). In a case of innocent misrepresentation, you are unlikely to get compensation, should it be too late to cancel the contract, return the goods and get your money back.

Safeguards when buying privately

- if the seller has advertised the goods, keep a copy of the ad in case it contains any description which turns out to be inaccurate

- look for other ads which give the same name, address and/or telephone number – a sign that you may be dealing with a trader, in which case your local Trading Standards Department will want to be informed

- be very wary of buying goods which you haven't inspected carefully; if you don't feel confident that you will be able to spot any faults, take along someone who will

- in any case, take a witness so that, if any of the seller's statements about the goods prove untrue, it's not just one person's word against another's (this is particularly important in Scotland, where the law requires evidence to be corroborated)

- ask the seller as many specific questions as you can about the goods, and make a note of the replies you receive. What you require are statements of fact, so that if the goods are faulty you may be protected by the law of misrepresentation. Opinions are not covered, so phrase your questions carefully; if you are considering buying a second-hand car, for example, don't be satisfied with remarks like 'It shouldn't give you any trouble' – ask specific questions such as when and where it was last serviced, how old the battery is, or whether it's been damaged in any accidents

- check whether the goods are still under a manufacturer's guarantee as this could prove helpful if they are faulty (see p 53).

Goods bought in the course of a business

If you buy goods in a professional rather than a private capacity, or you pretend to be doing so (to get a discount, say), then you are not a consumer in the eyes of the law, and your rights are significantly less protected than those of a private buyer. In particular, the contract (which might be the trade order or receipt you receive or sign) can have clauses excluding the implied terms of the Sale of Goods Act relating to description, merchantable quality and fitness for purpose. However, the general rules about exclusion clauses still apply (see p 4) and so the seller must have brought any such clause to your attention before you made the contract, and the clause would have to meet a test of reasonableness. Nor could the seller use such a clause to excuse a fundamental breach of contract. You are also protected by the laws of misrepresentation (see p 84) and negligence (see p 6).

Goods bought at auction

If you buy goods at an auction which turn out to be faulty, you may have no right to complain. This is because it is legal for auctioneers to exclude the Sale of Goods Act implied terms relating to description, merchantable quality and fitness for purpose from their contracts of sale. Such exclusions must be brought to your attention either in a prominent notice in the auction rooms or in the conditions of business printed in the catalogue; they often take the form of a statement such as 'Goods must be taken as seen' or the annotation 'a.f.' ('as found') against particular items. Consequently, it is important that you examine carefully any goods you wish to bid for (viewing is normally allowed the day before or on the morning of the sale). If, however, the auctioneer makes an untrue statement about the goods, then you are protected by the law of misrepresentation (see p 84).

Stolen goods

If you buy goods which you later discover are stolen, you will usually have no right to keep them, and will have to hand them back to their rightful owner. If you have spent any money on improving or repairing the goods, you may be able to claim this from the owner; get legal advice in such circumstances before handing them back. If the goods cannot be returned, you will have to pay the owner compensation. In either case, you can then claim the price you paid for them from the seller, on the basis that he/she had no right to transfer the goods to you. If you are unable to trace the seller, or get the money back, you will have to resign yourself to losing out.

There are two circumstances in which, if you buy something in good faith, you can keep it if it turns out to be stolen:

- if you buy it in an 'ancient market' (one established by Royal Charter or custom) or within the City of London, between the hours of sunrise and sunset, while the market is open to the public, and in accordance with the market's customs

- if you buy a motor vehicle, such as a car or motorbike, which you then discover is subject to a hire purchase or conditional sale agreement on which instalments are outstanding and which therefore belongs to the finance company (see 'Goods bought on credit,' p 71). However, this only applies if you buy it as a private individual; dealers and companies would not have a right to ownership. To avoid problems, you can ask your local Citizens' Advice Bureau, or a motoring organisation if you are a member, to check on your behalf, as they have access to a national record of all hire purchase agreements.

Hired goods

When you hire, rent or lease goods in England, Wales or Northern Ireland, the Supply of Goods and Services Act 1982 states that your contract with the supplier includes the same implied terms that apply under the Sale of Goods Act to purchase contracts. You therefore have the right to return the goods and claim compensation if they prove unsatisfactory. For example, if you hire a car to go on a fortnight's holiday and it breaks down after the first week, you can claim a refund of half the money already paid to the hire company, plus foreseeable additional costs such as that of hiring another similar car for the second week, and compensation for the inconvenience and disappointment suffered by you and anyone else directly involved.

Many agreements between consumers and traders for the hire of goods involve detailed written contracts, and it is important to read such documents carefully. In particular, look out for clauses covering the hire charge, payment terms, arrangements for servicing and repairs, and the minimum period of hire (regulations set out in the Consumer Credit Act 1974 allow you to end the contract after eighteen months, whatever the contract says, unless the rental payments exceed £300 a year, in which case you must observe the agreement you have made). If you don't understand any of the contract, don't sign it; ask the trader to give you a copy and get your local consumer adviser to run through it with you. If you think that any of the terms are unreasonable, see if the trader will agree to delete them.

You must take reasonable care of goods you have hired or rented, because you will be held responsible for any damage they suffer as a result of your negligence. It is therefore sensible (and some hire agreements make it obligatory) to insure the goods, unless your existing insurance policies extend cover to goods not owned by you. You are not liable, though, for fair wear and tear.

Goods received as a personal gift

When you receive a present, you do not enter into a direct contract
with the seller and so you do not have any rights under the Sale of
Goods Act, should the item prove faulty (except in Northern
Ireland, if you received the item from your husband, wife or parent
and it was bought specifically for you). If you know where the gift
was bought, you can try taking it back in the hope that, for the sake
of goodwill, the trader will agree to change it (this may also be
possible if you simply don't like it, or it doesn't fit you); otherwise,
unless you ask the present-giver to make the complaint, you may
have no redress.

Circumstances in which you may have a right to complain and make
a claim are:

- if the present is under a manufacturer's guarantee (see p 53)

- if the present causes injury or damage, as a result of a fault
  arising out of negligence (see p 60).

Getting help from a trade association

If you have a complaint about goods, you may find that a trade
association can help if you don't receive a satisfactory response from
the trader concerned and your local consumer adviser isn't able to
bring about a settlement. However, a trade association can only
investigate your claim and offer to conciliate if the dispute concerns
one of its members. Most traders who belong to a trade association
indicate this, for example by displaying the association's logo on
their premises or mentioning it in their promotional literature. If
you have a dispute with a trader who belongs to more than one
trade association, don't fire off letters to all of them or you'll risk
confusion and delay; write to whichever seems most appropriate for
your complaint.

A number of trade associations have drawn up codes of practice in
consultation with the Office of Fair Trading. These set out

standards which, though they do not have legal status, encourage their members to provide customers with benefits over and above their minimum legal rights. Most of the codes also give the dissatisfied customer the option to have his/her claim heard by arbitration, though this may not always be preferable to taking the trader to court (see 'Code of practice arbitration schemes', p 26). You can get copies of the codes direct from the associations (see 'Addresses', p 231) and free pamphlets summarising each code's guidelines in addition to general useful buying advice are published by the Office of Fair Trading (for how to obtain copies, see p 241).

The types of goods covered by codes of practice drawn up in consultation with the Office of Fair Trading are: mail-order catalogue goods (see p 75), party plan selling (see p 82), cars, motorcycles, electrical goods, furniture, shoes, glass and glazing, and photographic equipment.

CARS

A code of practice containing guidelines for the sale of new and second-hand cars, spare parts and accessories is supported by the Motor Agents Association and its Scottish counterpart, the Scottish Motor Trade Association (which deal with complaints other than those about new cars) and the Society of Motor Manufacturers and Traders (which deals with complaints about new cars). An arbitration scheme is available if you wish to use it.

For complaints about car repairs and servicing, see p 105.

MOTORCYCLES

A code of practice containing guidelines for the sale of new and second-hand motorbikes, spare parts and accessories is supported by the Motor Cycle Association and its Scottish counterpart, the Scottish Motor Trade Association (which deal with complaints about new bikes), the Motor Agents Association (for any complaints about its members) and the Motorcycle Retailers Association (for any complaints about its members). An arbitration scheme is available if you wish to use it.

For complaints about motorcycle repairs and servicing, see p 105.

ELECTRICAL GOODS

A code of practice containing guidelines for the sale of electrical goods is supported by the Radio, Electrical and Television Retailers Association (RETRA). It applies to domestic appliances such as washing machines, refrigerators, electric cookers and toasters (known in the trade as 'white goods') and electrical goods such as televisions, stereo equipment and radios (known in the trade as 'brown goods'). RETRA does not have an arbitration scheme, but it does have a conciliation panel which can make a recommendation; if you are unhappy with its verdict, you can still take the trader to court.

For complaints about the repair and servicing of electrical goods, see p 106.

FURNITURE

A code of practice containing guidelines for the sale of furniture is supported by the National Association of Retail Furnishers (representing four big trade associations) and the Scottish House Furnishers Association. If appropriate, the furniture in question can be examined by an independent expert (you will have to pay a fee for this service – £14 at the time of writing – but this will be refunded if your complaint is upheld). There is also an arbitration scheme, should you wish to use it.

For complaints about furniture repairs, see p 106.

SHOES

A code of practice containing guidelines for the sale of shoes and other footwear is supported by the Footwear Distributors Federation, the Multiple Shoe Retailers Federation and the Independent Footwear Retailers Association. All complaints about members should be sent to the Footwear Distributors Federation. There is no arbitration scheme, but you can opt to have the goods examined by the Footwear Testing Centre; you will have to pay a fee, as does the trader (at the time of writing, you pay £3.50 and the trader pays £6.50, as well as arranging for the shoes to be sent to the Centre) but your money will be refunded if the Centre upholds your complaint.

For complaints about shoe repairs, see p 107.

GLASS AND GLAZING

A code of practice containing guidelines for the sale of glass and glazing – single and double glazing, replacement windows, mirrors, patio doors or whatever – is supported by the Glass and Glazing Federation and its Scottish counterpart, the Scottish Glass Merchants and Glaziers Federation. An arbitration scheme is available for claims not exceeding £10,000. Under the code, you also have some protection if you pay a deposit to a member who then goes out of business, through a Deposit Indemnity Fund; this will cover you for deposits of up to 25 per cent on a 'supply and fixing' contract and 50 per cent on a 'supply only' contract, as long as the total contract price does not exceed £6,000.

For complaints about the installation of glass of all kinds, see p 111.

PHOTOGRAPHIC EQUIPMENT

A code of practice containing guidelines for the standard of photographic equipment is supported by the British Photographic Association (representing manufacturers of film and equipment) and the British Photographic Importers Association (representing importers of film and equipment). An arbitration scheme is available. However, the Photocode, as it is called, does not cover the majority of retailers.

For complaints about repairs and servicing, as well as film processing, see p 107.

Practical services

What do a builder, an optician, an insurance company and the Gas Board have in common? Very little, except that they all provide a service. Complaints about services can arise in such a wide range of circumstances that, instead of considering them all in a single section, Part Three starts by looking at general principles that apply to the majority of services, and then focuses on the more practical kinds: the repair and maintenance of goods; home-related services including those provided by tradesmen, builders, architects, surveyors and estate agents; public utilities (telephone and postal services, electricity, gas, coal and water supply); leisure services such as hotels, pubs and holidays; and travel services such as buses, trains and taxis. In Part Four, you'll find details of the other main groups of services: those concerned with health and welfare, education, law and finance.

Your rights under the Supply of Goods and Services Act

If you arrange with someone for a service to be supplied, you are usually covered by the law of contract (see p 2 for an explanation of the five essential features that make an agreement legally enforceable). The Supply of Goods and Services Act 1982 sets out three important implied terms that are assumed to apply to a contract for services, whether written, spoken or silent, unless anything more specific is agreed between the two parties. These are that the supplier carrying out the service must do so

- with reasonable care and skill

- within a reasonable time

- for a reasonable charge.

(This statutory law does not apply in Scotland, where contracts for the supply of services are covered by common law. In the majority of cases, however, the net effect is the same.)

Useful though these implied terms are if you have a complaint about a service, clearly much depends on how the word 'reasonable' is interpreted.

Reasonable care and skill

This implied term gives you the right to expect the normal standard reached by others following that particular trade or profession. Being 'new to the job' or only part-time cannot be used by a supplier as an excuse for falling below the average level of competence. However, if you employ someone who does not profess to follow that particular trade – for example, you pay a fireman to help you move house – then you must be prepared to accept a lower standard.

If a trader fails to repair goods successfully, you may still have to pay a reasonable charge for the work and any materials used, unless you can prove that the repair could have been carried out by any competent member of the same trade. Any parts or materials used to carry out a service must be fit for the purpose, of merchantable quality and as described (see 'Goods bought as part of a service', p 73).

'Reasonable care' includes the supplier's duty to look after a customer's property. If you suffer loss or damage, it is up to the trader to prove that this was not caused by his/her negligence. For example, if your car was stolen while at a garage awaiting a service, the garage would have to show that it took reasonable steps to prevent the theft.

Reasonable time

Unless you have agreed a specific completion date, you can expect the service to be carried out within a reasonable time – as defined by the average time taken by other members of the same trade or profession for doing the same job. For example, if you employ a roofing contractor to re-tile your terraced house and, after putting the scaffolding up, the workmen disappear for several weeks, you have a right to complain and get some form of compensation even if you rashly didn't agree a completion date for the job.

Reasonable charge

It is sometimes impossible to agree a price for a service in advance because the nature and extent of the work required are unknown. For example, if your car refuses to start, it could take a competent mechanic a few minutes or several hours to detect the cause, and the repair might require new parts. If you simply ask someone to find out what is wrong and put it right, you will have to pay whatever they charge you, as long as it is reasonable – that is, the price that any other member of that trade or profession would charge for doing the same job. A safer alternative is to ask them to investigate the problem and give you a quotation or estimate (see p 97).

If you have a complaint about the amount you are charged, check the bill carefully in case it covers any work you did not authorise; if necessary, ask the trader to give you a detailed breakdown of the costs. If you find that, for example, a garage has fitted new tyres to your car when servicing it without first checking that you wanted them, you do not have to pay for them (though the garage can then remove the new tyres and put back your old ones).

Evidence in a dispute over implied terms

If you have a complaint about the standard of skill or care provided, or the time taken, or the price charged for a service, and you did not agree any express terms that specified what you expected to get, it will be up to you to show that the supplier is at fault, by providing evidence of what could normally be expected. The best way to do this is to ask other suppliers in the same trade or profession to assess the standard of what has been done, or how long they would have taken, or how much they would have charged

– and get them to put their observations in writing. You may well have to pay for this but, if you succeed with your complaint and get compensation, you can add the expense to the amount you claim in damages.

A relevant trade association or professional body may also be able to help define what is 'reasonable' in any case.

If express terms are agreed

Many contracts for services include express terms, which can be spoken – for example, you ask your hairdresser to style your hair in a particular way – or written. You should be particularly careful about agreeing to any express terms when entering a contract for services because, under the Supply of Goods and Services Act, the implied terms that would otherwise apply can be superseded by any more specific terms agreed by the two parties. For example, if you agree to pay a particular amount for a service, you do not have the right to cancel the contract or demand a deduction if you find that the going rate is much less, even though you might be able to argue that the price you have agreed is not a 'reasonable charge'.

Generally speaking, disputes over express terms in service contracts are not about whether they are reasonable, but about how they are to be interpreted. If the contract is spoken, misunderstandings can easily occur. The more specific you can be about your requirements when discussing the service, the better; although the law gives you some protection if you've failed to do this, prevention is better than cure. Make sure that you have a witness to what is said; even better, confirm the terms in writing (see 'Evidence of a contract', p 5). The main points to agree are

- what the supplier must do or provide
- when the service must be carried out: if possible, agree starting and completion dates
- who will carry out the work (for example, will sub-contractors be used?) and who will be liable if something goes wrong

- the nature and quality of any materials required

- the price and payment terms: if the job includes various elements, get the costs broken down (see 'Estimates and quotations', below)

- if a price cannot be fixed, any upper limit or authorisation procedure

- the guarantee terms, if any (see 'Guarantees', p 101)

- your cancellation rights, if any.

If you are presented with written contract terms – often included on a standard order form or other document under the heading 'Conditions of business', or as part of an estimate or quotation, or simply in a letter – read them carefully. If you are unhappy with any clause, see if the trader will agree to delete it. If you don't understand anything, or you are not sure whether the terms are comprehensive, or you suspect that they are biased in the trader's favour, get a second opinion before you accept them (see 'Where to go for help and advice', p 131). Make sure that any revisions and additions to the contract are confirmed in writing; this includes any changes that arise during the course of the service, for example if extra work is needed that will add to the agreed price and possibly affect the completion date.

Estimates and quotations

Getting at least an idea of the price of a service before you commit yourself is essential, if only to make sure you can afford it. It is also usually sensible to 'shop around' for services, just as you would when buying goods. Finding out the price can be straightforward if the elements of the service are fairly standard, for example if you want to check the cost of having your coat dry-cleaned or the tariff for a night's stay in a hotel. It becomes more complicated when the nature and extent of the service depend on your individual requirements. Then you will have to ask the supplier to give you an estimate or quotation (but remember to ask whether you will have to pay for this).

Usually, an estimate is just a guide to the likely final price whereas a quotation is a fixed price; however, there is some confusion between the two terms, so check which you are getting. If you are given a fixed price, the supplier cannot charge you more unless the contract states circumstances in which the price can change, or you alter the terms of the contract, for example by asking for some additional work to be done; but neither can you claim that you should pay less, for example if the job turns out to be less complicated than was anticipated. If the supplier is not willing or able to quote you a definite price in advance, get an estimate. You can safeguard yourself by making it a term of the contract that the supplier must seek your written permission to exceed the estimated amount; otherwise, you will have to pay whatever is reasonable, even if the final bill is higher. However, if the difference is significant, you should ask the trader to justify the increase. If it is due to the addition of VAT, and the original estimate did not specify that the price quoted was 'subject to VAT' or 'exclusive of VAT', then you can refuse to pay the extra.

Inaccurate or misleading estimates often result from a failure by either party to allow for all the elements of a service, so that 'extras' bump up the final price. A quotation also has to be based on agreed requirements; if you realise later that you've forgotten something, you'll have to negotiate a new or additional price. To avoid misunderstandings, help you reach your buying decision and provide you with solid evidence of your contract:

* compile a list of the various aspects of the job, and ask for the estimate or quotation to show the different elements separately, distinguishing between the costs of labour, materials and VAT

* if getting several prices for comparison, make sure that you give the same information to each supplier

* when you receive quotes or estimates, compare them carefully with your original list in case anything has been altered or forgotten – for example, part of the price is based on a different type of material to the one you specified; and if there are any technical terms or product names that you don't understand or recognise, ask the supplier to explain or show you a sample

* check for how long each price will hold good, and what payment terms are being offered.

Completion dates

If a trader states the time a job will take (for example, a sign says 'four-hour dry cleaning service'), this is an express term and you can either cancel the contract or claim damages, as appropriate, if it is not observed (see also 'Complaints about misleading descriptions', p 103). If you specify a completion date and it is not met, you can claim damages for breach of contract, but their extent depends on whether you made it clear to the supplier that time was 'of the essence', and that there were particular reasons for the date. For example, if you are having building work carried out which, to qualify for a local authority grant, must be completed by a certain date, tell the builder this in writing; then, if it becomes necessary to make alternative emergency arrangements to get the work finished in time, you should be able to claim the additional cost as damages for breach of contract.

If you make an appointment for a service, for example you arrange to be at home one morning for the plumber to call, you may be able to claim damages if the appointment is broken, both for any financial loss you have incurred as a direct and foreseeable result (for example, lost wages) and for inconvenience; but tell the trader when making the appointment if you have to make special arrangements to be available. In practice, the easiest way to get the compensation is to deduct an appropriate amount from the final bill.

Advance payments

Be wary of making any advance payments for services. If a job is going to take some time – for example, you are hiring a builder for several months' work – you may have to agree to pay the bill in instalments. Get these linked to the completion of different stages of the job, and don't pay out more than the value of the work completed. If you are asked to pay a deposit when booking a service – for example, a package holiday or a hotel room – get a receipt for it and be clear whether and on what terms the money is returnable, and how much of the deposit you will forfeit if you cancel your booking. Consider taking out insurance if the amount involved is significant.

Each year, considerable sums of money handed over as prepayments for services are lost because the traders go bust. The Office of Fair Trading has investigated this problem and supports the idea of bonding schemes (which guarantee to refund all prepayments for outstanding contracts) but, with few exceptions (see the section on package holidays, p 127), this form of protection is rarely available. Some trade associations have their own schemes for safeguarding their members' customers. An alternative is to make any prepayment using a form of credit that allows you to claim compensation from the credit company (see 'Buying services on credit', p 101).

Choosing a supplier

Standards of service can vary considerably within a single trade or industry, particularly those that do not require any kind of qualification or registration – so much so that cautionary tales about cowboy builders and incompetent garage mechanics have become part of modern folklore. Although there's no foolproof – or rogueproof – method of finding someone competent and reliable, you can take certain basic precautions:

- ask friends and acquaintances for their personal recommendations; and, where appropriate, ask potential suppliers to give you the names and addresses of people for whom they've recently done similar work

- if you receive an unsolicited approach – for example, someone calls at your home and offers to mend your roof, or telephones you to sell you double glazing – don't commit yourself before checking up on them: get their name and address, ask them for references, and *never* part with any money in advance (see also the advice given on pp 81–84 about buying goods at home and by telephone, most of which applies equally to services sold by these methods)

- give preference to traders who belong to a trade association; although membership is no guarantee of standards, it is a fairly sure sign that you aren't dealing with a rogue, and the

association may have a code of practice and a complaints
procedure that could help you in the event of a dispute

- consult any relevant guide books, for example when choosing a
hotel or camp site.

Guarantees

When buying a service, you may be offered a guarantee, either for
goods supplied as part of the service (for example, spare parts used
to repair your car) or for the service as a whole (for example, for
damp proofing or wood preservation treatment). A guarantee
cannot take away your basic legal rights; in theory, therefore, it
should provide you with extra benefits. However, its terms may be
very limited or set out rigorous conditions for making a claim, so
read them carefully before allowing the existence of the guarantee to
influence your buying decision. Long-term guarantees, which can
last for twenty years or more, may look attractive, but they are
worthless if the trader goes out of business (and unscrupulous
traders can easily evade their responsibilities to guarantee holders
by periodically closing down, only to start up again in the same
trade under a new name). As you'll see later in this section, some
trade associations, aware of this problem, have set up insurance
schemes to back their members' guarantees.

Buying services on credit

If you buy services using some form of credit – for example, a credit
card such as Access or Barclaycard, or a bank loan – you may have
an additional means of obtaining compensation, should the supplier
fail to meet his/her legal obligations. This is because, under
Consumer Credit Act 1974, a credit company is equally liable, with
any trader with whom it has 'arrangements', for breach of contract
or misrepresentation, as long as the service cost more than £100 and
less than £30,000, and the credit agreement was for no more than
£15,000. However, you cannot claim redress from the lender if the
loan was a personal one, such as a bank overdraft, rather than credit

specifically negotiated to finance a particular purchase, because in such cases there is no arrangement between the creditor and the supplier. Nor can you claim if the service was paid for by a charge card, such as Diners or American Express, which is supplied on the basis that you pay off the full debt every month (however, if you fail to do this and the card company decides to charge you interest rather than cancel the card, then it will become liable for any service contract made after the interest charge is imposed).

If you agree to buy a service on credit – for example, you sign a loan agreement to pay for the installation of double glazing – you may be able to cancel the deal, because the same rules apply as when you buy goods on credit (see 'Cooling-off period', p 70).

Making a complaint about services bought on credit

- in all cases where the trader is liable, you should make your complaint in the usual way, in person or in writing as appropriate

- if your complaint is not accepted or you cannot get a satisfactory response, or if the trader has gone bust or disappeared, check whether you have a claim against the credit company (see the exceptions mentioned above)

- if you do, write to the company setting out the details of your complaint, the steps you have already taken to claim against the trader, and the redress you are seeking

- if you stop paying any instalments due on the service before your claim is settled, you may be in breach of your contract with the credit company, so it is usually best to keep up with the payments until your claim is settled

- if the credit company rejects your claim, or you are not happy with its offer, consult a consumer adviser (see 'Where to go for help and advice', p 13).

Complaints about misleading descriptions

When choosing a supplier, you may well be influenced by the way the service is described, for example in an advertisement or brochure, or in the supplier's own statements to you. The description may refer to the provision of a service ('24-hour plumbing service', 'riding lessons available'), any features of the service ('indoor heated swimming pool', '4-hour dry cleaning service') or any qualification or third-party recommendation of the service ('a member of the Federation of Master Builders', 'listed in *The good pub guide*'). If you have entered into a contract as a result of a description that turns out to be false, you may be able to sue the trader for breach of contract if the description amounts to an express term. Additionally, the Misrepresentation Act 1967 allows you to cancel the contract and get your money back if you discover the falsehood before the service is provided; or, if it's too late to cancel, to claim damages if the false statement was made deliberately or negligently (see 'Misrepresentation', p 84).

Traders who make false statements intentionally or recklessly (that is, without taking steps to check whether a description is true) can be prosecuted under the Trade Descriptions Act 1968. If you think an offence has been committed, you should contact the local Trading Standards Department.

If a trader disclaims responsibility for the accuracy of any descriptions – for example, a brochure states that 'All flight times are subject to change without prior notice' – then, like any express term, the disclaimer is valid only if it was brought to your notice before you made the contract.

Complaints about the repair and maintenance of goods

Part Two dealt with complaining if goods prove faulty; this section deals with complaints about the standard of workmanship, price or time taken to carry out any repair or maintenance work.

Following the standard procedure outlined in Part One, start by making your complaint to the trader, either in person or in writing. If you haven't already paid the bill, you are in a good position to negotiate and you may be able to get the trader to accept a reduced price for the job. This is not so easy if the trader still has your goods, and refuses to hand them back until you have paid up. Then you have two choices of action:

- pay the bill, or whatever the amount the trader will accept, but put it in writing that you are doing so 'under protest' and 'without prejudice to my legal rights' in case you decide it is worth suing for compensation

- take your complaint to a consumer advice agency or solicitor (see 'Where to go for help and advice', p 13), or to a trade association if the trader is a member (see below), and see if they can exercise some pressure to bring about a settlement.

If problems arise after you have paid the bill – for example, your washing machine develops the same fault that had supposedly been mended a couple of months before – you should notify the trader as soon as possible, stating the date on which the original repair was completed and the invoice number, if any. A dispute may arise if the trader inspects the goods and declares that the fault has another cause which could not have been detected during the original repair; it may then be necessary to get a second opinion from another trader. If the fault is due to the original trader's incompetence, you can have the repair done elsewhere and claim the cost as damages; but your claim must be reasonable, so get several estimates which you could provide as evidence. If you have suffered any loss as a result of the poor repair, for example the washing machine has ruined a load of sheets, you can add this to your claim.

Trade associations and codes of practice

If you find yourself in a dispute with a trader who belongs to a trade association – membership is usually indicated by a display of the association's name or motif on the trader's premises or a statement in the firm's promotional literature – then you can complain to the association and ask it to intervene if other attempts at reaching a settlement have failed. If the trader belongs to more than one association, write to whichever seems most appropriate to your complaint.

A number of trade associations have drawn up codes of practice in consultation with the Office of Fair Trading. These set out standards which, though they do not have legal status, encourage their members to provide customers with benefits over and above their minimum legal rights. Several of the codes give the dissatisfied customer the option to have his/her claim heard by arbitration, though this may not always be preferable to taking the trader to court (see 'Code of practice arbitration schemes', p 26). You can get copies of the codes direct from the associations (see 'Addresses', p 231) and free pamphlets summarising each code's guidelines in addition to giving useful advice on buying services are published by the Office of Fair Trading (for how to obtain copies, see p 241).

The types of repair and maintenance service covered by these codes are: the repair and servicing of cars, caravans, motorcycles and electrical goods; the repair of furniture and shoes; laundry and dry-cleaning; and photographic services including equipment repair and film processing.

CARS

A code of practice containing guidelines for the repair and servicing of cars is supported by the Motor Agents Association and its Scottish counterpart, the Scottish Motor Trade Association. A third association, the Vehicle Builders and Repairers Association, has a code of practice covering body repairs to cars and caravans. Both codes provide an arbitration scheme.

For complaints about new and second-hand cars, spare parts and accessories, see p 90.

MOTORCYLES

A code of practice containing guidelines for the repair and servicing of motorcyles is supported by the Motor Agents Association and its

Scottish counterpart, the Scottish Motor Trade Association, and the Motorcycle Retailers Association. An arbitration scheme is available.

For complaints about new and second-hand motorcycles, spare parts and accessories, see p 90.

ELECTRICAL GOODS

There are four codes of practice containing guidelines for the repair and servicing of electrical goods:

- the code supported by the Association of Manufacturers of Domestic Electrical Appliances (AMDEA), which covers British domestic appliances – washing machines, refrigerators, electric cookers, toasters – made by a member of AMDEA who accepts responsibility for servicing them

- the code supported by the Radio, Electrical and Television Retailers Association (RETRA), which covers domestic appliances and electrical goods such as televisions, stereo equipment and radios which are serviced or repaired by a member

- the code supported by the Electricity Council, which covers domestic appliances serviced or repaired by an Electricity Board in England or Wales

- the code supported by the South of Scotland Electricity Board and the North of Scotland Hydro-electric Board, which covers domestic appliances serviced or repaired by either of them.

Arbitration schemes are available except for complaints made to RETRA, which instead provides an independent customer conciliation service; if you are dissatisfied with its recommendations, you can still take the trader to court.

For complaints about new domestic appliances and electrical goods, see p 91.

FURNITURE

A code of practice containing guidelines for the repair of furniture is supported by the National Association of Retail Furnishers (representing four big trade associations) and the Scottish House Furnishers Association. If appropriate, the furniture can be examined by an independent expert; you will have to pay a fee for the service – £14 at the time of writing – but this will be refunded if your complaint is upheld. There is also an arbitration scheme.

For complaints about new furniture, see p 91.

SHOES

A code of practice containing guidelines for the repair of shoes and other footwear is supported by the St Crispin's Boot Trades Association and the National Association of Shoe Repair Factories (NASRF). There is no arbitration scheme but both associations will obtain a free test report for you (you will have to pay for postage of the shoes to the Association).

For complaints about new shoes and other footwear, see p 91.

LAUNDRY AND DRY-CLEANING

A code of practice containing guidelines for cleaning, laundering, dyeing and repairs is supported by the Association of British Laundry, Cleaning and Rental Services (ABLCRS); it does not, however, apply to launderettes or coin-operated cleaners. There is no arbitration scheme, but the Association's advisory service will investigate your complaint and can arrange for the article to be tested at one of several independent research establishments; you will have to pay a fee for this but, depending on the result of the test, this may be refunded in whole or in part (some members offer testing on a 'loser pays' basis).

PHOTOGRAPHIC SERVICES

A code of practice containing guidelines for film processing, the repair of photographic equipment and the service of professional photographers is supported by the National Pharmaceutical Association (representing retail pharmacists), the Association of Photographic Laboratories (representing film processors), the Institute of Photographic Apparatus Repair Technicians (representing repairers) and both the Institute of Professional

Photography and the Master Photographers Association (representing professional photographers). An arbitration scheme is available.

For complaints about new photographic equipment, see p 92.

Complaints about home-related services

Finding somewhere to live, and then keeping your home in good running order, can involve considerable expense. Among the people whose services you may at some point need to employ are tradesmen of various kinds such as plumbers, heating engineers, electricians, gas fitters, decorators, glaziers and dampcourse or wood treatment suppliers; builders; professional advisers such as architects and surveyors; and, if you're buying or selling your home, estate agents.

The Office of Fair Trading publishes a useful free pamphlet, *Home improvements* (for how to obtain a copy, see p 241), giving advice about how to avoid common pitfalls and setting out seven 'golden rules' you should follow when thinking about home improvements:

- before you start, decide exactly what you want done; and for larger jobs, consider getting advice from an architect or surveyor

- ask your local authority whether you need planning permission or building regulations approval and whether you can get a grant towards the work

- shop around before making your decision; get written estimates or quotations from at least two firms

- find out as much as you can about a firm before committing yourself: can it cope with the job? If in doubt, get a second opinion

- make sure your contract is in writing and gives full details of prices, cancellation rights, guarantees and when the work will be started and finished. Check whether any sub-contractors are to be used and who is liable if things go wrong

- be wary of parting with money in advance, especially if asked to pay a large deposit. Always query any price increases and ask why they weren't included in the original estimate

- if you have a problem, act quickly and get advice from your local consumer adviser.

In addition to contacting your local authority, you may also need to warn your insurance company (if you have separate policies for building and contents, warn both insurers); otherwise, if something goes wrong (for example, you are burgled while building work has created a temporary access to your home), you may not be covered. You may also need to consult your mortgage company, particularly if it holds the title deeds to your home in case these include any restrictions. It is also a good idea to tell your neighbours if the work is going to create any temporary mess or noise, so that you aren't on the receiving end of a complaint!

If making a contract with builder, consider using one of the pre-printed forms supplied by the Royal Institute of British Architects or the Royal Institution of Chartered Surveyors (see 'Addresses', p 231.)

When complaining, follow the standard procedure outlined in Part One by giving the supplier an opportunity to put faulty workmanship right or offer you compensation, as appropriate. If you are dissatisfied with the response and your local consumer adviser can't help, check whether the supplier belongs to a trade association or professional body to which you can complain; the addresses of those mentioned in the following pages are given at the end of the book (see p 231).

Plumbers

There are three organisations that can provide a list of members in your area and will investigate any complaints about them: the Institute of Plumbing (membership of which requires a certain level of practical experience and specialist knowledge; registered plumbers can use the Institute's symbol in advertisements and should carry a pocket certificate); and the National Association of Plumbing, Heating and Mechanical Services Contractors and the Scottish and Northern Ireland Plumbing Employers Federation (both of which have codes of practice and offer arbitration). Some plumbers belong to the Federation of Master Builders (see 'Builders', p 112).

Heating engineers

The Heating and Ventilating Contractors Association restricts its membership to heating contractors who have been trading for a minimum of two years, and can provide good financial and customer references. Work is guaranteed for twelve months and the Association operates a free guarantee protection scheme. If you have an unresolved dispute with one of its members, the Association will investigate and, if both parties agree, the claim can be settled by arbitration.

Electricians

There are three electricians' organisations that will investigate complaints about their members: the Electrical Contractors Association, which can provide a list of its members in England, Wales and Northern Ireland, and its counterpart, the Electrical Contractors Association of Scotland (both associations have standard of work and contract completion guarantee schemes); and the National Inspection Council for Electrical Installation Contractors (you can get a list of its members in your area from your Electricity Board showroom or Citizens' Advice Bureau). All members of these organisations are qualified and must follow the Institution of Electrical Engineers' wiring regulations.

Gas fitters

By law, anyone who fits or repairs a gas appliance must be competent and carry out work that complies with Gas Safety and building regulations, but there is no statutory professional qualification. Many fitters are registered with the Confederation for the Registration of Gas Installers (CORGI); their work is inspected at least once a year, so you can have some confidence in their competence (a list of registered fitters is available at your local reference library, Citizens' Advice Bureau or Gas Board showroom). If you have a complaint about a registered fitter, contact your local CORGI office (there is one in every gas region) which can investigate the problem and, if necessary, arrange an inspection.

If you have a complaint about a Gas Board fitter, see p 121.

Decorators

The British Decorators Association, which has a code of practice, will investigate complaints about its members and, if appropriate, arrange an inspection (it may also be able to inspect non-members' work in the event of a dispute over 'reasonable standards'). It offers an arbitration scheme.

Glaziers

The Glass and Glazing Federation and its counterpart, the Scottish Glass Merchants and Glaziers Federation, have a code of practice drawn up in consultation with the Office of Fair Trading, outlined in a free pamphlet, *Double Glazing* (for how to obtain a copy, see p 241). This covers all types of glazing work, including the installation of single and double glazing, replacement windows, mirrors and patio doors. Both federations will supply a list of their members, and investigate complaints about them. An arbitration scheme is available for claims not exceeding £10,000. Under the code, you also have some protection if you pay a deposit to a member who then goes out of business, through the Deposit Indemnity Fund; this will cover you for deposits of up to 25 per cent on a 'supply and fixing' contract, as long as the total contract price does not exceed £6,000. (The code also covers the sale of glass and glazing when installation is not included – see p 92.)

Dampcourse and wood treatment suppliers

The British Chemical Dampcourse Association, which has a code of practice, will supply a list of its members and investigate complaints about them, as will the British Wood Preserving Association. The associations have also jointly set up a separate Guaranteed Treatments Protection Trust, which for a small fee will register any long-term guarantee you are given by a member firm and cover you for any claim during the life of the guarantee, up to a maximum of twenty years, in the event of the member going out of business. For details, write to the Trust direct (see 'Addresses', p 231).

Builders

There are several organisations to which builders may belong, and which should be able to provide you with a list of members in your area.

The Federation of Master Builders is an association of small and medium-sized building firms, all of which have employer's liability and public liability insurance. The Federation has nine offices throughout England, Wales and Scotland which will supply a list of members in their area and which will handle complaints about ordinary members. Some members, who have provided good financial references and who have been trading for at least three years, are registered members of the Federation's Warranty Scheme; work carried out under the warranty, up to a maximum value of £30,000, is guaranteed for two years against defects caused by faulty materials or workmanship (though temporary work, including roof repairs other than complete re-roofing, is not covered).

The Building Employers Confederation has member firms of all sizes, and you can get a list of those in your area from one of its regional branches. It administers a guarantee scheme which applies to improvements and extensions costing from £500 to £25,000 carried out by a member (but only if you deal direct with the builder rather than through a professional adviser such as an architect). The guarantee, which costs you 1 per cent of the total contract price (minimum fee £20), covers the cost of completing the work if the builder becomes insolvent; and says that the builder will put right any faults that occur up to six months after practical completion, and rectify any serious structural faults that occur within a further two years. You also get full insurance cover for damage to the work while it is being carried out. The maximum you can claim under the guarantee is £5,000. In the event of a dispute with the builder, there is a conciliation and arbitration service.

If you are buying a house that is less than ten years old, or having a new one built, check whether the builder is registered with the National House Building Council (NHBC), which enforces and guarantees certain standards. The NHBC will inspect the finished house to check that it meets its requirements and, if satisfied, will issue a Notice of Insurance Cover. This says that any defects which arise during the first two years (or first year, in the case of certain fittings such as central heating boilers) because of the builder's failure to comply with the NHBC standards must be put right by the builder free of charge. The NHBC provides a conciliation and arbitration service in the event of a dispute; and it will pay up to 90 per cent of the cost of rectifying the defects if the builder refuses to comply with an arbitration award or goes out of business. The NHBC also provides insurance cover for any major damage caused by structural defects that occur in the following eight years, again if they are due to the builder's failure to comply with its standards. If you make a claim, you will be charged an investigation fee, but this is refunded if your claim is found valid or reasonable. If buying a 'second-hand' house, the NHBC guarantee will not cover claims for any defects which the seller should have told you about or which should have been spotted by you or your surveyor at the time you bought it; if the survey reveals any claimable items, get the seller to notify the builder or NHBC about them in writing, even if the remedial work cannot be carried out before the sale is completed.

Architects

All practising architects must have specific academic qualifications and be registered by the Architects Registration Council of the United Kingdom (ARCUK), which enforces a guide to professional conduct. Any architect who is reported to ARCUK for a failure to observe the guidelines may be investigated; possible penalties include a reprimand and even, in serious cases, removal from the register (so that he/she is prevented from practising). Many architects also belong to professional bodies with a similar code of conduct: the Royal Institute of British Architects (RIBA), the Royal

Society of Ulster Architects (RSUA) and the Royal Incorporation of
Architects in Scotland (RIAS). These bodies can recommend
suitable architects in your area and will investigate complaints about
their members, though this can take several months and the RIBA
and RSUA will intervene only if both parties in a dispute ask them
to do so. Sanctions for breaches of professional conduct include
reprimands and explusion.

The professional bodies and ARCUK cannot handle all disputes,
only those which involve allegations of professional misconduct
(though RIAS will also consider claims that an architect has simply
been inefficient); nor can they award compensation to injured
clients. If you are seeking damages, either for breach of contract or
for negligence, you must take legal action. It is always advisable to
seek expert advice before suing anyone for professional negligence –
that is, if you are claiming that the architect has caused you
financial or physical loss or injury, by action or advice that falls
below the standard of skill and care you could expect from other
architects in those circumstances – as such claims are often
complicated and potentially expensive.

Surveyors

All practising chartered surveyors must have specific academic
qualifications and belong to the Royal Institution of Chartered
Surveyors (RICS) which enforces a professional code of conduct by
means of various sanctions including reprimands and explusion. A
list of RICS members is available in many public libraries, and you
can also write to the Institution asking for recommendations of
suitable surveyors in your area; members identify themselves by the
initials FRICS or ARICS after their names (depending on whether
they are Fellows or Associates of the Institute).

Surveyors who do not belong to the RICS can still practise, but they
cannot call themselves chartered surveyors; instead, they may
belong to the Incorporated Association of Architects and Surveyors
(look for the initials FIAS or MIAS; also, your local reference
library should have a copy of the Association's Yearbook, which
gives a list of its members) or the Incorporated Society of Valuers
and Auctioneers (look for the initials FSVA or ASVA; and the

Society will answer telephone or written enquiries about members in your area). Both bodies have codes of conduct and will investigate complaints about their members alleging professional misconduct.

Be careful when employing a surveyor to carry out a structural survey that you specify whether you want a thorough technical inspection of the property or a more limited (and cheaper) survey which will note only major structural defects (known as the House – or Flat – Buyers Report and Valuation). This will affect your right to claim damages for breach of contract should you later become aware of defects not mentioned by the surveyor.

If you borrow money to buy property, for example from a bank or building society, the lender will usually insist on having a survey carried out; the charge for this will be passed on to you but you are not necessarily shown the surveyor's report. The main purpose of such a survey is to check that the valuation is correct, by assessing the overall condition of the property. It is advisable to pay for your own, more thorough structural survey as well (you may be able to get this carried out by the lender's surveyor, for a separate charge which will usually be slightly less that you'd pay to employ another surveyor); but if you haven't done this, you may still be able to make a claim for negligence against the lender's surveyor if you later become aware of major structural defects that should have been noticed during the valuation survey. If this occurs, get legal advice.

Estate agents

Estate agents are not required to have any specific qualifications or to register in order to trade, but they are obliged to obey a number of rules set out in a criminal law, the Estate Agents Act 1979. If they break this law, they can be prosecuted (usually by the local Trading Standards Department), and may be banned from trading. However, property shops and computer-listing companies, which charge a flat-rate registration fee to sellers, are probably not covered by the Act – the legal situation is currently unclear.

The main provisions of the Act are that an estate agent must tell you in advance (in speech or writing) the circumstances in which fees will have to be paid, and what they will be; must disclose any personal interest they or their associates have in a property; and must hold buyers' money, such as deposits, on trust in special client accounts, paying interest on any deposit of more than £500 if the interest due is £10 or more (in Scotland, the taking of pre-contractual deposits is forbidden). If you think that an estate agent has broken this law, or you have a complaint about either of the other two types of property-selling service, contact your local Trading Standards Department or consumer adviser.

Many estate agents belong to organisations which have codes of conduct and which will investigate complaints about their members; these are the Royal Institution of Chartered Surveyors and the Incorporated Society of Valuers and Auctioneers (for details, see 'Surveyors', above) and the National Association of Estate Agents (look for the initials FNAA and ANAA). All three organisations have insurance schemes to protect your money (against fraud, for example).

Before instructing estate agents to sell your property, read any document setting out their terms of business very carefully because you may otherwise get a poor deal. If you are giving an agent 'sole agency' (this is the usual type of agreement in areas of the UK north of a line drawn roughly between Bristol and the Wash), consider putting a time limit on the agreement so that if, say, you don't get an offer within a month, you can take your custom elsewhere. Check that you will pay the agent's fee only if your property is actually sold (some contracts make the fee payable once a willing and able buyer is introduced to you; others impose a cancellation penalty, should you decide to withdraw the property for any reason). Never give an agent 'sole selling rights'; otherwise, you may have to pay the fee even if you find a buyer yourself.

If you are dealing with an estate agent as a buyer rather than seller, you may wish to complain if you find that the particulars of properties you are sent are inaccurate, especially if as a result you have wasted time and money going to see somewhere unsuitable. Unfortunately, such inaccuracy is all too common because descriptions of property are not covered by the Trade Descriptions

Act. You can sue the agent for misrepresentation (see p 84) but this is possible only if you have actually bought the property on the basis of a misleading factual statement, and in any case estate agents often include disclaimers in their particulars, denying responsibility for any inaccuracies.

Complaints about public utilities

Each of the organisations and corporations that provide what are commonly called public utilities – British Telecom, the Post Office, the Electricity and Gas Boards and the Water Authorities – has a complaints procedure, and several have codes of practice. Coal, though supplied by individual traders, is dealt with under this heading as it is a nationalised industry. Useful addresses are given at the end of the book (see p 231).

British Telecom

British Telecommunications plc, to give it its full title, has worked out a code of practice in consultation with the Office of Fair Trading. This is explained in a free booklet obtainable from your local Citizens' Advice Bureau or British Telecom area office (whose address appears on your telephone bills); the code is also printed in telephone directories. When using its services, you enter into a contract with the company; since August 1985, all applicants for a service (for example, to rent an exchange line) have been provided with a copy of the conditions of service, but if you don't have one, or you don't understand it, you can call in at your local British Telecom office.

If you have a complaint about the standard or price of the service – for example, you think your quarterly bill is wrong, or the line is often noisy – start by telephoning your local area office during working hours. Faulty lines can be reported at any time by telephoning the local fault repair service (the number is given in your telephone directory or separate code book); under the terms of the standard contract, British Telecom aims to clear most faults within two working days after the day on which they are reported, but if it takes longer you should tell your area office which will adjust the rental charge on your next bill. You can also call the operator to claim refunds for poor quality calls – wrong numbers, crossed lines, getting cut off, faint or noisy lines – and for money lost in public payphones. If your telephone equipment is to blame, your rights depend on whether you have bought or rented it from British Telecom or another supplier, and the terms of the contract you made (most equipment rented from British Telecom is maintained free of charge; for details, see the code of practice booklet).

If you are dissatisfied with the way your initial complaint is handled, write to the General Manager of your area office. If dissatisfied with the response you receive, find out (ask at your local post office) whether there is a Post and Telecommunications Advisory Committee in your area, which may be able to take up your complaint with British Telecom's management. You can in any case pursue the matter further within British Telecom yourself by writing to the Secretary of the Advisory Committee on Telecommunications (there are separate ones for England, Wales, Scotland and Northern Ireland). You can also get advice and assistance from the Office of Telecommunications (Oftel), an independent body set up to ensure that British Telecom and all other telecommunications suppliers meet their legal obligations.

If the dispute is still not resolved, get legal advice about your case; you may be able to sue British Telecom or, if your claim relates to one of the services covered by the code of practice and you are claiming no more than £1,000 in compensation, you can opt instead for arbitration (there is a registration fee which will be refunded if the arbitrator upholds your claim). If you apply for arbitration, you must do so within twelve months of the cause of your complaint, unless exceptional circumstances prevent you.

The Post Office

A code of practice worked out by the Post Office in consultation with the Office of Fair Trading and the Post Office Users National Council (POUNC) is described in a free booklet available from your local post office. Although there is no contract between the Post Office and its customers, you still have the right, in certain circumstances, to claim for items lost or damaged in the inland post. Unfortunately, you cannot normally claim redress for the most common type of complaint, late delivery, though you can express your dissatisfaction in writing to your local Head Postmaster (if possible, enclose the envelope or outer wrapping with your letter giving details of when and where the item was posted and when received). If you can show that the Post Office's failure to provide a service for which postage or a fee was paid was caused by negligence, you can claim a refund of that postage or fee.

If you have a complaint about lost or damaged post, get a copy of form P58 'Enquiry about a missing or damaged letter or parcel'; complete it and either hand it in or post it to the local Head Postmaster. If you are applying for compensation for damage, keep the article and all the packing, as evidence. If you are applying for compensation for loss, you will have to produce evidence in the form of a certificate of posting (obtainable free from the post office at the time of posting) for the Post Office to be legally liable. The amount of compensation you can claim will depend on whether you sent the item by ordinary mail service, or you used one of the special services which make the Post Office liable for higher claims. These include the recorded delivery letter service, the registered letter service and the compensation fee parcel service (for inland mail) and the insured letter and parcel services and registered letter service (for overseas mail); details are given in the code of practice booklet, or you can ask for specific advice at your local post office.

You may have to wait up to six weeks (or more, if your complaint concerns overseas mail) for the Head Postmaster's response, though your letter or compensation claim will generally be acknowledged within one week of its receipt. If you are dissatisfied with the response, you can write to the Regional Director (there are seven in England and one each in Wales, Scotland and Northern Ireland), and you can also discuss your claim with a local consumer adviser or, if there's one in your area, the Post and Telecommunications Advisory Committee (ask for details at your post office). You can also get advice and assistance from the Post Office Users National Council, an independent body which may take up your case (there are separate councils for England, Wales, Scotland and Northern Ireland). If the dispute is still not resolved, get legal advice. If your claim concerns an inland postal service, you may be able to sue the Post Office, or you can opt for arbitration (in which case you should apply direct to the Secretary of the Chartered Institute of Arbitrators). If your claim concerns an overseas postal service or a postal order, the Post Office is not legally liable, but you can have your complaint considered by a member of a panel set up by the Chartered Institute of Arbitrators whose recommendation, though not legally binding, will normally be accepted by the Post Office.

Don't delay in making your complaint; if you decide to start court proceedings you must do so within twelve months of the date on which the lost or damaged item was posted, and applications to the Chartered Institute of Arbitrators must be made within eighteen months of the postal date. If calculating the precise amount of compensation is likely to take time, you can indicate on the compensation application form that the value is approximate and will be confirmed or adjusted later.

Electricity

Whether your complaint is about the accuracy of your electricity bill, an appliance you have bought from an Electricity Board showroom or the repair and maintenance work carried out by an Electricity Board employee, start at local level: either telephone the customer accounts office (whose phone number appears on your electricity bills) or complain in person at your local showroom. If you are dissatisfied with the response, write to your Area Electricity Consultative Council, an independent body representing customers' interests which may be able to arrange a settlement of the dispute; its address appears on your bills, otherwise ask at your local showroom. If this proves ineffective, either you or the Consultative Council can take the complaint further, to the Electricity Council (except in Scotland, which doesn't have one), which will consider your claim in a hearing. If you are still dissatisfied, you can write to the Secretary of State for Energy, who has the power to instruct Electricity Boards.

If you suspect your meter is faulty, you can have it checked by the

Board (you may have to pay for this but you will be refunded if your complaint is shown to be justified); if still not satisfied, you can have it examined by an independent meter reader from the Department of Energy, whose decision is final.

If your complaint concerns faulty goods bought from an Electricity Board showroom, your rights are protected in law by the Sale of Goods Act and other relevant consumer legislation (see Part Two) and you may be able to sue the Board for damages if you are not offered adequate compensation. If it concerns servicing or repairs to electrical appliances carried out by a Board, you are also given the alternative of arbitration, under the code of practice mentioned on p 106; for details, read the free leaflet, *Electrical goods*, published by the Office of Fair Trading (for how to obtain a copy, see p 241).

Another code of practice regulates the Boards' right to cut off your electricity supply if you have failed to pay your bills; you can get a leaflet explaining the code from your local showroom. If you think the code has not been observed, get in touch with your Area Electricity Consultative Council or a local consumer adviser.

Gas

As with electricity, so with gas: whatever the nature of your complaint, start at local level by contacting your Gas Region office (its address and a telephone number for queries about bills are given on your bill) or by visiting your local British Gas showroom. If you are dissatisfied with the response, write to your Regional Gas Consumers Council, an independent body representing gas consumers' interests; its address also appears on your bills, otherwise ask at your local showroom. It may in turn refer the matter to the National Gas Consumers Council which can obtain a final decision from the Secretary of State for Energy.

If your complaint is not settled by your Regional Gas Consumers Council, you may be able to take legal action if you are claiming compensation for faulty goods bought from a gas showroom or for any repair, servicing or maintenance work carried out by the Board.

The Gas Boards, like the Electricity Boards, are obliged to follow the code of practice relating to disconnection; you can get a leaflet explaining the code from your local showroom. If you think the code has not been observed, get in touch with your Regional Gas Consumers Council or local consumer adviser.

The National Gas Consumers Council publishes a free booklet, *Help and advice from the Gas Consumers Councils*, which you may find useful (copies can be obtained from your local showroom, Citizens' Advice Bureau or other advice agency).

Coal

Unlike gas and electricity, coal, though produced by a nationalised industry, is supplied to consumers by individual traders. If you have a complaint, start by giving the supplier an opportunity to put matters right; if appropriate, for example you suspect the coal merchant of giving short weight, contact your local Trading Standards Department. If you want to take the complaint further, most coal merchants belong to the Approved Coal Merchants Scheme, which has a code of practice they must follow; complaints about them can be made to one of the scheme's eleven Regional Secretaries (for the appropriate address, ask your coal merchant or local consumer advice agency, or contact the scheme's head office in London). If you are still not happy, contact the Domestic Coal Consumers Council, an independent body set up to represent consumers' interests. You can also seek help from a regional office of the Solid Fuel Advisory Service.

In Northern Ireland, there is no Approved Coal Merchants Scheme at the time of writing; instead, disputes with coal merchants should be referred to the Northern Ireland Coal Advisory Service, or the Trading Standards Branch of the Department of Economic Development for Northern Ireland.

Water

The water industry in England and Wales is controlled by ten autonomous water authorities (in Scotland, it is the responsibility of the regional councils, and in Northern Ireland that of the Department of the Environment for Northern Ireland). Each local water authority has its own bye-laws, including rules and restrictions about the design of domestic water systems (these will be observed by good plumbers); you can obtain a copy from your local office, whose address appears on your water rates bill.

Your bill for water is normally based on the rateable value of your property, with extra charges being levied for non-domestic water use (for example, if you have a garden hose pipe or swimming pool); it may show separate charges for water supply, sewerage and environmental services. If you wish, you can have a meter installed as an alternative means of calculating your water supply charge. You do not have to pay for sewerage if you are not connected to the public sewer (for example, if you have a septic tank or cesspool).

Any complaint about water should be made to the responsible local water authority (your water rates bill will give an address and phone number for enquiries). If you are not satisfied with the response, your local councillor may be able to help (see p 17); and if your complaint concerns maladministration by the authority – for example, you have been given faulty advice or you feel that an official has been inefficient or rude – then you or you councillor can complain to the Commissioner for Local Administration (there are three in England, and one each in Wales, Scotland and Northern Ireland; for details, see p 154).

Complaints about leisure services

When you have set out with the aim of enjoying yourself, and perhaps been prepared to fork out quite a hefty sum in the process, it is particularly disappointing and upsetting to have to complain about the service you receive. Depending on the amount of money you have wasted and inconvenience you have suffered, you may feel that making a complaint will merely increase the unpleasantness of the experience. Even so, partly for the sake of those who come after you, resist the temptation to keep your dissatisfaction to yourself; it is often only by customers making complaints that those supplying a service become aware of their shortcomings, or that rogue traders can be detected and controlled.

In addition to the general guidance given at the beginning of this section, which applies to all complaints about leisure services, here is some more specific advice about the commonest types of leisure service.

Restaurants

Meals provided by restaurants and other catering establishments are covered by the laws relating to the sale of goods (see pp 62 and 63). However, there is often also a service element – and, indeed, a service charge. If such a charge is indicated clearly on a menu, you are legally obliged to pay it unless the standard of service falls below that which you could reasonably expect from an establishment of that type, in which case you can claim compensation by deducting all or part of the charge from the bill. However, you should indicate your dissatisfaction at an earlier stage whenever possible (for example, by asking to see the manager or head waiter if you have had to wait an unreasonably long time to be served).

Hotels

Establishments in the UK offering accommodation are divided in law into two groups: hotels, which are those that offer travellers food, alcoholic drink and, if requested, sleeping accommodation without prior arrangement (these are covered by the Hotel Proprietors Act 1956) and establishments which do not meet the qualifications, for example because they don't have a liquor licence, or require advance booking (a group that includes boarding houses, bed-and-breakfast places, private hotels and most pubs). This distinction affects your rights in two areas in which a complaint might arise: a refusal to serve you, and the loss or theft of, or damage to, your property.

A hotel can refuse your custom only if it is fully booked, or if you are obviously drunk or look disreputable, or if the proprietor has reasonable grounds for suspecting you won't be able to pay the bill. It must also provide you with food and drink on request, and if they are available, at all reasonable times. If a hotel fails to meet its

obligations, you can report it to the Trading Standards
Department. Other establishments, however, do not have to accept
your custom or provide food or drink on request (as long as they are
not breaking the racial or sex discrimination laws – see p 226).

If any of your property, including money, is lost, stolen or damaged
while on a hotel's premises, then you will usually have a right to
claim damages from the hotel (exceptions are vehicles and any
property left in them, and live animals, for which a claim can be
made only if you can prove the hotel has been negligent). The only
way in which a hotel can limit its liability is by displaying a clear
notice in the reception or entrance area (so that you can see it before
you enter into the contract – a notice in a bedroom is insufficient),
limiting its liability for loss or damage to the property of those
staying in the hotel, and to a total of £50 for any one article and
£100 for any one guest. However, this exclusion clause is not
effective if you can prove that the hotel was negligent or if you left
or offered to deposit the article for safe keeping. Other
establishments, however, are not liable for lost, stolen or damaged
property unless you can prove negligence.

If you have booked a room in a hotel or other establishment,
perhaps specifying certain requirements – for example, you want a
double bedroom with private bath, overlooking the sea – then you
have made a contract as soon as your booking is accepted, whether
or not you pay a deposit; if the establishment is fully booked when
you arrive or unable to meet any of the agreed requirements, you
can claim compensation for breach of contract. If the establishment
does not match up to the way it has described itself or its services,
then you can report it to the Trading Standards Department which
may decide to prosecute under the Trade Descriptions Act, and you
may be able to claim damages for breach of contract or
misrepresentation (see 'Complaints about misleading descriptions',
p 103).

When booking accommodation, you may be required to pay a
deposit. If you later decide to cancel, you are breaking the contract
and the proprietor is entitled to keep your money, and even to claim
additional damages as compensation for the profit he/she has lost
(this may be as much as two-thirds of the price you would have

paid). However, this loss must be kept to a minimum and so your room should, if possible, be re-let.

If you have an unresolved dispute with a hotel, in addition to the usual sources of help and advice mentioned in Part One, you can contact the relevant National Tourist Board which may be able to conciliate.

For complaints about hotels booked as part of a package holiday, see p 127.

Pubs and wine bars

Assuming that the establishment does not qualify as a hotel (see above), its proprietor can refuse to serve you without giving any reason, as long as the refusal is not based on racial or sex discrimination (see p 226). It is also illegal for a child under fourteen to be allowed into a bar, which is any part of licensed premises used primarily for the sale or consumption of alcoholic drinks; but this does not include other areas, for example those used mainly for eating, where the law allows even children over five to drink alcohol, as long as they do not buy it for themselves. People over fourteen but under sixteen can enter a bar, but cannot buy or drink alcohol; when over sixteen but under eighteen, they can buy or drink beer, cider or perry – but not wine – as long as it is to be drunk with a meal.

Wine, unlike cider, beer and spirits, does not have to be served in standard measures. Some wine bars specify the amount they serve if you order a glass, and you can complain, and even report them to the Trading Standards Department, if you get less; but otherwise all you can do if you get a mean measure is to register your dissatisfaction and take your custom elsewhere.

For other complaints about drink or food served in a pub or wine bar, see pp 62 and 63.

Clubs

Whether a club is privately owned and run by its members – many sports clubs operate in this way – or belongs to a proprietor who runs it as a business to make money, its members are bound by the club rules, which form part of the contract they enter when joining. A club can reject your application to become a member, but you will have the right to complain if you are refused on the grounds of

- your race (unless it is a genuinely private members' club with fewer than twenty-five members; or it is for members of a particular group to which you don't belong – for example, if you are Welsh and the club is for Scots only – as long as the distinction is not based on people's colour)

- your sex (unless it is a private members' club, rather than a proprietor's club).

For complaints about discrimination, see p 226.

Anyone who is injured on a club's premises, whether or not they are a member, can sue any club employee or member whose negligence caused the injury, and may also be able, in the case of the former, to sue the employers, for example the members of the club's committee.

Package holidays

When you buy a package holiday, you make a contract with the tour operator, even if the deal is made through a travel agent. The terms of your contract will be contained in the booking conditions set out in the tour company's brochure or in a separate booking form; express terms may also be contained in advertisements and statements made to you by the travel agent, and in the form of brochure illustrations. As with other contracts, you must read any written terms very carefully; unfortunately these are usually set out in columns of horribly small print. You are unlikely to be able to get any of them changed, but you can at least compare different companies' deals, and be aware of your legal position should anything go wrong. You can of course introduce additional express terms by stating your specific requirements, for example that you want a double room with bath and balcony overlooking the sea, in a quiet hotel with a choice of international and local food; if the operator accepts your booking on that basis, you can claim damages if any of your terms are not met. To cover yourself, make sure they are set out in writing, whether on the booking form or in a separate letter.

A tour operator is liable for any breach of contract, and cannot pass the responsibility on to its sub-contractors, for example the management of a hotel. However, most booking conditions include a clause excluding the operator's liability for certain matters beyond its control (for example, airline strikes). Whether such exclusion clauses effectively remove your right to complain to the operator and claim compensation for any loss you have suffered depends on whether the operator can prove that the clause is reasonable (see 'Exclusion clauses', p 4); the less specific the circumstances to which the clause refers, the greater are your chances of getting judgement in your favour. If an exclusion clause is reasonable, check whether you can claim against another party, for example the airline (see 'Airlines and airports', p 134) or your insurance company.

When claiming damages for breach of contract, you can claim not only for any difference in the value of the service you received and the price you were charged (for example, to compensate you for being given a poorer standard of accommodation than you had booked or been led to expect) but also for any disappointment, distress and inconvenience you and any other members of your party have suffered. This means that, if your holiday has been entirely ruined by the operator's failure to observe the contract's terms, you may be able to claim damages in addition to a complete refund.

A breach of contract may occur before you go on holiday – for example, if the tour is cancelled because of insufficient bookings, or the hotel is changed. Even if the operator is able to offer you an equivalent alternative, you can insist on cancelling the contract and getting your money back. If no satisfactory alternative is offered and you have to pay more to book a similar holiday with another firm, you can claim the extra expense as damages; if it is too late to find an alternative, you can claim compensation for your disappointment.

A more common cause for pre-holiday complaints is the addition of surcharges to the quoted price. A number of operators now

guarantee prices, but others include a clause in their contracts
allowing them to pass on to customers increases in the cost of fuel
or to reflect changes in the exchange rate. Even so, you can insist
that the operator justifies the surcharge; and, if you are not
convinced but don't want to jeopardise your holiday, you can pay
up 'under protest', so reserving your right to claim a refund later.

In most cases, however, causes for complaint arise while you are on
holiday. You may reach your destination only to find that your hotel
is overbooked; sometimes facilities described or illustrated in the
brochure are not available, or the hotel's food and service are sub-
standard. Whether a term of the contract has been broken or you
simply feel you were misled, for example by a brochure illustration,
you should complain as quickly as possible. Most package tour
companies have local representatives whose job is to try to sort out
any problems on the spot; otherwise, if you are staying in a hotel,
talk to its manager. The next step is to contact the tour operator's
area office, if there is one, and talk to its manager. At all stages,
keep a note of dates and times, and what is said or done in response
to your complaint as well as any costs you incur and time you waste
coping with the problem. Collect evidence to support your case
such as signed statements from other guests or photographs. You
may be offered alternative accommodation; if it is of inferior
quality, or less conveniently or attractively situated, you can either
reject the offer, return home, and claim a refund and compensation,
or you can accept 'under protest' (make this clear in writing),
reserving your right to claim damages later on.

When you get home, see your travel agent as soon as possible; if
you didn't use one or your agent proves slow or unhelpful, write to
the tour operator direct. If you can, state the amount of money you
are claiming (your local consumer adviser can help you to calculate
what is reasonable). If the tour operator points out an exclusion
clause in the contract, get legal advice as to whether it could be
successfully defended; if there's any doubt, persist. If you get an offer
of a discount off your next holiday with the company, or a token
refund 'as a gesture of good will', don't accept if you have a right to
claim more (you can keep any cheque you are sent but don't bank it –
this could be construed as an acceptance of the offer – unless it is 'in
full and final settlement', in which case you should return it).

If, despite your letters, you get nowhere, check whether the tour operator is a member of the Association of British Travel Agents (ABTA). The Association has a code of practice which is described in a free pamphlet published by the Office of Fair Trading, *Package holidays* (for how to obtain a copy, see p 241). It will investigate complaints about its members, free of charge; and it also offers an arbitration scheme as an alternative to court action, though you must normally apply within nine months of the date of your return from holiday, and you cannot claim more than £1,000 per person or £5,000 for several people listed on the same booking form. The Association can also help if you have a claim against a travel agent member, for example, if the agent failed to pass on your booking to a tour operator and you didn't discover the error until the holiday was fully booked, or if the agent gave you false information.

If you used credit to buy your holiday, check whether you can make a claim against the credit company (see 'Buying services on credit', p 101); however, this will be possible only if the payment was made direct to the tour operator or using ABTA's special credit card charge form, not to the travel agent (unless of course your claim is against the agent).

As well as or instead of pursuing your claim in civil law, you can report a tour operator to your Trading Standards Department if you suspect an offence has been committed under the Trade Descriptions Act (see 'Complaints about misleading descriptions', p 103); if the operator is successfully prosecuted, the criminal court may award you compensation.

If the worst happens, and one of the companies involved in your holiday – travel agent, airline, tour operator – goes out of business, so that you lose your deposit or are stranded in your resort, you may be protected. First, if your booking has been confirmed, you are safe even if the travel agent goes bust. Even without the confirmation, if you've been dealing with an ABTA agent you will, if necessary, be offered an acceptable alternative holiday or else given a refund. Similarly, if you've booked a holiday with an ABTA tour operator who goes bust, either you will be offered an alternative holiday or, if you are already on holiday, ABTA will help to get you home if it is impossible for your holiday to continue as planned. Additionally, if your holiday includes air travel, you will probably be protected by the bonding scheme that covers all companies with an Air Travel Organisers Licence (ATOL) (this is backed up by the government-run Air Travel Reserve Fund); this will apply if you have bought either a package holiday or a seat on a charter flight (to find out whether a company has an ATOL, telephone the Civil Aviation Authority). If your holiday is by coach, you may be covered by the bonding scheme run by the Bus and Coach Council.

Complaints about travel services

Railways

When you buy a train ticket, you enter into a contract with the relevant supplier (British Rail, unless you are travelling by London Underground, in which case it is London Transport, or you are in Northern Ireland which has an independent rail system). The contract has certain conditions which are referred to on the ticket; these apply regardless of whether you have seen them (they should be available for inspection at the ticket office), and include clauses excluding or limiting the railway boards' liability for damages. For example, if British Rail loses or damages your luggage, the conditions limit its liability to £500 per passenger; and they also deny your right to claim compensation for inconvenience if you have reserved a seat but have to stand because someone else with a reservation has taken it (though you can claim a refund of the reservation fee). However, in the event of a dispute, it would be up to the railway board to prove that any exclusion clause was reasonable (see 'Exclusion clauses', p 4).

Unfortunately, the passenger has little or no chance of obtaining redress for two of the most common causes of complaint – fare increases and cancellations or delays to scheduled services. Timetables carry a notice saying that the service described is not guaranteed; however, if a failure to provide the service forces you to make alternative arrangements at extra expense – for example, to hire a taxi to get you home because the last train is cancelled at short notice – you might succeed in claiming the cost from the railway board.

If you have a complaint about a British Rail service, start by speaking to the station manager or else write to the area manager, whose address is usually displayed in the booking office. If you are dissatisfied with the response you receive, write to the Transport Users Consultative Committee for your area (its address will be displayed in your station); it cannot handle complaints about ticket prices, but will investigate poor service or proposed reductions of, or alterations to, the service. If you feel the matter is of national rather than purely local importance, you can write to the Central Transport Consultative Committee.

Complaints about the London Underground should be made to London Regional Transport's Director of Press and Public Relations; if you are still dissatisfied, to the London Regional Passengers Committee; and finally to the Chairman of London Transport.

Buses and coaches

Bus and coach services are supplied by local authorities, national companies and private contractors. All are regulated by the Department of Transport which, through local Traffic Commissioners, issues licences to operators and drivers. If you have a complaint, your first step is to write to the manager of the appropriate local office of the company or organisation running the service.

The National Bus Company (NBC), which runs services in England and Wales, has subsidiary companies responsible for different parts of the country, as does its Scottish equivalent, the Scottish Bus Group (SBG). Addresses to which complaints should be sent can be obtained from the relevant local bus or coach station. If you are dissatisfied with the response, you can write to the NBC's or SBG's General Manager at head office. Complaints about NBC's National Express service should be made in writing to its headquarters in Birmingham (this also applies to express services run jointly with private companies).

If complaining about a local authority service, write to the authority's Transport Manager; if this doesn't get results, write to the Chairman of the authority's Transport Committee (you can also seek support from your local councillor – see p 17). In London, buses are run by London Transport and you should follow the complaints procedure already outlined (see 'Railways', above).

If your complaint is not handled satisfactorily by the responsible body, you can write to the Traffic Commissioners for your area; they will consider all aspects of a service, including the routes operated, the fare structure (though not the level of prices as such), the competence of drivers, and alterations to services. The Commissioners have the ultimate sanction of refusing or revoking a licence.

As with complaints about rail services, your legal right to redress depends in part on the terms of your contract, as set out in the operator's conditions of carriage which are usually referred to on the ticket. However, any exclusion clauses are subject to a test of reasonableness (see 'Exclusion clauses', p 4), so take legal advice if you think you may have a claim.

Taxis and minicabs

Taxis are vehicles that have been licensed by the local authority (in London, by the Metropolitan Police) to ply for hire. Their fares are regulated, and a taxi driver cannot charge more than the amount shown on the meter (unless there is a new tariff displayed in the cab to show recent price increases); if a driver agrees to take you further than the distance covered by the meter, you must negotiate a price in advance. A taxi driver can refuse to take you outside his/her operating area; London taxis, which operate within the Metropolitan Police area, can also refuse to accept journeys of over six miles, or which will take over one hour, or which require detours to drop off other passengers. A taxi does not have to stop when hailed but, if parked in a taxi rank or stationary and awaiting passengers (though not, for example, if stopping to drop off a fare), the driver must generally agree to be hired unless the destination you give entitles him/her to refuse.

If you want to make a complaint about a taxi driver – for example, you think you were overcharged or treated rudely – you will have to be able to identify him/her, so take the cab's licence number (displayed on the rear of the taxi and in the passenger compartment) and, if possible, the driver's badge number. Write, as soon as possible, quoting these numbers and briefly explaining your complaint, to the licensing authority (letters about London taxi drivers should be sent within seven days of the incident to the Public Carriage Office – listed under 'Police' in the telephone directory). If your complaint concerns a taxi's failure to collect you at an agreed time, you can also take legal action to claim compensation for breach of contract.

An alternative to the taxi service is provided by private minicabs, which are not allowed to ply for hire – to use their service, you must either telephone or call in at their office – but which may be required by the local authority to obtain a licence in order to operate. There are no fare regulations, so you should always ask for a firm price to be quoted in advance. If you have a complaint about a minicab driver, you should take it up first with the firm concerned; if you agreed a collection time but were let down, you can claim compensation for breach of contract. In districts where minicabs have to be licensed, you can also complain to the local authority; licensed cabs must carry an identification disc.

Airlines and airports

When booking a seat on a scheduled flight, you are accepting the conditions of carriage offered by that airline; but, as always, any exclusion clause would have to meet a test of reasonableness (see 'Exclusion clauses', p 4). The most common causes for complaint about airline services are delays, overbooking and luggage problems.

Commonly, airlines do not accept liability for delays caused by factors beyond their control – for example, severe weather conditions or strikes. However, if the airline fails to take all possible measures to avoid the delay – for example, your flight is held up by repairs to faulty equipment which has not been properly maintained – you can claim compensation for any foreseeable losses (for example, the cost of staying overnight in a hotel or of extra meals and drinks). In practice, most airlines will arrange accommodation or distribute meal vouchers as necessary.

Overbooking is clearly the responsibility of the airline, and if you have booked a seat on a particular flight you can claim compensation for breach of contract if you are turned away, even if the conditions of carriage state that a booking or reservation does not constitute a guarantee of a seat. Alternatively, British and several foreign airlines operating out of the UK have a scheme whereby they will get you to your destination within four hours (on overseas flights – for domestic flights, within two hours) of the arrival time of the flight you booked; or, failing that, will pay you compensation, including a refund of part of your fare. If you accept this, you won't be able to make a further claim at a later date but it is usually better to accept the immediate offer rather than get involved in legal wranglings.

If your luggage is delayed by an airline and you incur expenses as a result – for example, you have to buy toilet items or nightclothes, and make a special journey to the airport to collect your luggage when it finally turns up – you can claim these costs back. An airline is also liable to pay compensation for lost luggage unless it can show that it took all reasonable measures to prevent the loss, but compensation is limited to a maximum amount per kilogram (£13.80 at the time of writing) and so you may be wiser to take out insurance against such a calamity. If the luggage has been damaged while in the airline's care, you should complain at once if this is evident or, if you discover it later, within seven days of collecting the item; otherwise, you lose your right to claim compensation.

If you have a complaint about an airline service, see the airline's staff at the airport. If necessary, take the matter further by writing to the company's Customer Relations Officer at its head office. If still dissatisfied, you can write to the Air Transport Users Committee which will investigate your claim and try to conciliate.

If you have a complaint about an airport's services, you can ask to speak to the manager of the relevant department (for example, the restaurant manager if you have been served poor food). Alternatively, at any of the airports run by the British Airports Authority (Heathrow, Gatwick, Stansted, Glasgow, Prestwick, Aberdeen and Edinburgh), you will find comment cards distributed in the terminal, or you can speak to the staff at the BAA information desk (in the arrivals area). Written complaints should be addressed to the public relations department at the airport. If you are dissatisfied with the responses you receive, you can write to the Secretary of the airport's Consultative Committee who may take the matter up with the airport's management.

For complaints about aircraft noise, see p 195.

Public, professional and financial services

The general principles that apply to the majority of services were considered at the beginning of Part Three (see pp 93–103). In Part Four, the focus is on health services (including complaints about doctors, dentists, opticians and pharmacists, hospital staff, mental health services, and alternative therapists); social services; education services (including complaints about teachers, school facilities, school allocation and examination results); lawyers (solicitors and barristers); and financial advisers and institutions (insurance companies and brokers, accountants, stockbrokers, licensed dealers, banks, building societies and credit agencies).

In several of the areas covered in this section, you may not be paying, directly at least, for the service about which you wish to complain, and you won't have entered into a contract with the supplier of the service. However, regardless of whether any contractual obligations exist, you are always protected by the common law of duty of care (see p 6) and, if you suffer injury or loss as a result of some's negligence, you can sue them in the civil courts for damages. In the context of this section, you would generally be claiming for 'professional negligence'; that is, you would be alleging that you had suffered (financially, physically and even, in some cases, psychologically) as a result of the person's failure to carry out his/her job with the skill and care normally expected in such circumstances from other members of that profession. The onus would be on you, as claimant, to prove the allegation; as this can be extremely difficult, you should always get legal advice before embarking on such a claim. If you do decide to sue for negligence, you must do so within six years of the event (three if claiming for personal injury) except in some cases when the period runs from the date when you became aware that you had a claim.

If you do have a contract with the person or organisation supplying a service – for example, you employ a solicitor or an accountant, or you open a bank account – then you may be able to sue them for breach of contract if they fail to observe the terms of your agreement (see 'The law of contract', p 2 and 'Your rights under the Supply of Goods and Services Act', p 93).

Additionally – or alternatively, if you are unable to prove negligence or breach of contract – you can often report someone with whose service you are dissatisfied to a controlling body which, though it usually won't be able to award you compensation for any loss or distress you have suffered, may be able to sort matters out or, if appropriate, reprimand or penalise the person or organisation concerned. Some bodies – for example, the Family Practitioner Committees and their Scottish and Northern Ireland equivalents – will consider complaints about the quality of service provided, since it is they that are directly employing the person concerned. Professional bodies – for example, the General Optical Council or the Law Society – are concerned with professional misconduct; they have rules regulating the behaviour of their members and may even expel a member for gross misconduct, so severely limiting or even denying his/her right to continue working in that profession. If disciplinary measures are enforced against a member of a profession, this can be useful evidence to support any claim you make in the courts.

Complaints about health services

Health services of various kinds are supplied in three different ways:

- by self-employed people (general practitioners, pharmacists, opticians and dentists) who carry out some or most of their work under contract to the National Health Service (NHS)

- by staff employed by the NHS in hospitals or within the community (such as consultants, nurses, midwives and health visitors)

- by self-employed people (who are often, but seldom necessarily, medically qualified) who offer private treatment.

These groups are not mutually exclusive; for example, many general practitioners (GPs), opticians and dentists split their time between NHS and private work, and you can obtain private treatment within an NHS hospital.

Who handles complaints?

Whenever possible, start by giving the person concerned an opportunity to explain or amend whatever is causing your dissatisfaction. If you are not happy with their response, one or more of the following bodies may be able to help.

COMMUNITY HEALTH COUNCILS (CHCS)

Community Health Councils are local bodies set up by government to represent the interests of NHS users (in Scotland, the equivalent bodies are the Local Health Councils; in Northern Ireland, the District Committees). They will consider comments and suggestions as well as complaints about any NHS services and can advise you about your right to NHS treatment; in some cases, they may agree to act on your behalf in a dispute, for example by appearing at a Family Practitioner Committee hearing (see below). The address of your local CHC should be listed in the telephone directory under 'Community'; otherwise, ask your GP, post office, hospital or Family Practitioner Committee office. Ring to check its opening times before you visit.

FAMILY PRACTITIONER COMMITTEES (FPCS)

These are the NHS bodies responsible (in England and Wales) for administering and supervising the health services carried out under the NHS's contracts with self-employed GPs, dentists, opticians and pharmacists (in Scotland, the appropriate bodies are the Area Health Boards; in Northern Ireland, there is one body, the Central

Services Agency). If you have a complaint about the *standard of service* you have received while being treated under the NHS – for example, your doctor failed to visit you when your medical condition required it, or an optician charged you for an eye test which should have been free – then you should write to the Administrator of your local FPC; the address is usually listed in the telephone directory under 'Family' and is given on your NHS medical card; otherwise, ask at your local main post office or CHC.

Complaints to the FPC should be made within eight weeks of the event in question (six weeks for a complaint to a Scottish Health Board). If you miss the deadline, you will have to satisfy the FPC that the delay was reasonable, and it will then have to get the consent of either the person you are complaining about or the Secretary of State for Social Services to agree that your case should be considered. Complaints can be made either by the patient or by someone acting with the patient's authority, or on their behalf (for example, if the patient is unable to complain because of illness, infirmity, age or youth, or if the complaint concerns someone who has died.

If there is a chance of sorting the problem out informally, the FPC may ask both parties to attend a meeting; otherwise, if you insist on formal investigation or the complaint is serious, your letter will be considered by the chairman of the appropriate Service Committee (there are separate ones for GPs, dentists, opticians and pharmacists). If he/she decides that the FPC should investigate your allegation, a copy of your letter of complaint will be sent to the other party, who is then given four weeks in which to provide a written reply, a copy of which is sent to you. If you are unhappy with the explanations given, the chairman decides whether the case should be discussed by the whole Service Committee (which may then come to a decision – if you disagree with its findings, you can appeal to the Secretary of State for Social Services) or whether a hearing should be held (this may also be recommended by the Service Committee).

At the hearing, both parties can call witnesses, and you can be represented by an unpaid 'friend' (this could be a member of your CHC) but not by a solicitor (though you can get legal advice on the case). The Committee will then draw up a report and make recommendations; if these are accepted by the FPC, copies of the report will be sent to both parties in the dispute and to the Secretary of State for Social Services. If your complaint has been upheld, the other party (your GP or whoever) may

- receive a warning

- have a limit imposed on the number of patients on his/her NHS list

- have part of his/her NHS pay withheld

- be referred to an NHS tribunal which may withdraw his/her right to work for the NHS.

You will not receive compensation though, if the complaint concerns NHS work for which you paid a fee (for example, for some dental treatment), the money may be refunded to you. If either party is dissatisfied with the FPC's decision, there is a right of appeal to the Secretary of State for Social Services.

THE HOSPITAL AND DISTRICT ADMINISTRATORS

If you have a complaint about the *general, rather than medical, service* you have received under the NHS while a hospital in- or out-patient – for example, about aspects of the hospital's routine or the standard of food, or being kept waiting an unreasonable time, or being treated rudely or inconsiderately by hospital staff – you can write to the Hospital Administrator if the ward Sister or consultant in charge of your treatment is unable to sort matters out.

If you are unhappy with a Hospital Administrator's reply, or you are no longer attending the hospital (in which case you must act within one year of the events about which you are complaining), write to the District Administrator at the District Health Authority (in Wales, write to the Health Authority for your area; in Scotland, to the relevant Area Health Board; in Northern Ireland, to the Central Services Agency). Your telephone directory should give its address, under the name of your nearest large town or the county in which you live; otherwise, ask at your hospital or CHC. Your complaint will be investigated and, if necessary, a formal enquiry will be held. This process may take some time, but you will eventually be told what steps, if any, are being taken as a result of your complaint.

REGIONAL MEDICAL OFFICERS

If you have a complaint about the *medical competence* of a doctor, nurse or other qualified NHS employee – for example, your illness has been incorrectly diagnosed or you feel you have not received appropriate treatment – you should start by arranging a meeting with the consultant in charge of your case (if you are still in hospital, the ward Sister will do this for you; otherwise, write or telephone). If you are not satisfied with the explanation given (which should be confirmed in writing), you can write to the Regional Medical Officer (in Wales, the Medical Officer for Complaints); the hospital or your local CHC should have the address. He/she will look into the case, and reply to your complaint in writing. If you are still dissatisfied, you may wish to take legal advice to see whether you can pursue your complaint through the courts; alternatively, you can ask the Regional Medical Officer to arrange for a 'second opinion', in which case two independent consultants will talk to you, and to the medical staff concerned, and (if you consent) may carry out a physical examination of you. If they uphold your complaint, you will be told, in writing, what steps are being taken as a result, but you will not receive any compensation.

THE HEALTH SERVICE COMMISSIONER

Also known as the NHS Ombudsman, the Commissioner is an independent official appointed by government to investigate claims of *maladministration* by NHS officials. If you have made a complaint to the relevant health authority – for example, the District Administrator – but are dissatisfied with the way it has been handled, you can write direct to the Ombudsman (this must be done within one year of the event in question, unless there are exceptional circumstances to justify the delay).

The Ombudsman cannot investigate all types of complaint; those outside his/her jurisdiction include complaints about the diagnosis or treatment of an illness (known as 'clinical judgement'), complaints which you have taken, or plan to take, to court or a tribunal, and complaints about GPs or other self-employed practitioners under contract to the NHS. If you are unsure whether your case falls within the Ombudsman's jurisdiction, either get advice from your CHC or write to the Ombudsman with a summary of the facts and ask for an opinion. If you decide to make a formal complaint, guidance is given in a leaflet available from CHCs, Citizens' Advice Bureaux and District Health Authority offices (or their Welsh, Scottish and Northern Ireland equivalents – see above); and your CHC can also help you write the letter.

When the Ombudsman has carried out an investigation, a report is published setting out the conclusions reached and, if necessary, making recommendations; you will receive a copy, as will any other individual or government department named in the complaint. The Ombudsman has no power to enforce any recommendations, and cannot award compensation; but you may, as a result, receive an apology from the health authority concerned. If the authority rejects the Ombudsman's report or recommendations, you can do little other than expose it publicly (for example, by getting a local newspaper to run a story on the case); but beware the law of libel, though the Ombudsman's report is itself protected from legal action.

PROFESSIONAL BODIES

There are a number of professional bodies to which you can complain if you feel that one of their members has been guilty of *professional misconduct* – for example, by behaving rudely, attending you while under the influence of alcohol or drugs, making an indecent assault, or disclosing confidential information (except if authorised or legally obliged to do so). If a complaint is upheld, the consequences can be serious for the member concerned, but you won't be awarded any compensation; on the other hand, if your allegation is dismissed, you could be sued by the member for defamation (though only if you made the complaint maliciously).

You can complain to the relevant professional body whether its member was treating you on the NHS or privately. For further details, see the comments on specific health services below (and for addresses, see p 231).

ADVISORY ORGANISATIONS

In addition to the sources of help and advice mentioned in Part One, such as Citizens' Advice Bureaux, there are some specialist organisations you can contact. The Patients Association, which is financed partly by government grant and partly by members' subscriptions, can answer written or telephone enquiries about your rights as an NHS or private patient. The College of Health, an organisation set up by a number of consumer activists and members of the medical profession, publishes a regular magazine (obtainable on subscription only) and a range of booklets, can answer members' written queries about the health services, and will provide details about relevant self-help groups. A charitable organisation called Action for the Victims of Medical Accidents may be able to help if you think you have suffered injury as a result of negligence on the part of a doctor or other medical practitioner; it can put you in touch with solicitors specialising in such claims, and maintains a panel of medical experts who are prepared to give an objective opinion of what has happened to you.

General practitioners (GPs)

■ If you simply feel that your GP is *unsympathetic*, consider changing doctors (for advice on how to do this, contact your local CHC, Citizens' Advice Bureau or FPC).

■ If you want a second opinion, ask your GP to refer you to a specialist. If your request is refused, you cannot go to a specialist direct, so you will have to change doctors or consult another GP privately.

■ If you are dissatisfied with the *standard of service* you have received from your GP, and you are an NHS rather than private patient, complain to the FPC (see p 139).

■ If you have suffered injury or loss which you think was caused by the doctor's failure to exercise professional standards of skill or care, get legal advice about suing for *professional negligence* (not only the patient can make a claim; for example, the widow of a man who has died as a result of medical negligence can sue those responsible).

■ If you think the GP has been guilty of *professional misconduct*, write to the Registrar of the General Medical Council (GMC); you will be required to make a sworn statement and, if the GMC considers it should investigate the matter, it will obtain the GP's comments and either refer the complaint to the Preliminary Proceedings Committee or, in serious cases, to the Professional Misconduct Committee. The GMC's final sanction is to remove the GP from its register of doctors; this prevents him/her from practising within the NHS (though not from providing private medical treatment).

■ If you have been treated on a private rather than NHS basis, you may be able to sue the GP for breach of contract, but seek legal advice first.

Dentists

■ There is no formal procedure for changing your NHS dentist, and you can do so after any course of treatment. Always specify in advance if you want NHS treatment.

■ If you want a second opinion, either ask your dentist to refer you to a specialist, or simply go to another dentist (you can do this even though you have signed a form for a course of treatment).

■ If you are dissatisfied with the *standard of service* you have received from your dentist, and you are an NHS rather than private patient, complain to the FPC (see p 139).

■ If you have suffered injury or loss which you think was caused by the dentist's failure to exercise professional standards of skill or care, get legal advice about suing for *professional negligence*.

■ If you think the dentist has been guilty of serious *professional misconduct*, write to the Registrar of the General Dental Council. If the GDC considers your allegation may be justified, it will investigate and, if serious misconduct is revealed, may remove the dentist from its register, so preventing him/her from practising.

■ If you have been treated on a private rather than NHS basis, you may be able to sue the dentist for *breach of contract*, but seek legal advice first.

Opticians

■ There is no formal procedure you must follow if you want to consult a different optician to the one you've been using.

■ If you have been prescribed spectacles but, after a couple of weeks, find you can't get used to them, and your optician can't resolve the problem, ask your FPC for permission to have another eye test on the NHS (you can go to another optician for this). If the original prescription or the lenses are found to be faulty, you can have new lenses at no charge (as long as you request this within about three months of the first sight test).

■ If you are dissatisfied with the *standard of service* you have received from your optician, and you are an NHS rather than private patient, complain to the FPC (see p 139).

■ If you have suffered injury or loss which you think was caused by the optician's failure to exercise professional standards of skill or care, get legal advice about suing for *professional negligence*.

■ If you think the optician has been guilty of *professional misconduct*, write to the Registrar of the appropriate professional body:

● the General Optical Council (if complaining about an ophthalmic optician – that is, someone qualified to test eyesight and prescribe lenses, but not to treat any medical eye problems)

● the General Medical Council (if complaining about an ophthalmologist – that is, a doctor specialising in eye disorders such as a hospital eye consultant or surgeon)

● the Orthoptists Board of the Council for Professions Supplementary to Medicine (if complaining about a registered orthoptist – that is, someone specialising in treating eye defects such as squints).

There are several other bodies that may be able to help with a complaint. The Association of Optical Practitioners runs a complaints bureau to which you can turn for help if you have an unresolved dispute with any individual ophthalmic practitioner, whether or not he/she is a member. The Federation of Ophthalmic and Dispensing Opticians, to which many of the chains of opticians belong, will consider allegations of professional misconduct by its members (write to the Director General), as will the British College of Ophthalmic Opticians (write to the General Secretary).

■ If you have been treated on a private rather than NHS basis, you may be able to sue the optician for *breach of contract*, but seek legal advice first.

Pharmacists

■ With the exception of hospital in-patient prescriptions, you can take your prescription to any pharmacist.

■ If you are dissatisfied with the *standard of service* you have received from your pharmacist, and your complaint concerns medicines dispensed under the NHS, complain to the FPC (see p 139).

■ If you have suffered loss or injury which you think was caused by the pharmacist's failure to exercise professional standards of skill or care, get legal advice about suing for *professional negligence*. However, if you are claiming that the wrong medicine was prescribed, your claim would probably be against the doctor, not the pharmacist. If you are claiming that the medicine itself is to blame, even though correctly prescribed and dispensed, then your claim is against the manufacturer.

■ If you think the pharmacist has been guilty of *professional misconduct*, write to the Law Department of the Pharmaceutical Society of Great Britain (in Northern Ireland, to the Department of Health and Social Services), with which all qualified pharmacists are registered. Complaints that a medicine was 'not of the nature and quality demanded' should also be addressed to the Society, and this could lead to a pharmacist being prosecuted under the Medicines Act 1968.

■ If you have been supplied with medicines by a pharmacist on a private rather than NHS basis, you may be able to sue for *breach of contract*, but seek legal advice first.

NHS hospital and community staff

■ Many hospitals have their own complaints procedures which are described in their guidebooks; otherwise, ask a member of staff.

■ If the cause for your complaint arises while you are staying in hospital, speak to the ward Sister. If it concerns your medical treatment, she can arrange for the consultant in charge of your case to discuss it with you.

■ If you have a complaint about the *standard of general rather than medical service* provided, write to the Hospital Administrator; if dissatisfied with the reply, write to the District Administrator (see p 141).

■ For complaints about *medical competence*, whether of a nurse, doctor or member of one of the supplementary medical professions such as a dietician or physiotherapist, write to the Regional Medical Officer (p 142).

■ If you have suffered injury or loss which you think was caused by a member of staff's failure to exercise professional standards of skill or care, get legal advice about suing for *professional negligence*. If the treatment in question was carried out on the NHS, the health authority is liable as well as any individuals alleged to have been negligent, if they can be named. If the treatment was carried out on a private basis, even though in an NHS hospital, the health authority is not liable if your claim is against the consultant rather than a member of the hospital's NHS staff.

■ If you think a member of a hospital's medical staff has been guilty of *professional misconduct*, write to the appropriate professional body:

● the General Medical Council (for complaints about doctors, including registrars and consultants) – see p 145

- the National Board (there is one each for England, Wales, Scotland and Northern Ireland) for Nursing, Midwifery and Health Visiting (for complaints about registered members of those professions) – it will investigate your complaint if you name the person concerned and make a sworn statement; if it feels you have a case, it will refer the allegation to the United Kingdom Central Council which in serious cases may remove a nurse, midwife or health visitor from the register, so preventing him/her from practising within the NHS (and midwives must be registered to practise at all)

- the appropriate Board of the Council for Professions Supplementary to Medicine (for complaints about registered orthoptists, chiropodists, occupational therapists, physiotherapists and dieticians – there are also Boards for radiographers and medical laboratory scientific officers but you are unlikely to need to complain about them) – again, you will have to make a sworn statement in order for your complaint to be investigated; in serious cases, the Boards' final sanction is to remove someone's name from the register, so preventing him/her from practising within the NHS or claiming to be 'state registered' (though not from providing private medical treatment).

Professional associations may also be able to help with complaints about one of their members, for example the Society of Chiropodists, the Chartered Society of Physiotherapy and the British Association of Occupational Therapists.

■ If you undergo medical treatment without giving your consent and/or being given an explanation of the likely benefits and potential risks of the treatment, you may be able to bring a claim for assault. For minor forms of treatment such as X-rays, your consent may be 'implied'; otherwise, you will be asked to sign a form (though this does not exclude your legal rights). Exceptions when medical staff need not obtain a patient's informed consent include emergency cases when the patient is unconscious or unable to communicate, and to delay treatment would endanger life; some forms of treatment for compulsorily detained mental patients (see below); and the treatment of notifiable infectious diseases.

■ If you have been treated on a private rather than NHS basis, you may be able to sue for *breach of contract*, but seek legal advice first.

Mental health services

The majority of patients with a mental illness are treated by their GP, often with the use of drugs (for example, to control depression or anxiety). Some are referred to a non-medical counsellor such as a clinical psychologist or a social worker, others to a psychiatrist, and treatment may be provided on the NHS or privately. Psychiatric treatment does not usually require a stay in hospital, and the vast majority of those patients who are admitted, either to the psychiatric wing of a general hospital or to a mental illness hospital, enter on a voluntary (informal) basis. A small proportion, however, are compulsorily admitted, or may be compulsorily detained.

Either before or when a patient is admitted as an in-patient, whether informally or compulsorily, the hospital should provide the patient and his/her relatives with information on their rights. The legal position of an informal psychiatric patient is technically little different to that of a patient undergoing hospital treatment for any other kind of illness; for example, he/she has to consent to treatment and can leave the hospital at any time. However, a doctor in charge of an informal patient can apply for a compulsory detention order, under the provisions of the Mental Health Act 1983, to prevent self-discharge in certain circumstances. A compulsorily detained patient has fewer rights than an informal patient; for example, many forms of treatment can be given without his/her consent, though, if the patient is capable of understanding an explanation of the treatment, this should always be given and consent sought.

The rules and regulations about the treatment of the mentally ill as set out in the Mental Health Act 1983 are detailed and complex, and you should seek specialist advice if you are unsure of your or your relative's or friend's rights in a particular dispute; either contact your local Citizens' Advice Bureau or GHC, or write to the National Association for Mental Health, also known as MIND (or the Scottish or Northern Ireland Associations, as appropriate). Meanwhile, here are some general guidelines on how to complain.

■ If you are being treated by your GP, follow the complaints procedure described on p 144–145.

■ If you are being treated in an NHS hospital, as either an out-patient or a voluntary or compulsory in-patient, follow the procedures described on p 148 for complaints about the standard of service or medical treatment (if necessary, relatives can do this on a patient's behalf). If this proves unsatisfactory, complaints concerning the care of compulsorily detained patients can be made to the Mental Health Act Commission, a body set up by government to monitor the care and treatment of those detained under the Act.

■ A detained patient must be discharged on the order of his/her nearest relative (though seventy-two hours' notice has to be given), unless the hospital issues a 'barring certificate'. Either a detained patient or, in certain cases, his/her nearest relative can apply for discharge to the Mental Health Review Tribunal (in Scotland, to the Mental Welfare Commission); patients must be given details of how to apply, and if necessary helped by a member of the medical staff or a social worker to complete the application form. The patient can be represented at the hearing by a friend or legal adviser but legal aid is not available for tribunals; however, MIND's legal department may be able to help, or to suggest suitable solicitors who might be willing to give advice under the legal advice and assistance scheme (see p 21), and provide free or cheap representation at the tribunal hearing.

■ One crucial difference between the means of redress available to patients receiving treatment for mental illness and other patients concerns the right to take legal action. Under the Mental Health Act 1983, any detained patient or his/her relative wishing to sue hospital staff or anyone else for actions carried out under the provisions of the Act – for example, for injury caused by negligence in the course of treatment – has to get the permission of the High Court before starting proceedings. To obtain this permission, he/she must show that there are reasonable grounds for the claim. Similarly, the police are not allowed to prosecute anyone for ill-treating or neglecting a mental patient without first obtaining the permission of the Director of Public Prosecutions. However, these restrictions do not apply to cases brought against health authorities.

■ The Health Service Commissioner (see p 142) can consider complaints alleging maladministration by NHS officials made by mental patients or their relatives, but not if an application has been made to a Mental Health Review Tribunal.

Alternative therapists

Most alternative medical treatment is provided on a private basis only (homoeopathy and acupuncture are the exceptions, and these are practised by only a small minority of NHS GPs). Practitioners do not have to be registered, and anyone can set up as an osteopath or herbalist, for example. It is therefore advisable to obtain treatment either from a medically qualified doctor who practises the therapy you require or from a member of an appropriate professional organisation which imposes certain standards on members (for example, the British Chiropractors Association, the General Council and Register of Osteopaths and the British Homoeopathic Association). Advice and information about alternative therapies can be obtained from the Institute for Complementary Medicine, which will answer telephone or written enquiries and has also set up some local information centres which carry directories of qualified practitioners in acupuncture, chiropractic, homoeopathy, medical herbalism and osteopathy.

If you have a complaint about alternative medical treatment provided on the NHS, you should follow the procedures described on p 144 (if a GP is concerned) or p 148 (if you were treated in hospital – there are a few, including the Royal London Homoeopathic Hospital, offering homoeopathic therapy). The professional organisations referred to will investigate complaints about their members, though you won't be able to get any compensation as a result; if you wish to claim damages, for negligence, fraud or breach of contract, you will have to start civil proceedings.

Complaints about social services

A wide range of social services is provided by most local authorities
(in Northern Ireland, by the four Health and Social Services
Boards), aimed at helping those in the community in particular
need. Typically, they are concerned with the care and protection of
children (such as adoption and fostering schemes, community
homes, day nurseries and child-minders for the under fives, and the
detection and prevention of child abuse), the elderly (for example,
day centres, residential accommodation and home helps), the
disabled, the mentally handicapped and the mentally ill. They may
also provide emergency help for one-parent families in need, or
battered wives. Social workers with a range of qualifications and
experience are employed, and may specialise in a particular area
such as mental illness.

However, although local authorities are authorised by Act of
Parliament to provide such services, they are in many cases not
legally obliged to provide them. The availability of any service in
your area will depend on your local authority's own policy and the
amount of money it has to pay for such services. If a service is
provided, but the demand exceeds the supply – for example, for
places in a local authority residential home for the elderly – there
may be a waiting list, and applicants may also have to meet certain
qualifying criteria.

To check which services are provided in your area, and whether you
qualify, contact the Social Services Department of your local
authority or ask at your Citizens' Advice Bureau. If you feel that a
particular service should be introduced, or made more widely
accessible, contact your local councillor (see p 17) and consider
setting up a pressure group (see 'When group action is appropriate',
p 38). You can also seek help from one of the many organisations
that aim to improve the welfare of particular groups of people, such
as Help the Aged, the National Association for Mental Health
(MIND), Shelter, the Child Poverty Action Group, the Disabled
Living Foundation and the National Council for One-parent
Families. Your Citizens' Advice Bureau should be able to make
further suggestions.

If you have a complaint about an individual social worker, or the
Social Services Department, write to the local authority's Director
of Social Services. If you are dissatisfied with the response, ask your
local councillor to help. If this doesn't get results, you may be able
to complain to the Commissioner for Local Administration,
otherwise known as the Local Ombudsman. For complaints about
benefit payments see p 203.

THE COMMISSIONER FOR LOCAL ADMINISTRATION

There are four local Ombudsmen, one each in England, Wales and
Scotland and one in Northern Ireland (whose official title is the
Commissioner for Complaints). However, the Ombudsman can
consider only complaints alleging maladministration – for example,
that your application for a social service was not handled according
to the official procedure, or was delayed by inefficiency, or that you
were discriminated against. If you are not sure whether your
complaint comes within the Ombudsman's jurisdiction, either ask
your Citizens' Advice Bureau or write to the Ombudsman with a
summary of the facts, asking for an opinion.

Your formal written complaint must be sent to the Ombudsman by
a councillor of the local authority concerned (though it doesn't have
to be your own councillor), unless he/she refuses, in which case you
can write direct; and the Ombudsman must receive the letter within
twelve months of the event in question. A free leaflet giving details
of how to make your complaint is available from Citizens' Advice
Bureaux, most main libraries and local authority offices. An
investigation is carried out and, usually after some months (during
which time you may be contacted by the Ombudsman's office for
further information), a report is issued setting out the
Ombudsman's findings. A copy is sent to you, the local authority
and anyone else named in the complaint; and the local authority is
obliged to make the report available for three weeks for public
inspection (unless the Ombudsman has ruled otherwise),
advertising this fact in the local press. If the report upholds your
complaint, the Ombudsman makes recommendations about what
should be done; these are not enforceable but, if the local authority
fails to take any action within a reasonable time, the Ombudsman
makes the failure public in another report.

Complaints about education services

The majority of children in the United Kingdom are educated in state schools according to general policies set out in Acts of Parliament and associated regulations (in Scotland and Northern Ireland, the education systems differ in various ways from those of England and Wales, so some of the following information does not apply). The responsibility for providing and supervising the schools lies with the local authority, except in inner London where it lies with the Inner London Education Authority (ILEA). Each local education authority (LEA) has an Education Committee, responsible for determining its specific policies, the majority of whose members are councillors but which must also include representatives of other interested parties such as the Church, teachers and, in some cases, parents; and an Education Department, responsible for the administration of those policies, headed by a Chief Education Officer. At school level, responsibility for carrying out an LEA's policies and deciding what constitutes a suitable education for the pupils attending that school lies primarily with the head teacher; however, influence can also be brought to bear on, or by, the school's governors (who must, by law, include two parents of children attending the school).

The law gives each LEA considerable powers to determine the nature of the education service it provides, and so policies and procedures can differ quite significantly from one part of the country to another; moreover, schools within a single LEA may have important differences, for example in the curriculum offered. By law, all LEAs must ensure that information about each school is made available (you can obtain details from the LEA Education Department or the schools themselves). If you have particular requirements, for example you want your child to study a certain subject, you should check in advance which schools can meet them. You do not have a right to specify which school your child should attend, but you can express a preference (that said, one of the commonest causes for complaint is the allocation of school places – see below).

How to complain

If you have a complaint about the school your child is attending –
for example, about the quality of teaching or facilities provided, the
absence or presence of subjects on the school curriculum, or the
methods of discipline used – start by telephoning or writing to the
member of staff concerned and/or the head teacher and arrange a
meeting to discuss the problem. If you are not satisfied with the
head's response, write to the local Education Department (if your
complaint is shared by a number of other parents, write a joint
letter). At this stage, you might also wish to contact a school
governor (for names and addresses, ask your school head or
telephone the LEA) and also the secretary of the school's parent–
teacher association, if one exists, as they might also be able to
exercise some pressure. If the Education Department can't sort
matters out to your satisfaction, write to the chairman of the LEA's
Education Committee and/or your local councillor (see p 17). If it
appears that the problem is caused by lack of money – for example,
the school is not providing enough copies of set books, or the school
buildings are dilapidated – you can also try enlisting your MP's
help, because issues of government policy may be involved
(although local authorities are responsible for funding educational
services in their area, their capacity to raise money through the rates
in order to do this is subject to government control, through the
rate support grant).

If you consider that an LEA has behaved unreasonably, you have a
right to complain to the Secretary of State for Education, who has
the power to instruct the LEA to take particular action; in practice,
however, the Minister seldom overrules an LEA's decision. If you
think there has been maladministration (for example, the LEA has
taken an unreasonable amount of time to investigate your
complaint), you can complain to the Commissioner for Local
Administration (see p 154 for details).

CHOICE OF SCHOOL

Although parents have a statutory right to state a preference about which school they wish their child to attend, they do not have the final choice because an LEA can disallow it on certain rather vaguely defined grounds. Disputes often arise because a school is popular and there are too many applicants (at least in the eyes of the LEA, which will be trying to protect other schools in its area from becoming depopulated). Some primary schools operate a first come, first served system or give preference to children with older brothers or sisters at the school. Priority may be given, at all stages of education, to children living within a school's catchment area (whose boundaries are drawn up by the LEA, and may vary from year to year, though they must be set at least nine months before admission date).

Whatever reason is given, you have a right to appeal against the denial of your preference. The appeals procedure operated by your LEA, including the deadline you must meet, will be set out in the information details about individual schools; usually, you have to complete a form setting out the reasons for your preference. Those that in the past have proved most likely to influence an LEA to change its mind include

- religious convictions (for example, you want your child to go to a Roman Catholic school)

- medical reasons (if a shorter journey is involved, for example, or you feel your child would suffer psychologically from attending a large school), in which case try to get written evidence from a doctor

- the attendance at the preferred school of an older brother or sister

- the unique opportunity for your child to study a particular subject

- (in Wales only) your wish for your child to be taught in Welsh.

You will be notified of the date of the appeals hearing, and can either attend in person – most appeals tribunals allow you to appoint a representative, such as a friend or teacher, if you prefer – or submit your case in writing. A letter setting out the panel's decision, and its reasons, will be sent to you; if you are dissatisfied, you can appeal either to the Secretary of State for Education or to the Commissioner for Local Administration, depending on the grounds of your appeal.

'SPECIAL NEEDS' ASSESSMENT

It has been estimated that around 15 per cent of children, in addition to the 2 per cent or so in special schools for the mentally and physically handicapped, have a significant learning difficulty compared to other children of their age. The causes may be physical (such as poor eyesight or hearing, or an accident), emotional (disrupted family life, for example) or mental; and the child's need for special help with his/her education – usually provided within the ordinary school, sometimes within a special unit – may be pointed out by the school staff, a doctor or a parent.

If you disagree with a school's assessment of your child, or feel that insufficient help is being provided, you can ask the LEA to organise a formal assessment, which you have the right to attend. Alternatively, if such an assessment is proposed and you feel it is unnecessary, you have around four weeks in which to notify the LEA in writing of the reasons for your objection. If the assessment is made, you have a right to appeal against its findings; and if, after further discussions with the LEA and any professional on whose evidence the LEA's decision was made, you still disagree, you can appeal to a local committee (the same one that handles disputes about choice of school). If you don't accept its findings, you can appeal to the Secretary of State for Education; you may be able to enlist your MP's help at this stage, and also, if you are claiming that your child is in need of special facilities which the LEA is failing to provide, the help of a relevant organisation such as the Royal Society for Mentally Handicapped Children and Adults (MENCAP).

EXAMINATION RESULTS

If your child does unexpectedly badly in a GCE or CSE examination, and you wish to query the result, you should make an appointment to discuss the matter with the head teacher. There is no right of appeal but the head may agree to contact the examining board concerned and ask for the exam papers to be re-checked (you will probably have to pay a fee for this).

If someone taking an exam has a particular problem that could affect his/her performance – an attack of migraine, or a recent emotional upset such as a death in the family – this should be made clear at the time to the invigilator supervising the exam (if possible, produce a medical certificate); otherwise it cannot be taken into account when the papers are marked.

Independent schools

Schools with more than five pupils (with certain exceptions) must register with the Department of Education and Science, and fulfil certain basic requirements. However, the specific obligations of a private school to the children in its care and their parents are those set out in its prospectus and other documents. If a school fails to meet its obligations, it can be sued for breach of contract. Additionally, parents have a right to complain to the Secretary of State for Education if the school fails to provide adequate suitable premises (including accommodation, if it takes boarders) or suitable and efficient teachers, or if either the proprietor or any teacher is morally or physically unfit for the post.

Advisory organisations

In addition to the sources of help and advice mentioned in Part One, there are many specialist organisations you can contact. The National Children's Bureau will supply a list of the names and addresses of those concerned with your particular interest or problem (covering not only education but many other aspects of children's and young people's lives). The Advisory Centre for Education (ACE) publishes a number of free leaflets as well as a bi-monthly magazine, *ACE Bulletin* (available on subscription only) and can answer telephone or written enquiries about a wide range of educational issues. The Children's Legal Centre offers a free advice and information service (either write or telephone on a weekday between 2 pm and 5 pm), covering all aspects of law and policy affecting children and young people in England and Wales; it may be able to take up your case with a local authority or other responsible body.

Complaints about lawyers

The legal profession is divided into two groups, solicitors and barristers (the latter are called advocates in Scotland), each with its own form of training and its own professional body. Solicitors handle the bulk of legal work and are also responsible for choosing and instructing a barrister, should one be needed; consequently, the majority of complaints about the legal profession are directed at solicitors.

Solicitors

The procedure to follow when complaining about a solicitor depends on the nature of your complaint, which will usually fall into one of the categories outlined below. In most cases, start by complaining in person or in writing to the solicitor handling your work in case he/she can offer an adequate explanation or suggest ways of compensating you for any loss or distress you have been caused. If dealing with a firm of solicitors, you can take your complaint further by writing to one of the senior partners (for names, look at the firm's stationery – partners are usually listed in order of seniority).

PROFESSIONAL NEGLIGENCE

If you have suffered loss as a result of a solicitor's failure to exercise professional care or skill – for example, someone you have engaged to advise you on a claim for damages misses a legal deadline so that you forfeit your rights to start civil proceedings – you can sue him/her for professional negligence. The exception is if you feel a solicitor was incompetent in the way he/she represented you in court or at a tribunal or hearing (the same applies to barristers – see p 165).

As always when making a claim for negligence, you should get legal advice. If you cannot find another solicitor willing to help you, consult your local Citizens' Advice Bureau; alternatively, contact the solicitors' professional body, the Law Society, by telephoning one of its local offices or writing to the Secretary, Professional Purposes, at its head office, and asking to be put in touch with one of the solicitors on its negligence panel, who will give you an hour's free advice about your claim (this applies to England and Wales only, though a similar scheme is available in Scotland). If he/she agrees to take on your case, you will have to pay (but ask whether you are eligible for legal aid – see p 20).

All solicitors are obliged to have insurance to meet negligence claims, and most are settled out of court.

BREACH OF CONTRACT

As always, any claim for breach of contract depends on the terms, express and implied, of your agreement. However, you cannot refuse to pay your solicitor just because he/she has failed to sort out a problem successfully, unless you can show that any competent solicitor would have been able to do so.

PROFESSIONAL MISCONDUCT

All practising solicitors are licensed each year by their professional body, the Law Society, and have to follow its guidelines on conduct. If you feel your solicitor has behaved unprofessionally, write to the Secretary, Professional Purposes, at the Society's head office, setting out the basis of your complaint and authorising the Society to send a copy of your letter to the solicitor. The types of complaint that the Society can investigate include

- persistent delay in replying to letters

- a failure to keep a client's business confidential

- a failure to account to a client for money held on his/her behalf

- dishonesty

- overcharging (see below)

- taking advantage of a client's age or inexperience

- acting in a dispute for two parties with conflicting interests.

If the solicitor fails to give an explanation that satisfies either the
Law Society or you, the complaint may be considered by the
Society's Professional Purposes Committee. If it is upheld, the
solicitor may be reprimanded, restricted in the way he/she is
allowed to practise or, if a financial misdemeanour is suspected,
subjected to an accounts investigation. In certain cases, the solicitor
may also be called before a disciplinary tribunal; if found to have
committed a serious breach of conduct, he/she may be fined,
suspended from practising for up to five years, or even 'struck off'
the Solicitors' Roll. It is not within the power of the Law Society to
award compensation to any client; however, if you have lost money
as a result of the fraud or dishonesty of your solicitor or another
member of his/her firm's staff, the Law Society can pay you back
out of its compensation fund.

If you are dissatisfied with the way the Law Society has handled
your complaint, you can write to the Lay Observer, who acts as a
kind of ombudsman. He/she will investigate and make a written
report, copies of which are sent to you, the Law Society and the
solicitor named in your complaint. The Lay Observer may
recommend that the Law Society reconsider your case, but cannot
enforce this.

OVERCHARGING

There is nothing to stop you asking a solicitor to estimate or quote
in advance for handling a particular piece of legal work for you, and
indeed it is advisable to do so. In most cases, you are unlikely to be
given a fixed price because the extent and nature of the work
involved are difficult to assess; however, if you get an estimate, you
can make it part of your contract that the solicitor must obtain your
agreement in writing to exceed the estimated fees or some other
limit that you specify, should the need to do so become apparent.
Otherwise, you will have to pay a 'reasonable charge'.

If you feel the bill you have received is unreasonable, there are
recognised procedures for having it checked which, in England and
Wales, depend on whether it covers 'non-contentious' work (that is,

work not involving court proceedings) or contentious work, and
whether you have already paid it.

■ If the bill is for non-contentious work, and you have not paid it,
you can insist that the solicitor submits it to the Law Society to be
checked (this will not cost you anything). The Society investigates
and, usually after three or four months, issues a 'remuneration
certificate', stating what it considers to be a fair and reasonable
price (fortunately for the client, it can only confirm or reduce a bill,
not increase it). If either party rejects the certificate, they can apply
to have the bill 'taxed' (the procedure applied to bills for
contentious work – see below).

Alternatively, if you simply refuse to pay the bill, the solicitor must
inform you of your right to apply for a remuneration certificate and
give you twenty-eight days to instruct him/her to apply for one
before suing you for the unpaid fees. However, informing you of
this right may take the form of a statement on the back of the bill,
referring to the relevant legislation (the Solicitors Act and the
Solicitors Remuneration Order), and it is easy for a dissatisfied
client to fail to grasp the implications of this notice. If you've
missed the deadline, you can usually still apply to have the bill
taxed.

The remuneration certificate procedure is not available to clients of
solicitors licensed by the Law Society of Scotland, which will not
investigate disputes about fees.

■ If the bill covers any contentious work, or you have paid it, you
can apply to have it 'taxed' – that is, assessed by a High Court
official. He/she has power to reduce a bill but, unless it is reduced
by a fifth or more, you will have to pay the cost of this assessment.
If you decide to opt for taxation, ask at your local court office for
details of how to apply.

If a solicitor has deducted his/her fees from money due to you – for
example, the proceeds of a property sale – you cannot be said to
have paid the bill and can still ask the solicitor to apply for a
remuneration certificate, as long as you do so quickly.

GENERAL INEFFICIENCY

Your complaint about your solicitor may be that you feel he/she has been rather half-hearted about pursuing your case, or has failed to keep you fully up-to-date with progress, or to explain the issues clearly. Until recently, there was little hope of obtaining redress for any inconvenience and annoyance caused by a solicitor's inefficiency, if it didn't actually cause you financial loss or amount to a breach of contract or professional misconduct. However, legislation likely to come into force in the first half of 1986 widens the Law Society's powers to allow it to investigate complaints of 'inadequate professional service'. Although the Society will not be able to award compensation as such, it will be able to order a solicitor to remit part or all of his/her fees, and/or take action to put matters right if this is possible.

Before contacting the Law Society, it is worth writing to a more senior partner in the firm with details of your complaint. You can also consider taking your custom elsewhere. Unfortunately, if you do this before the work is completed, you may end up paying twice for the one job; or, if you refuse to pay part or all of the first solicitor's bill, you may find that you can't get him/her to release the necessary papers.

Barristers

As your solicitor is responsible for selecting and briefing any barrister needed to work on your case, your first step if you have a complaint about the barrister is to express your dissatisfaction to your solicitor. In most cases, he/she will pursue the matter if your complaint seems justified; otherwise, you can decide to take it further yourself.

Although barristers practise as individuals rather than as partners in a firm, they usually share offices (known as chambers) with several other barristers, one of whom acts as Head of Chambers. If you write to the Head, he/she can make an informal investigation of your complaint (the chambers system does not exist in Scotland or Northern Ireland, however). The next step is to make a formal complaint in writing, within twelve months of the events concerned, to the barristers' professional body, the Bar Council, giving the name and business address of the solicitor as well as the barrister involved in the case, details of where and when any court proceedings took place, and an explanation of why you are complaining (the complaints procedure is clearly described in brief guidance notes available from the Bar Council). Your complaint will be considered by the Professional Conduct Committee which can reprimand the barrister or, if serious misconduct is indicated, report him/her to a disciplinary tribunal; the tribunal has the power to reprimand, suspend or, in extreme cases, disbar the barrister (thus preventing him/her from practising).

You have little chance of obtaining compensation from a barrister through legal action. In particular, neither you nor your solicitor can bring a claim for negligence relating to the barrister's performance in court (known as advocacy work), though this restriction does not apply to non-advocacy work (for example, advising how a case should be conducted or a point of law interpreted).

Complaints about financial advisers and institutions

This group includes insurance companies and insurance brokers, accountants, stockbrokers, licensed dealers, banks, building societies and credit agencies. The basis of your dealings with these organisations and individuals is your contract with them, the terms of which may be set out as 'Conditions of business' on the back of an application form or contained within promotional literature, advertisements and the like, or be agreed in conversation or correspondence. If you have a complaint, start by reading back through the relevant papers to check what was agreed before getting involved in endless letter-writing; if there is anything you are unsure about (for example, how to interpret the legal jargon beloved by insurance policy writers), seek advice (see 'Where to go for help and advice', p 13).

Insurance companies

If you have a complaint about your insurance company – for example, it has rejected part or all of a claim or is taking an unreasonably long time to settle it – take the matter up with the manager of the branch that issued the policy, either in writing or by making an appointment to discuss it in person. If dissatisfied with the explanation given or action taken, write to the company's chief executive at its head office; the address should be on the policy document, and you can find out his/her name by either telephoning the company or looking it up in *The insurance directory and year book* (your local reference library should have an up-to-date copy). If this fails to get results, and a consumer adviser can't exercise sufficient pressure on your behalf, your next step depends on whether your complaint concerns a general non-life policy (for example, one covering your home and its contents, your car or your holiday arrangements), a Lloyd's policy or a life insurance policy.

GENERAL POLICIES

The Association of British Insurers (ABI) will investigate complaints made by any of its members' policy-holders, although it cannot enforce its recommendations. If you are unhappy with its findings or the way it handles your complaint, or if your company does not belong to the Association, telephone or write to the Insurance Ombudsman Bureau to see if it can help (a free leaflet about this service is available from the Bureau). The Ombudsman can investigate your complaint only if it concerns a personal policy issued by one of the insurance companies that supports the Bureau (to find out whether yours does, ask the company or write to the Ombudsman), and only if you appeal no later than six months after the company has informed you of its final decision on the matter. Give brief details of the dispute as well as the company's name and the policy number.

If the Ombudsman decides that the case falls within his/her jurisdiction, and that a full investigation is required, the insurance company will be asked for the relevant files, and expert advice may be sought; in some cases, you may be asked to attend a hearing. If the Ombudsman cannot bring about an amicable settlement, he/she will reach a final decision, a copy of which will be sent to you and

the company; this may include the recommendation that the
company pays you a certain amount, and all member companies
have agreed to abide by the Ombudsman's awards, up to a
maximum of £100,000 (or £10,000 a year in permanent health
insurance cases). You are free to reject the Ombudsman's decision
and consider other action, such as suing the company for breach of
contract, but do take legal advice before doing so.

If your company does not support the Insurance Ombudsman
Bureau, check whether it uses the Personal Insurance Arbitration
Service (PIAS), a scheme run by the Chartered Institute of
Arbitrators which has the approval of the Office of Fair Trading.
You, as complainant, must make the application to the Institute
(though the insurance company's agreement to arbitration will then
be sought), and the service is free. However, the arbitrator's
decision is legally binding, and you cannot then take legal action
through the courts if you are dissatisfied with the result, so get
advice before you commit yourself to this course of action (see
'Arbitration schemes', p 25). For details of the PIAS, write to the
Institute, giving brief details of your complaint so that it can
confirm that your case lies within the scheme's scope (legally
complicated disputes or those involving claims above certain limits
cannot be settled by this method, though the Institute may be able
to offer an alternative form of arbitration).

LLOYD'S POLICIES

If you take out a Lloyd's policy, you must do so through an
insurance broker, and it is to him/her that you should make your
initial complaint. If the matter is not settled satisfactorily as a
result, you can write to Lloyd's Consumer Enquiries Department.
If it cannot bring about a settlement, you may have to consider
taking legal action (neither the Insurance Ombudsman Bureau nor
the Personal Insurance Arbitration Service have the authority to
intervene).

LIFE INSURANCE POLICIES

Many companies offering life insurance belong to the Association of
British Insurers which may be able to act as a conciliator in a
dispute. Appeals for an independent assessment can be made to the

Personal Insurance Arbitration Service or, in some cases, to the Insurance Ombudsman Bureau (see 'General policies', above). However, the Insurance Ombudsman cannot intervene in disputes over an industrial life policy – the name for personal life policies sold by representatives who call on people at home and collect premiums at intervals of two months or less. Instead, complaints should be made to the Industrial Assurance Commissioner, a government-appointed official who is empowered to investigate and bring about a binding settlement.

Insurance brokers

Insurance policies are often sold through an intermediary, for example if you consult an insurance broker or a policy is arranged for you by a building society or a bank. You may also deal with a company agent or representative. If you are unhappy about the service you have received from an insurance adviser, and he/she is uncooperative when you make a complaint, write to the company whose policy the adviser sold you or was offering; get in touch with the local office first and, if still dissatisfied, write to the company's chief executive at the head office (see p 166 for how to get a name).

If dealing with a broker who belongs to the British Insurance Brokers Association (BIBA), write to its consumer relations department. The Association will investigate and try to bring about a settlement; and, if the broker appears to have been negligent or unprofessional, the case may be considered by a disciplinary committee, and the broker may be expelled from the Association.

If the broker is not a BIBA member, or if you are unhappy with BIBA's handling of your complaint, write to the Registrar of the Insurance Brokers Registration Council (IBRC), the professional body with which anyone calling him/herself an insurance broker must be registered. The IBRC has powers to discipline brokers found to have breached its code of conduct and, in serious cases, may strike them off the register; it can also offer some compensation if you have lost money as a result of a broker's fraud, dishonesty, negligence or insolvency.

If you have been dealing with a Lloyd's broker, write to Lloyd's Consumer Enquiries Department.

If you have been dealing with an unregistered broker (for example, someone describing themselves as a financial consultant or insurance adviser), check whether he/she belongs to a trade association such as the Institute of Insurance Consultants which may be able to conciliate.

Accountants

If you are unhappy with the service you have received from your accountant, and have given him/her an opportunity to explain or put matters right, write to the senior partner (assuming you are dealing with a firm rather than a self-employed individual). If this proves ineffective, check whether the accountant belongs to a professional body. All chartered accountants are members of the Institute of Chartered Accountants in England and Wales (or its counterparts, the Institute of Chartered Accountants in Scotland, and the Institute of Chartered Accountants in Ireland, which has an Ulster branch). Unlike many professional bodies already discussed in Part Four, the Institutes will investigate claims that a chartered accountant has been incompetent or inefficient, as well as complaints alleging professional misconduct. If your complaint is upheld, the accountant may be reprimanded or even, in serious cases, expelled, but you will not receive any compensation.

Similar disciplinary measures can be taken to penalise their members' professional misconduct by the Chartered Association of Certified Accountants, the Institute of Cost and Management Accountants, the Chartered Institute of Public Finance and Accountancy and the Institute of Chartered Secretaries and Administrators (whose members, though not accountants, may offer book-keeping services).

If you have suffered financial loss as a result of your accountant's negligence or dishonesty, get expert legal advice about suing for damages.

Stockbrokers

If you have a complaint about your stockbroker – for example, he/
she has failed to carry out your instructions when buying or selling
shares on your behalf or has given you poor investment advice – and
you are not satisfied with the broker's explanation or offer to make
amends, write to the Complaints Section at the Stock Exchange. It
will try to conciliate and, if the stockbroker appears to have broken
any of the Stock Exchange's rules, will conduct a formal
investigation; it may, as a result, reprimand or even expel the
broker. Additionally, if you have lost money, you might be awarded
compensation from a fund set up by the Stock Exchange, which will
supply details of when and how to claim. However, a stockbroker is
not liable simply for giving bad advice, unless you can prove
negligence, or for failing to point out the risks you may be taking in
a particular transaction.

Licensed dealers

Licensed dealers are individuals and firms regularly buying and
selling shares and other investments on behalf of clients, who hold a
government licence allowing them to do so. Many belong to a
professional body, the National Association of Security Dealers and
Investment Managers (NASDIM), and have agreed to abide by its
rules. NASDIM will supply a list of its members in your area, and
investigate any complaints against them; penalities for professional
misconduct range from reprimand to expulsion.

Licensed dealers who do not belong to NASDIM receive their
licences direct from the Department of Trade and Industry, and are
listed in a directory published each summer by Her Majesty's
Stationery Office; updates are given in the Department of Trade's
monthly magazine, *British business* (your local reference library
should hold these publications). If you have a complaint, write to
the Companies Legislation Division of the Department of Trade
and Industry.

Banks

If you have a complaint about any aspect of your bank's services, take it up with the individual or department immediately concerned, either by telephone, in person or in writing; for example, if you have a query about items shown on your statement, you may be able to clear it up over the telephone by speaking to the branch accountant. If the responsible member of staff cannot help, write to the branch manager or arrange an appointment to discuss the matter in person; or, if it concerns a bank department (for example, home loans or insurance), write to the department head. If these people cannot solve the problem, or you are dissatisfied with the way your complaint is being investigated, write to the bank's head of customer relations or the chairman, at head office.

If your persistent attempts to get the bank to put matters right meet with a series of inadequate or unreasonably slow responses, you can appeal to the Banking Ombudsman, under a recently introduced scheme financed by seventeen High Street banks. The Ombudsman can deal only with personal complaints (not those of businesses), and there is an upper claims limit of £50,000. The Ombudsman will investigate and, if unable to bring about an amicable settlement, will reach a decision; this will be binding on the bank, but you can reject it and take legal action. However, before suing a bank, always get expert legal advice.

Building societies

If you have a complaint about a building society, whether you are a borrower or an investor, start by writing to the manager of the branch handling your account. If he/she does not sort the problem out to your satisfaction, write to the society's head of public relations or chief executive at its main office. If this doesn't get results, check whether your society belongs to the Building Societies Association (BSA), which can investigate complaints about its members and make recommendations, though these are not legally enforceable.

If it is not a BSA member, you can complain to the Chief Registrar of Friendly Societies, who may be able to act as a conciliator if the dispute is about the way you have been treated by your society (he/she cannot, for example, investigate disputes about the wording of a mortgage deed).

Credit agencies

This heading covers many types of trader and organisation, since credit can be obtained in a number of ways: from your bank (as a loan or overdraft facility), from a credit card company such as Access or Barclaycard, from a company offering hire purchase, conditional or credit sale agreements, from a finance company offering personal loans, or from a money-lender. Whenever you enter into a credit agreement, check its terms very carefully and if there is anything you don't understand, get advice. If you have signed an agreement but then change your mind, you may be able to cancel it (see 'Cooling-off period', p 70).

Most credit agreements for sums falling between a lower and upper limit (£50 and £15,000 at the time of writing) are covered by the Consumer Credit Act 1974; the Office of Fair Trading (OFT), which enforces the Act's regulations and issues (or withdraws) licences to traders providing credit or goods on hire, publishes a useful free booklet, *Shop around for credit*, explaining how the law protects you and advising on how to avoid problems (for how to obtain a copy, see p 242). If you have a dispute with a credit agency which you suspect is rather disreputable, it is worth checking whether it has a licence; you can either visit the OFT's Credit Licensing Office in West London to inspect the register or enquire by post (there is a small fee for this). Unlicensed traders are generally committing a criminal offence and any agreements they make are unenforceable; you should report such cases to the Office of Fair Trading or to your local Trading Standards Department.

If you foresee difficulties in keeping up payments on a loan, explain the problem to the credit agency and see if it will agree to a new arrangement (the OFT booklet already mentioned contains helpful advice about coping with debt). If you think that you are being charged an extortionate rate of interest, consult a local consumer adviser; you may be able to get the rate cut by applying to the county court. If you are being harassed by a lender – for example, you receive persistent telephone calls, or your employer is contacted – you can report the matter to the police or your local Trading Standards Department.

If you use a credit broker to arrange a loan for you, but he/she fails to do so within six months, there is a limit to the fee you can be charged (£3 at the time of writing). If you want to investigate why you have been refused credit, you have a right to inspect a credit reference agency's files (see p 225 for further details).

5 The individual, the community and the state

The previous sections of this book have been primarily concerned with the kind of complaint we make as consumers. This section focuses on disputes arising out of our rights and responsibilities as citizens. On the most personal level, it looks at the conflicts that can develop between neighbours, and between landlords and tenants. Moving out from the home, it considers aspects of the local environment – how to complain about the quality or quantity of public amenities, how to object to planning proposals, and how to protest about noise and pollution. It also looks at the financial aspects of citizenship – how to complain about your tax or rates bill, or the decisions or treatment you receive when you claim welfare benefits. Next, it looks at problems in the workplace, and how employees can seek redress for unfair treatment. Then it describes procedures for complaining about advertising and the media, which play such an important role in our society. Finally, issues of civil liberty are considered, including complaints about the agencies of law and order (the police and the prison system), complaints about invasion of privacy, and complaints about discrimination.

Complaints about neighbours

The behaviour of neighbours can have a considerable impact on the quality of our lives, and it's very easy, particularly when living cheek by jowl with several other households in a block of flats or a heavily built-up area, to come into conflict. A disagreement can quickly deteriorate into a running battle from which it is difficult to escape, short of moving home. Although the law imposes certain

obligations on neighbours towards each other, and provides various
ways in which these can be enforced, it is in everyone's interest to
sort out problems informally and amicably, even if, in order to do
so, you have to accept a compromise. Unfortunately, it is usually
the more reasonable, considerate neighbour who gets the poorer
end of the bargain.

If your tactful approaches pointing out the problem – for example, a
request to turn a radio down, or repair faulty guttering overflowing
on to your property, or keep a pet under control – are rejected, you
may find that a letter, indicating your wish to sort matters out
informally rather than invoking the law, will help. If you do decide
to take legal action, this will also be evidence that you have behaved
reasonably. Before invoking your legal rights, however, you need to
know what they are.

The basis of many complaints about neighbours is that they are
doing, or not doing, something that affects your use and enjoyment
of your property. It may affect only you, or others in the
neighbourhood as well. In law, you have a right to make an official
complaint if the cause amounts to a 'nuisance'; but, in a legal
context, this word has a more precise meaning than when used in
everyday speech. In deciding whether something amounts to a legal
nuisance, those enforcing the laws (local authority bye-laws as well
as Acts of Parliament) have to consider whether either party's
behaviour is 'unreasonable'. This makes it impossible to state
precisely how the law applies to your individual complaint, though
the following advice should give you some idea of your rights. For
more specific advice, consult a Citizens' Advice Bureau or solicitor.

Noise and other types of nuisance

People vary in their sensitivity to noise, and what one person
considers an infuriating din can be quite acceptable to another. As
far as the law is concerned, whether noise constitutes a nuisance
depends on how the average reasonable person would react to it.
Not only the level of noise but also its timing and duration are taken
into account; for example, someone playing their stereo at full blast
during the day is much less likely to be committing a nuisance than
someone who plays theirs through the night, and people who hold
an occasional noisy party will probably not be considered

unreasonable though, if they held one every Saturday night, they might be. Statements from other neighbours affected by the noise are useful evidence that your objection is not unreasonable, as is a doctor's certificate if you or your family's health suffers as a result of the noise, for example because of frequent disruption to sleep. You have three options when making an official complaint about noise.

■ Complain to the Environmental Health Department of the local authority (in Northern Ireland, the Public Health Office). Although it will usually send someone round, this won't happen immediately; so if the noise is intermittent rather than, say, continuous noise from industrial premises, and particularly if it occurs outside working hours, it may be difficult to ensure that the official hears it – hence the importance of evidence to support your complaint. If the local authority decides that a nuisance probably does exist, it will usually make an informal approach to the person responsible; if this fails, it may serve a 'notice of abatement', though only after a department official has heard the noise him/herself. If the noise continues despite this notice, the local authority may decide to prosecute, under either the Control of Pollution Act 1974 or one of its own bye-laws, by starting proceedings in the magistrates' court (or its Scottish equivalent, the sheriff's court); if found guilty, the accused will be fined.

■ If the local authority refuses to take any action, you can complain yourself to the magistrates' court. This is one of the relatively rare occasions when you might want to bring a private prosecution – that is, start criminal proceedings against someone rather than leaving it to the police or another state body. The main drawback of bringing a private prosecution is that you will have to pay the accused's legal costs if he/she is acquitted.

Telephone your local magistrates' court (listed under 'Courts' in the telephone directory) and find out when applications for summonses are heard. Take any evidence with you as you will have to convince the magistrate or clerk of court hearing the applications that you have a reasonable case. The summons (which is issued by the court on your behalf, at no charge) will specify the date of the hearing, which you should attend together with any witnesses you intend to call; you can also take a friend or adviser (though he/she cannot represent you). If the defendant is found guilty, he/she can be fined; if the noise still doesn't stop, further fines can be imposed for every day it continues.

■ As a last resort, you can start civil proceedings (see p 31) to seek an injunction (that is, a court order telling the defendant to stop or restrict the noise) and, in some cases, to make a claim for compensation for the distress or injury to your physical or mental health that you have suffered as a result of the noise. However, this course of action will almost certainly cost you money, so take expert legal advice before undertaking it.

The police will do little to help if you are disturbed by noise, even if it occurs in the middle of the night when there's no chance of getting the local authority to respond. However, they will have to investigate if you warn them that there is likely to be a 'breach of the peace' as a result of the disturbance (in other words, a fight is likely to break out).

Although noise is the commonest type of nuisance about which neighbours complain, other intangible intrusions such as smells can be tackled in this way. Trees can also cause a nuisance, for example if your neighbour's tree overhangs your property. In such a case, though, you should not have to take legal action; if the neighbour refuses to prune the tree, write to him/her setting out the grounds for your complaint and a deadline after which you will prune the tree yourself (you should offer to return the cut branches). If a neighbour's tree cuts out light but doesn't overhang your property, you have no means of redress unless it cuts out light into your building and the property has what is known as a 'prescriptive right to light', acquired by twenty years' continuous access to that light.

Pets and livestock

If you have a complaint about the noise or smell created by pets or livestock owned by a neighbour – for example, constant barking from a dog kept locked up all day – you should follow the guidelines outlined above for dealing with a nuisance. If someone's pet injures you or causes damage to your property, your right to

redress will usually depend on whether you can show that the owner
was negligent. The law is stricter about the keeping of livestock –
for example, cattle, sheep, goats and poultry – and of animals
belonging to classified dangerous species; in any case where such
animals cause damage, the owner is liable even though he/she took
all steps to prevent it. If a pet, though not one of a dangerous
species, is likely to cause damage or injury in certain circumstances,
the owner should take extra precautions to prevent this (assuming
he/she knows about the risk). However, the owner will not be liable
if the person suffering injury or damage provoked the animal, or
was aware of the risk and ignored it, or was a trespasser.

If you think a neighbour is ill-treating an animal, get in touch with
the Royal Society for the Prevention of Cruelty to Animals
(RSPCA) or its Scottish equivalent, the SSPCA. You can also bring
a private prosecution, under the Protection of Animals Act 1911. If
a neighbour persistently allows a dog to foul the footpath, contact
the Environmental Health Department of the local authority, which
may decide to prosecute the owner (again, private prosecutions are
allowed).

Damage to your property

If your neighbour carries out work on his/her property (for
example, to a party wall), as a result of which your property is
damaged, you can sue for compensation. Similarly, if damage
occurs because an adjoining property has been allowed to fall into
disrepair, you can make a claim if you can show that the owner has
been negligent. However, if a single incident is to blame – for
example, a bath in someone's flat overflows and water leaks into the
flat below – you are unlikely to get compensation through the
courts; instead, your building or contents insurance policy, if you
have one, should cover you.

Boundaries

The documents you receive when you buy property usually contain
a plan showing its boundaries. Disputes can arise about the precise
position of a boundary, but often a fence, wall or hedge will be

accepted by both parties as the dividing line. An argument may then arise as to who owns the fence, wall or hedge and has responsibility for its upkeep. If the title deeds are not clear on this point, and neither neighbour has appeared to lay claim to ownership by carrying out maintenance work in the past, you will usually have to agree to treat it as a party boundary; in that case, neither neighbour can do anything to their side of the structure that will affect the other's, and both must contribute to the cost of any repair carried out.

If someone owns a boundary fence or wall, he/she is under no obligation to repair it unless it is in a dangerous condition and could injure the neighbour or damage his/her property.

Complaints about landlords and tenants

Privately rented accommodation

The law relating to private letting and renting is extensive and complex, and it is impossible to give any detailed advice here. If you find yourself in a dispute, whether you are a landlord with a troublesome tenant or a tenant with a lousy landlord, you should seek expert advice. Your local Citizens' Advice Bureau or local authority housing aid centre (if one exists) may be able to help, or else refer you to a solicitor or other adviser specialising in this field; and housing is often one of the problem areas handled by legal advice centres and law centres, if there is one in your area (see 'Where to go for help and advice', p 13). You can also seek advice from Shelter (in London, its Housing Action Centre is known as SHAC).

If you are a tenant, the extent to which you are protected by law (as set out in various Rent Acts and other regulations) depends on the kind of tenancy you have. Most people renting private residential premises are protected (exceptions include those with genuine holiday lets and tenants who run a business from their rented homes). This protection may be full or restricted; the main difference between the two is that fully protected tenants have far greater protection against eviction.

In addition to the way in which the law affects dealings between landlords and tenants, there will usually be some sort of contract, whether written or spoken. It may set out more specifically each party's rights and obligations, but it cannot legally exclude those set out in law.

Disputes between private landlords and tenants generally arise in one of the following areas.

RENT

If you feel that you are being charged an excessive rent, you can apply to the local Rent Officer (listed under 'Rent' in the telephone directory) to have a fair rent assessed and registered. You must fill in an application form and the Rent Officer will usually inspect your accommodation. Factors taken into account are the floor area rented, the age and condition of the property, and its location. If you want to check before applying that your application has a chance of success, you can inspect the Rent Officer's register to see what rents have been registered recently for similar properties in your area.

Either party can appeal against the Rent Officer's decision (you should do so within twenty-eight days of notification) to the Rent Assessment Committee; if it decides to alter the figure, it usually increases it in the landlord's favour. If the registered rent is higher than the rent agreed in the contract between the landlord and tenant, then the tenant pays the lower amount until the expiry of the contract.

The main problem that tenants can encounter if they get their rent registered is that they antagonise their landlords; this is important if you have restricted protection, as you may then be evicted.

EVICTION

Even if you have a restricted protection tenancy, your landlord cannot simply order you out of your home. First, he/she must serve a 'notice to quit' on you which has to meet certain legal requirements to be valid:

- it must be in writing

- it must give you at least twenty-eight days' notice, and the expiry date must coincide with the end of a completed tenancy period or the first day of a new one (for example, if you are a monthly tenant and you receive the notice on the 15th of a month, you must be given until the last day of the following month or the first day of the month after that)

- it must refer to your rights under the Rent Acts, if your tenancy is covered by them.

Even if the notice to quit is valid, a landlord cannot evict a tenant who stays on after the expiry date without first obtaining a court order. This will be granted only if the landlord can show that one of the grounds allowed in law for repossessing the property exists, and (except when the landlord is an owner–occupier) that it is reasonable for the tenant to be evicted in the circumstances. In most cases, if a court order is made, the tenant will have at least twenty-eight days' notice; in some cases, for example when the ground for eviction is rent arrears, the order may be suspended to allow the tenant a certain time to pay.

HARASSMENT AND ILLEGAL EVICTION

If a landlord evicts a tenant without following the correct legal procedure or uses methods of harassment in order to make it difficult for the tenant to stay or in any way exercise his/her legal rights, the tenant can take legal action. Examples of harassment include changing the locks, turning off the power supplies, physical assault or verbal abuse, depriving the tenant of services included in the contract, or demanding access to the rented accommodation under false pretences or unreasonably frequently. If you are not sure whether your landlord's behaviour amounts to harassment, seek advice from a Citizens' Advice Bureau or housing aid centre, or telephone your Town Hall and ask whether the local authority has a harassment or tenancy relations officer.

The main remedy for tenants who have been illegally evicted or harassed is to start civil proceedings in the county court, seeking an injunction to stop the landlord's illegal behaviour and damages to compensate for any injury or damage to property, any expenses incurred (for example, the cost of alternative accommodation), and inconvenience or distress (if the damages claimed exceed £5,000, the case will have to be heard in the High Court). It is important to act quickly in such cases, and you should seek legal advice as soon as you think you have a claim.

Harassment and illegal eviction are criminal offences, and a tenant could bring a private prosecution (see 'Noise and other types of nuisance', p 176); however, this is potentially much more costly than civil action and you will generally not get any compensation. Theoretically, the police could prosecute; in practice, however, they avoid involvement in landlord–tenant disputes unless some other offence such as assault is involved. The other state body that could start criminal proceedings in such a case is the local authority, but it usually declines to do so. In any case, the penalties imposed by magistrates' courts for illegal eviction and harassment are seldom severe (usually a relatively small fine).

REPAIRS AND MAINTENANCE

Under the Housing Act 1961 (and its Scottish equivalent, enacted in 1966; Northern Ireland has no equivalent law), landlords have certain minimum obligations to repair and maintain rented accommodation unless it has been let as a fixed term tenancy of seven years or more. These include the upkeep of the exterior and structure of the property, the plumbing and drainage systems including sanitary installations, gas and electricity fittings and fixed water and space heating appliances. However, the tenant also has an obligation to take reasonable care to prevent damage, and not call in the landlord for trivial maintenance jobs that any tenant could reasonably be expected to do.

In addition to the statutory requirements, the contract between a landlord and tenant will usually set out responsibilities for repair and maintenance on either side. In the absence of an express agreement to the contrary, the law adds some minor implied terms, for example that the landlord will be responsible for the safety of any common parts such as a hallway or staircase.

The majority of complaints about the repair and maintenance of rented property are made by tenants whose landlords have failed to carry out their legal obligations. Always start by informing your landlord in writing of the repairs required, and ask for them to be carried out. Allow a reasonable time for this to happen; if some but not all of the necessary work is done, make a note of what was completed and when, and what was omitted.

If your landlord ignores your notification and request, you have four choices of action.

■ Contact the Environmental Health Department of your local authority (in Northern Ireland, the Public Health Office), which will send someone round to inspect the property. Give the council official a list of the defects (for example, a copy of your original letter to the landlord). If the local authority considers that they constitute a nuisance under the Public Health Act, it can serve a notice on the landlord to carry out the work. If this is ignored, the authority can take the landlord to court and get an order instructing him/her to do the repairs by a certain date; alternatively, it may carry out the repairs itself and reclaim the cost from the landlord. Any defect that constitutes a risk to someone's health or safety comes under the Act, for example a leaking roof, damp, a rickety stair rail or loose slates that might fall and injure a passer-by.

■ Start civil proceedings against the landlord with an application to the county court for an order instructing the landlord to carry out the repairs for which he/she is legally responsible; you might also wish to bring a claim for damages.

■ Bring a private prosecution under the Public Health Act if the local authority will not do so (but take legal advice first).

■ Get the repairs done yourself and deduct the cost from the rent. However, to safeguard yourself, make sure you have given the landlord ample opportunity to carry out the work, and give notice in writing of your intention to take this course of action; also, get at least two estimates for the work as evidence that the deduction is reasonable. It's best to get legal advice in such circumstances, as non-payment of rent is one of the grounds for eviction.

Housing association accommodation

Most housing associations are registered with the government-run Housing Corporation, to which complaints can be made if the tenant has an unresolved dispute with an association. In the first place, though, complaints should be taken up with the association's housing manager.

RENT

Registered housing associations must charge a fair rent that has been assessed by the local Rent Officer; you can check yours by examining the Rent Officer's register. If you discover that you are being charged more, you can deduct the excess already paid from future payments; and if you find that no rent has been registered, you can apply for this to happen (for details, see 'Rent', p 180).

EVICTION

The majority of housing association tenants have considerable protection against eviction (exceptions include long-term tenants with a fixed-term tenancy of over twenty-one years and those granted a tenancy of less than twelve months as a 'homeless person'). The procedure for eviction is very similar to that followed by private landlords, involving a formal notice to quit and a court order to regain possesion of the property (see 'Eviction', p 180). In addition to showing that one of a number of specific grounds for possession exists, the association often has to show that suitable alternative accommodation is available for the tenant.

REPAIRS AND MAINTENANCE

The rules for privately rented accommodation apply (see p 180).

RIGHT TO BUY

Whether a housing association tenant has the right to buy the freehold (or, in the case of flats, a long leasehold) of his/her home depends on the type of association (for example, those registered as charities or which have not received government funds do not have to give tenants this right).

Council accommodation

Although council housing is theoretically available to any citizen, it is usually in short supply and a local authority can impose various criteria when considering applications such as a minimum period of residence in the area. Priority is often given to people in special need such as homeless parents with small children. Details of a council's selection policies must be available for public inspection, and you can also demand to see the file relating to your application (contact the local authority's Housing Department).

Whether you feel your application for council housing is not being properly considered or you are an existing tenant with a complaint, start by writing to the local authority's Director of Housing (in Northern Ireland, complaints are handled by the local offices of the Northern Ireland Housing Executive, the body responsible for state housing). If you are dissatisfied with the response, see if your local councillor can help. Complaints about the way in which the authority has handled your application or complaint can be passed on to the Commissioner for Local Administration (see p 154 for further details).

RENT

A council tenant has to pay the rent demanded by the council and cannot apply to the Rent Officer to have a 'fair rent' fixed. However, the rent must be 'reasonable', and tenants must be notified of any intended increase at least four weeks in advance.

EVICTION

Most council tenants have considerable protection against eviction (exceptions include council employees and 'homeless persons' granted a tenancy of less than twelve months). The procedure a council must follow is very similar to that followed by private landlords (see 'Eviction', p 180). In addition to showing that one of a number of specific grounds for possession exists, the council often has to show that suitable alternative accommodation is available for the tenant.

REPAIRS AND MAINTENANCE

The same rules apply as to privately rented accommodation (see p 182). As a council cannot start criminal proceedings against itself, you may have to consider bringing a private prosecution. Before doing so, discuss the other courses of action with your local councillor or a consumer adviser.

RIGHT TO BUY

All council tenants have a right to buy their homes, under the Housing Act 1980, as long as they have been in occupation for at least three years and have a 'secure tenancy' (the most widespread type). The council fixes the market price of the property, and the tenant is then given a discount, on a rising scale increasing with the number of years the tenant has lived there. If you disagree with the market price figure, you can appeal to the District Valuer, who is a government official (you must do this within three months of the council fixing the price); your council's Housing Department will supply the appeal application form.

Complaints about the local environment

Local authority amenities

Many aspects of your local environment come under the care of the local authority. There are two or three tiers of local government, depending on where you live; for most of the country, these are the county council (in Scotland, the regional or island council), the district council and, in rural areas, the parish council (in Wales and Scotland, the community council). Greater London has a system of borough councils.

If you have a complaint about a local authority service, write to the department responsible for providing it. If you're not sure which council office to contact, the Town Hall or the staff at your local Citizens' Advice Bureau or library should be able to point you in the right direction. If you are dissatisfied with the department's response, contact your local councillor. In some cases, you may be able to take legal action as a last resort; and, if maladministration is involved, you can complain to the Commissioner for Local Administration (see p 154). If the issue is one of public importance, consider taking group action (see p 38).

REFUSE COLLECTION

This is the responsibility of district councils (in London, borough councils). Household refuse must be collected regularly, and at no charge; a charge can be levied for other types of waste, for example building rubble or garden waste. You can be required to put refuse in a particular type or size of container, or to leave it out at a specified convenient pick-up point. If the council fails to maintain a collection service, you can 'serve notice' on it to do so, in writing, by telephone or in person; if it ignores this, you can apply to the magistrates' court for an order instructing it to carry out its legal duties.

PUBLIC PARKS AND RECREATION FACILITIES

A council can pass and enforce bye-laws restricting the way in which any of its parks or recreation facilities are used, for example specifying opening times or prohibiting certain types of behaviour (such as organised games or the holding of public meetings). If you feel any such bye-law is unreasonable or is not being properly enforced, or if you are dissatisfied with the standard of upkeep of a public park or recreation facility, telephone or write to the Parks or Recreation Department, or to your parish council if you have one.

Anyone who suffers personal injury while using council recreation facilities (for example, a child injured while playing on a public slide) may be able to make a claim for negligence; if you think this applies to you, seek legal advice.

ROADS AND PAVEMENTS

Most local public roads and pavements are maintained by the county council, though minor roads may be the responsibility of the district council; motorways and trunk roads are maintained by the Department of Transport. Privately owned and maintained 'unadopted' roads, as they are called, are the responsibility of those whose properties front on to the road, who usually pay for the upkeep by means of a service charge or levy.

Local authorities have a duty to inspect public roads and pavements regularly and to make good any damage to their surface; some distribute special forms through public libraries and other neighbourhood information centres, inviting local residents to bring such damage to their attention. The local authority is also responsible for keeping streets and pavements clean and free from obstruction, and for maintaining adequate street lighting (unless this is done by the parish council). If an authority fails to carry out its obligations, you can apply to a magistrates' court for an order requiring it to do so. If you suffer injury or damage to your property as a result of the poor condition of a road or pavement – for example, you trip over a broken paving stone or your bicycle overturns in a pothole – you may be able to sue the responsible authority for negligence (this also applies to accidents on a private road, in which case you can sue its owners). However, if the council can show that it took reasonable steps to prevent such an accident (for example, by regularly carrying out inspections), you are unlikely to succeed.

Local authorities (usually the district council) are also responsible for removing abandoned vehicles from public land; to report one, telephone or write to the Environmental Health Department.

TRAFFIC CONTROL

Part of a local authority's responsibility for roads includes the control of parking and traffic, and the improvement and encouragement of road safety. If you feel that a particular stretch of road is dangerous, or that a pedestrian crossing is required, or that parking restrictions are unreasonable, you'll probably find that group action is the most effective way of getting the authority to take action. Complaints should be made to the Planning and Transportation Department.

Planning proposals

Changes to the area in which you live – for example, proposals to alter the appearance or change the use of an existing building, or to construct a new block of flats or a factory, or to build a new road – are controlled by the local authority, which is responsible for giving or denying planning permission. This system allows members of the public to register their objections and to attempt to influence the planners' decisions. Most of the following information is concerned with how you can complain if you object to someone else's planning proposals; but there is also advice on how to appeal if you are the person whose proposal has been rejected.

The way in which you should complain about a planning proposal depends partly on the stage at which you find out about it, and partly on whether your objection is shared by others. There are two basic tips to follow:

- the earlier you make your objections known, the greater chance you have of getting plans scrapped or changed

- when plans affect a number of people, group protest is far more likely to get results than submitting individual objections (see 'When group action is appropriate', p 38).

FINDING OUT WHAT IS PROPOSED

Once a local authority has reached a decision about an application for planning permission – a process that usually takes no more than eight weeks – it's too late to complain about the plans. It is therefore essential to find out about them in advance, and then to act quickly. If one of your neighbours has made the application, you may know about the plans already, but applicants are under no obligation to warn or contact those who will be affected (except in Scotland, where immediate neighbours have to be informed of planning applications in advance). Fortunately, most local authority planning departments contact people who will obviously be affected by a proposed development and seek their opinions (and in conservation areas, the council is obliged to do this by posting a notice on or near the site concerned). Many councils also supply lists of planning applications to local newspapers for publication. Otherwise, if you want to check whether there are any planning applications in the pipeline for your immediate area, you can telephone the district or borough council's Planning Officer; although not obliged to do so, he/she will often tell you. You also have the right to inspect the planning register at the council offices and to see all the plans that have been submitted.

If you want to get advance warning of changes that may occur in the longer term, and to discover what the local authority's intentions are as distinct from the specific proposals submitted by private individuals or businesses, find out from the Planning Department whether the council has a local plan. This sets out the policies and existing proposals for the use of buildings and land in the council's area likely to take effect over the following ten years or so. Though councils are not obliged to have local plans, most do, and they have to observe a set procedure when drawing them up that gives members of the public a chance to state their views and objections. First, a plan is prepared in draft form; if the council chooses, it can invite comments at this stage (usually there is a deadline of six weeks), and it may hold public meetings at which anybody, directly affected or not, can raise questions, express worries or make suggestions for improvements. Then, when all comments have been considered, the council draws up a final plan and puts it on deposit; at this stage, it must insert notices in local newspapers, informing members of the public of their right to send in written objections or comments, and giving details of where and by when to send them (again, you'll usually have six weeks to respond). At this stage, you can also demand a public inquiry (see 'Taking group action', p 192).

COMPLAINING ABOUT A NEIGHBOUR'S PLANNING PROPOSAL

If your neighbour intends to change the appearance of his/her building or to use it in a different way – for example, by building an extension or extra storey, or by turning part of a home into business premises – then he/she will almost certainly require planning permission (if work starts and you suspect that planning permission has not been obtained, you can check the planning register and, if you're right, report the matter to the district or borough council's Planning Department).

Objections to a planning application should be made in writing as soon as possible to the Planning Department, which will pass them on, together with its own recommendation, to the Planning Committee. The committee, which is made up of councillors, makes the final decision; if you feel strongly about the plans, you can also approach the committee direct by writing to its chairman (the Planning Department will give you his/her name and address). You may also find your local councillor sympathetic and willing to talk to other committee members on your behalf.

In most cases, you will be able to attend the meeting at which the Planning Committee discusses the application and hear the arguments for and against it; the chairman may also invite you to address the committee, but you have no right to do so. Once the decision is made, only the applicant has the right to appeal against it.

THE APPLICANT'S RIGHT TO APPEAL

If you have applied for planning permission but it has been refused, or the council has imposed conditions or restrictions which you feel are unreasonable, or you haven't received a decision within eight weeks (unless you agreed to allow them extra time), you should start by contacting the development control section of the Planning Department. If you can't reach a satisfactory conclusion by informal discussion, you can appeal to the Secretary of State for the Environment (or his/her counterparts in Wales, Scotland and Northern Ireland), as long as you do so within six months of receiving the council's decision (or six months after the eight-week deadline for a decision has been passed). The Planning Department can give you a copy of a free booklet on the appeal procedure; and you must obtain an official appeal form from the Department of the Environment (or the Welsh Office, the Scottish Development Department or the planning division of the Department of the Environment for Northern Ireland, as appropriate).

There are two kinds of appeal: written representations, in which the inspector appointed to consider the case reads full statements submitted by you and by the local authority and makes a site visit (a decision will normally be reached within four months if this procedure is followed) and a public inquiry, which allows you to present your case in person, call witnesses and cross-examine the local authority's planners (a decision will normally be reached within six months if this procedure is followed). In either case, you may wish to seek advice about how to present your case most effectively and a solicitor can represent you at the inquiry if you wish. However, professional help can be expensive, so check whether there is a voluntary planning aid service in your area (the council's Planning Department or your local Citizens' Advice Bureau should have details).

TAKING GROUP ACTION

If you think that others may have reason to share your objection to a planning application or local authority proposal, you should seriously consider some form of group action (for advice on how to canvass initial support and then organise a pressure group, see pp 40–48). Instead of submitting individual letters of complaint, write a joint letter or send in a petition. As well as lobbying the chairman of the Planning Committee and other councillors (and the clerk of your parish council, if your area has one), seek support from independent bodies such as your local Civic or Amenity Society, if one exists.

If you feel the issue seriously affects a whole community or is even of regional or national significance – for example, you are objecting to a proposal to build a major road that will cut through an area of outstanding natural beauty, or a new shopping complex that will ruin the character of an area – you can write direct to the Secretary of State for the Environment (or his/her counterparts in Wales, Scotland and Northern Ireland) and ask for a public inquiry; again, either write a joint letter or get others to write as well, as this will influence the Secretary's response. If an inquiry is set up, you'll need to get expert help on preparing and presenting your case. Start by contacting a relevant national organisation, for example one of the many concerned with the environment (the National Council for Voluntary Organisations may be able to make suggestions; or consult *The environmental directory*, published by the Civic Trust).

Preparing a case can be extremely time-consuming and expensive; your group will have to pay for a solicitor if it wishes to employ one, as legal aid is not available for public inquiries, and obtaining experts' reports or paying witnesses' expenses can be costly. Moreover, you can win the public inquiry battle and still lose the planning war because the inspector who holds the inquiry can only make recommendations to the local authority; the final decision, which may ignore those recommendations, rests with the Secretary of State for the Environment.

WHEN PUBLIC WORKS AFFECT YOUR PROPERTY

If a local authority goes ahead with a development that affects the value of your property, you may be able to seek redress for 'planning blight', as it is known. There are two main types of planning blight:

- if your home is threatened by a compulsory purchase order, in which case you can demand that the council buys it from you at full market price (if you dispute the sum it offers you, you can appeal to the Lands Tribunal)

- if vibration, noise, smells or fumes created by new public works – a power station, for example, or a new road – reduce the value of your property by over £50, in which case you can claim compensation from the council for nuisance (it is best to get a surveyor to assess the reduction, and you can claim a refund of the survey fee from the council). If the amount you claim is disputed, the District Surveyor will inspect the property and, if you are unhappy about his/her estimate, the case will be heard by the Lands Tribunal. For further details, get a copy of the free booklet, *Your home and nuisance from public development*, from your council or local Citizens' Advice Bureau.

To make a claim for planning blight, contact the Planning Department and ask for a 'blight notice'.

If you do not qualify for compensation for nuisance, you may be able to claim a reduction in your rates (see p 201).

Noise and pollution

The law's attitude to intangible nuisances such as noise, vibration and smells, and the means of redress it provides if you have a complaint, have been outlined in the section on complaints about neighbours (see 'Noise and other types of nuisance', p 175). This section looks at some other common sources of nuisance when those responsible are not known individuals who can be approached informally; and at how you can take action about suspected pollution of your local environment.

BUILDING SITES

Local authorities are authorised, by the Control of Pollution Act 1974, to control the way building work is carried out in order to limit the noise it creates. A certain amount of noise is unavoidable, but you may feel that the work is being carried out at unreasonable times of the day. You can also complain if you feel that an unnecessary amount of dust is being produced. To make a complaint, telephone the Environmental Health Department of your local council (in Northern Ireland, the Public Health Office); if it agrees with you, it can serve a notice on the builder imposing restrictions on the work. If these are not observed, notify the council which may then decide to start criminal proceedings in the magistrates' court. If it is unwilling to do so, take legal advice about starting proceedings yourself.

ROAD TRAFFIC

The local authority is responsible for the routing and control of traffic. If you feel that, for example, your residential road is being used by too many noisy and smelly commercial vehicles, contact the council's Planning and Transportation Department; if your neighbours share your concern, you can send a petition. See your local councillor about it in case he/she can wield any influence on your behalf.

If the level of traffic noise you hear in your home increases because the local authority builds a new road or adds an extra carriageway to an existing road, you may be eligible for an insulation grant (whether your home qualifies depends on a noise test carried out by the council). You may also be able to get a discretionary grant if traffic noise has increased because a road has been widened or its position changed. For details, get a copy of the free booklet, *Insulation against traffic noise*, from your council or Citizens' Advice Bureau.

AIR TRAFFIC

Most airports have regulations which control the level of noise that aircraft using the airport can make, and there may also be limitations on the times of day that certain types of aircraft can operate. However, aircraft are exempt from the laws controlling nuisance; unless the noise or vibration from an aircraft causes damage to your property, you cannot seek legal redress or compensation, even if the noise means you can't sit out in your garden without being deafened. Some airport authorities provide insulation grants to residents living within a specified distance of the airport; contact the authority if you think you may be eligible.

POLLUTION

Pollution can take many forms; noise and refuse have already been mentioned in this section, but to many people the most worrying form of pollution is the introduction of excessive amounts of chemicals into the air, water and soil, particularly by those working in industry and agriculture. Some legal controls exist, as a result of the introduction of such laws as the Clean Air Act and the Control of Pollution Act; these are usually enforced by the local authority's Environmental Health Department, to which you can complain about any specific local sources of pollution. The water authorities (see 'Water', p 122) are responsible for dealing with the pollution of waterways, and control the discharge of waste into rivers and estuaries; to report a case of suspected water contamination, telephone the relevant authority's pollution department (listed under 'Water' in the telephone directory).

Pollution is often not simply a local problem, as recent research into the phenomenon called 'acid rain' has emphasised, and this makes its detection and control difficult and expensive. A number of national and international environmental organisations collect evidence and carry out research, as well as campaigning for additional legal sanctions or voluntary controls. The Council for Environmental Conservation, an umbrella organisation for conservation groups, has an inquiry service which will give advice on where to get information about a particular pollution problem, and many of the organisations have local branches from which you can seek support in a local environmental campaign. You could also consult the Civic Trust's *Environmental directory* (mentioned on p 192).

Complaints about tax, rates and welfare benefits

Having considered elsewhere in this book how to complain about some of the services provided by the state – for example, education, health care, the transport system and housing – this section looks at how to complain about the means by which central and local government raise much of the money to pay for those services: taxation. It also looks at the system by which money can be passed back to the citizen, in social security payments: the largest single form of government expenditure.

Income tax assessment

Most employed people pay income tax through the 'Pay-as-you-earn' (PAYE) system, which means that deductions are made from their salary or wages through the year by their employers (who act as tax collectors). These deductions are based on the rate of tax applied to their level of earnings, less various tax-free allowances. The allowances for which you qualify depend on your personal circumstances – for example, whether you are single or married – and are indicated in your tax code. The taxman obtains the necessary information to work out your tax code by sending you a tax return, a form on which you give information about your earnings from your job and any other sources of income such as a pension or savings, and about your outgoings. If your financial affairs are straightforward, you probably won't be sent a tax return every year; instead, the tax man will assume that your personal circumstances, in so far as they affect your code, have not changed, and will simply amend the code to take account of any changes made by government to the level of allowances.

You will usually be sent a notice of coding shortly before the beginning of a new tax year (6 April). It shows the allowances you will be given, any other source of income, and the difference between the two which (minus the last digit) is your code. Check these figures carefully; if you think they are wrong, write to the Inspector of Taxes for your tax district (the address is given on the notice) as soon as possible. You can get help on how to check your code from the *Tax-saving guide* issue of *Which?* magazine, published each March by Consumers' Association (see p 17).

At the end of the tax year, you may be sent a notice of assessment. This sets out the income you are supposed to have received during that year from your job and any other sources; the deductions and allowances given; the amount of tax paid; and the amount of tax actually due. When you are taxed through PAYE, you will usually receive a notice of assessment only if the Inspector of Taxes decides that you have overpaid or underpaid tax (if the former, you'll get a cheque in repayment, either with the notice or shortly after; if the latter, you'll get a demand for the amount you owe). However, you can always ask for one if you want to check that your tax has been correctly assessed. If you are not taxed through PAYE, for example you are self-employed or your income is obtained from sources other than a job, then you will always get a notice of assessment (and the following procedure applies in all cases).

If you disagree with any of the figures, write to the Inspector of Taxes as soon as possible, and certainly within thirty days; otherwise you'll lose your right to appeal unless you can show that there was a sufficient reason for the delay – for example, you were away on holiday or ill in hospital (if the Inspector rejects your reasons, you can appeal to the General Commissioners – see below). Use the appeal form supplied with the notice, which also allows you to apply for a postponement of payment of tax which you consider is not due; if you don't apply, the taxman will chase you for the full payment demanded, even though you have lodged an appeal. Leaflets explaining the appeal procedure are available from your local Inland Revenue office.

Most appeals are settled informally in correspondence with the Inspector of Taxes. If a meeting is likely to be helpful, but your tax office is some distance away, you can ask for your file to be sent to the local tax office and one of its staff will discuss any problems with you. However, if you and the Inspector of Taxes are unable to agree about the amount of tax you owe, you can appeal further, to the Tax Commissioners. There are two types:

- Special Commissioners, who are tax experts appointed by the Treasury; they will automatically consider any appeal involving a claim that the 'income' section of a tax return was filled in incorrectly, and also handle more complex tax disputes

- General Commissioners, who are lay volunteers advised on legal matters by a paid clerk; they will automatically consider any appeal involving a PAYE code or failure to claim a personal allowance, and hear the majority of appeals (in some cases, you may be able to opt instead for the Special Commissioners, but this is seldom in your interest).

Your appeal will be considered at a formal hearing, at which both you and the Inland Revenue will be asked to explain your views and provide any necessary evidence; witnesses can be called as well as documents produced. Preparing your case carefully is essential and will be time-consuming; it can also be expensive if you employ a professional such as a qualified accountant or solicitor to advise you and, if you wish, represent you at the hearing (legal aid is not available and each side pays its own costs, regardless of the Commissioners' final decision). It is therefore advisable to seek advice before embarking on an appeal; your local Citizens' Advice Bureau may be able to help, or refer you to a specialist.

The only way in which you can appeal against the Commissioners' decision, which will be given at the end of the hearing, is if you appeal on a point of law (their decision on points of fact is final); then you will have to take your case to the High Court (in Scotland, the Court of Session), and this can prove very expensive if you lose, as you will then almost certainly have to pay the Inland Revenue's costs as well as your own.

COMPLAINTS ABOUT INLAND REVENUE STAFF

If you feel that your tax inspector is behaving unreasonably (for example, by demanding information which you feel is irrelevant), start by giving him/her a chance to explain. A personal conversation is often more likely to clear up any misunderstandings than a further exchange of letters, so telephone the tax office (be ready to give the reference number shown on your notice of coding, tax return or notice of assessment) and speak to the person responsible, or arrange a meeting. If, after this, you are still dissatisfied, you can write to the District Inspector (whose name appears on the tax office's stationery); write 'For the personal attention of' before his/her name on the envelope and the letter, and be sure to explain clearly the basis of your complaint or disagreement with the inspector. If you are not satisfied with the reply you receive, you can write to the Regional Controller responsible for your tax office (which will give you his/her name and address). As a last resort, you can ask your MP to pass on a complaint to the Parliamentary Commissioner for Administration, whose role is similar to that of the Local Commissioners for Administration (see p 154) except that he/she investigates allegations of maladministration by government departments and official Crown bodies (a free leaflet about how and when to complain to the Parliamentary Ombudsman is available from Citizens' Advice Bureaux and major libraries, or direct from the Ombudsman's office – see 'Addresses', p 231).

Value-added tax (VAT)

Unlike income tax and taxes on capital such as capital gains tax and capital transfer tax, which are assessed by the Inland Revenue, VAT is the responsibility of Customs and Excise. If you think that a trader has been wrong to charge you VAT or has calculated it incorrectly, but he/she denies this, you can contact your local Customs and Excise office for advice; if it confirms that you are right but you still can't get the trader to agree, ask the VAT office to write to the trader.

Most complaints about VAT come from traders themselves. The appeal procedure is outlined in a free booklet, *The VAT guide*, issued to anyone who applies to register for VAT; further details are given in a leaflet, *Appeals to value-added tax tribunals*, which is available, together with appeal forms, from VAT Tribunal centres and local VAT offices. An appeal to a VAT Tribunal must be made within thirty days of the decision with which you are disagreeing; alternatively, you can ask the VAT office to reconsider and, once it has done so, you'll have twenty-one days to lodge an appeal to the Tribunal if the original decision is confirmed, or thirty days if the original decision is revised. The Tribunal's decision is final unless you wish to appeal against it on a point of law to the High Court (in Scotland, the Court of Session); but this can prove very expensive, so take expert advice before embarking on this course of action.

Rates

Rates are a form of property tax levied by local government to help pay for the services it provides. The rates for your home are calculated on the basis of its gross value, which is the notional amount a tenant would pay in rent if it was let unfurnished. This is dependent on a number of factors including its floor area, the number of habitable rooms, the age and type of building and its location, and the figure is calculated by Valuation Officers employed by the Inland Revenue. Certain standard deductions are made from the gross value to set the rateable value.

Once your home's rateable value has been assessed, it will remain at that figure until any general revaluation takes place, unless there are any physical alterations to the property or changes in the surroundings that affect it. However, as ratepayers are all too aware, the rates bill still tends to go up every year because the local authority can increase the rate-in-the-pound. This is the figure set by the local authority according to the amount of revenue it wishes to raise, by which a property's rateable value is multiplied in order to calculate the rates bill. For example, if the rateable value of your property is £325, the rate-in-the-pound might go up from 180 pence one year to 192 pence the next, resulting in an increase in your rates bill of £39. There is no right of appeal against an increase in the rate-in-the-pound, though you can tackle your local councillor about it if you feel it is excessive.

APPEALING AGAINST THE RATEABLE VALUE

If you move into a new property which has not been rated before, or if you carry out any improvements, such as building an extension, that affect the rateable value, you may wish to dispute the Valuation Officer's assessment of what the new rateable value should be. When you receive the Valuation Officer's proposal, you have twenty-eight days (from the proposal date) to object in writing (a short letter briefly giving your reasons is sufficient). If you miss this deadline, you can still object by appealing against it as an existing assessment.

There are three grounds for applying to have the existing rateable value of your property reduced (in Scotland, the rules are different; the Land Valuation Assessor at your local Inland Revenue office will be able to give you details):

- it is over-valued in comparison to similar properties in the area

- since it was last valued, a change has occurred that in effect has reduced its value

- when it was last valued, a relevant factor was either miscalculated or overlooked.

In order to check whether your home is over-valued, you should note the addresses of several properties in your immediate area which you feel are comparable to yours and then find out their gross values from the valuation list kept at your local council offices. However, finding genuinely comparable properties can be tricky because of the range of factors that affect the valuation, and you'll have to do a lot of research work to prepare an appeal that has a real chance of success. If your neighbours also want to appeal, you might be able to share the work.

You have a greater chance of success if you can show that a change has occurred to make your property less attractive, were it to be let. This might be a significant increase in noise (from heavy traffic or nearby properties such as a school or pub, for example), a deterioration in the immediate environment, a reduction in local amenities, or a loss of light or privacy affecting one or more rooms (for example, because of a neighbour's new extension or the construction nearby of a new block of flats). It does not have to be a permanent change (for example, you can appeal if major building works nearby are creating a lot of noise and dust) but it must last for several months at least.

Examples of when you might dispute the accuracy of the valuation are if you suspect that the floor area was inaccurately measured, or notice that your garden shed is described as a garage.

Whatever the grounds, write to the Valuation Officer (if you wish, you can use a standard proposal form which he/she can supply); the address is given in information accompanying your rates bill, or look under 'Inland Revenue' in the telephone directory. Simply say that you feel the existing assessment is incorrect and excessive (you'll be able to give your full reasons at a later stage). Your proposal for alteration will be acknowledged, and in due course your property may be inspected.

If the Valuation Officer does not accept the grounds for your appeal or you cannot agree about the size of the reduction, you then have the right to appeal to the local Valuation Court (in Scotland, the local Valuation Appeal Committee); this will happen automatically if you do not withdraw your proposal within fourteen days of the Valuation Officer's decision. You will be asked to attend a hearing at which the Valuation Panel (three local people, all volunteers) considers the arguments on both sides; the Valuation Court is open to the public, so you can attend any similar appeals hearings in advance to get an idea of what happens. In most cases, you are wise to accept the Panel's decision (you can ask it to explain its reasons). If you wish to take the matter further, you can appeal within twenty-eight days to the Lands Tribunal; however, you will probably need professional help at this stage, which could be expensive, and it will certainly be time-consuming, so seek expert advice before embarking on this course of action.

If the rateable value of your home is reduced, notify the water authority (this is not necessary in Scotland, where water charges are included in the rates bill), as you'll receive a corresponding reduction.

APPLYING FOR A RATE REBATE

The rating system is in many ways an unfair form of taxation, because it ignores the number of people living in a house and so making use of the local authority's services; neither does it take into account their financial circumstances, as income tax does. To compensate for the problems that can arise as a result, housing benefit to pay part or all of the rates is available on a means-tested basis. Whether you are eligible depends on the size of your rates bill, the number of people in your household, and the money coming in. If you are getting supplementary benefit, you are automatically eligible for housing benefit; otherwise, you must complete an application form (available from your local Citizens' Advice Bureau, which can help you to complete it, or from the Director of Finance at your local Town Hall). The benefit is usually granted from the first day of the month in which your application was received, so don't delay if you think you may be eligible.

RATE RELIEF FOR THE DISABLED

If you or anyone in your household is disabled and as a result you have made any improvements to the property that would normally add to its rateable value (for example, you have installed an extra bathroom on the ground floor), or if you have had to buy a property with extra space or special features to accommodate the needs of the disabled person, you can apply for rate relief on the extra rates you'd otherwise have to pay. Your local authority offices can give you an application form, as well as a free leaflet explaining how the relief is calculated.

Welfare benefits

Whether you have a right to claim one or more of the many types of welfare benefit provided by the state usually depends not only on your need but also on whether you meet certain qualifications. Some, such as sickness and invalidity benefit, unemployment benefit, maternity allowance and the state retirement pension, are available only if you have contributed sufficient National Insurance payments (these are therefore known as contributory benefits). Others, such as supplementary benefit, family income supplement, child benefit and housing benefit, are available only if your financial means fall below a certain level and, except in specific cases, you are not in full-time employment but are available for work (these are known as means-tested benefits). Some benefits, such as attendance allowance, invalid care allowance and mobility allowance, are available simply according to need (though that need has to be proved, and the benefits are generally low).

You can get information about which benefits are available, and advice about whether you qualify and how to apply, from your local Citizens' Advice Bureau or social security office (listed under 'Health and Social Security, Department of' in the telephone directory); the DHSS publishes various free leaflets about individual benefits, as well as a booklet, *Which benefit?*, which you may find helpful.

When you apply for a welfare benefit, make sure that you give all the relevant information or you may lose out on your rights. If your application is refused, ask the social security office to explain why it has decided you are not eligible, if it hasn't already done so. If you are in any doubt about the answer, get advice from your local Citizens' Advice Bureau or from a legal advice or law centre, if there's one in your area. If your application is accepted but you disagree with the amount awarded, write to the social security office asking it to check its calculations. It is now common practice for details of the calculations to be attached to the notification of the decision, so you can do some checking yourself – if necessary, with help from one of the advice centres already mentioned.

If you cannot reach agreement with the social security office about either your entitlement or the amount payable, you have the right to appeal to the local Social Security Appeal Tribunal. You must do so in writing within twenty-eight days of the date of the decision, either by letter or using a special form (included in a leaflet, *How to appeal against a decision made by a social security office or unemployment benefit office*, available from DHSS offices, libraries and post offices). If you miss the deadline, your appeal may be rejected, so give your reasons for the delay as these may be accepted by the Tribunal's chairman. The social security office will consider your form, and may at this stage decide to accept your claim; otherwise, you will be notified of the date of the tribunal hearing.

Help with making an appeal can be obtained either from one of the general advice centres or from a specialist agency such as the Child Poverty Action Group or Age Concern; and you can take someone with you to the hearing to help explain your case. The decision of the tribunal panel, which consists of a chairman and two other people (none of whom are employed by the DHSS or the Department of Employment) will be sent to you in writing, a few days after the hearing. You will have to accept it unless you wish to appeal against it on a point of law, and to do this you will need expert legal advice (check whether you are eligible for help with legal expenses – see p 20); in such a case, your appeal will be heard by the Social Security Commissioner.

COMPLAINTS ABOUT DHSS STAFF

If your complaint relates to the treatment you have received from staff at your social security or unemployment benefit office, or the way in which either your application or your appeal has been handled, or you feel there has been inefficiency, you should first of all write to the manager of the office you've been using. Ask at the office for his/her name, and write 'For the personal attention of' on the envelope and the letter. Explain briefly, clearly and politely the basis of your complaint. If you are dissatisfied with the reply you receive, you can write to the Regional Controller responsible for your area (ask the local office for the name and address). You can also ask your MP for support. If this doesn't get results, and you feel that your complaint is serious, ask your MP to take the matter up with one of the Ministers of State at the Department of Health and Social Security, or you can write yourself; and, if you consider there has been maladministration, you can appeal through your MP to the Parliamentary Commissioner for Administration (see p 199).

Complaints about employment

The legislation relating to employment is extensive and in many cases extremely complex, and it is impossible to give any detailed

advice here though the following general guidelines may be useful.
You should therefore contact one of the sources of help and advice
mentioned below if you have a complaint that you cannot resolve
amicably with your employer.

Your contract of employment

The basis of an employee's rights and responsibilities is his/her
contract of employment and, like most contracts, this need not be
in writing. However, with few exceptions, an employee must be
supplied with a statement of the contract's main terms and
conditions (known as 'written particulars') within thirteen weeks of
starting work, or at least notified that the particulars are contained
in some comprehensive statement covering all employees which is
easily available for inspection. Although written particulars do not
constitute the contract, they are useful evidence in the event of a
dispute.

The written particulars must refer to the work rules you are
required to observe (these may be detailed in a separate document),
and the procedure by which they will be enforced, and should tell
you how to appeal against any disciplinary action you feel is unfair.
They must also tell you to whom you should make a complaint
about any aspect of your job.

Employment protection laws

Your rights as an employee do not depend solely on your contract of
employment. Various employment protection laws require
employers to meet certain minimum standards and requirements in
their treatment of employees, or risk legal action. However, not all
employees qualify for every type of protection; sometimes it
depends on the length of your employment, and several groups of
workers (part-time employees, for example) have significantly fewer
rights. Moreover, you can forfeit what rights you have if you fail to
take action within the legal time limit, which is usually three
months (see 'Applying to an industrial tribunal', p 209).

Where to get help and advice about your rights

There are various people and organisations to which you can turn if you feel you have been treated unfairly by your employer. If you belong to a recognised trade union, speak to your union representative. You can also consult a law centre, if there's one in your area, or a Citizens' Advice Bureau; if they feel you need specialist advice, they may be able to suggest a suitable solicitor (see also 'How to get help with legal expenses', p 20). If you are alleging racial or sexual discrimination, you should contact either the Commission for Racial Equality or the Equal Opportunities Commission (see 'Complaints about discrimination', p 226). Last but not least, you can get advice from the Advisory Conciliation and Arbitration Service (except in Northern Ireland, where you should contact the Labour Relations Agency instead).

THE ADVISORY CONCILIATION AND ARBITRATION SERVICE (ACAS)

ACAS is an independent body with regional offices in England, Scotland and Wales, set up to encourage and help employers and employees to resolve any disputes voluntarily, without recourse to law or industrial action. You can contact an ACAS office by letter or telephone if you need information about any aspect of employment law, or advice about how to pursue a complaint; and you can ask it to conciliate if you have an individual dispute relating to your rights in employment law and you don't want to negotiate directly with your employer. If you apply to an industrial tribunal (see p 209), ACAS will automatically be informed of your claim and will usually attempt to bring about an amicable settlement before the case is heard by the tribunal.

Taking legal action

Most claims by employees against employers are heard by industrial tribunals. These are statutory bodies each consisting of a chairman (a solicitor or barrister) and two lay people, one from a panel nominated by the Trades Union Congress (TUC) to represent employees, the other from a panel nominated by the Confederation of British Industry (CBI) to represent employers. Tribunal proceedings are less formal than those of a court, though either party can choose to be represented at the hearing by a solicitor, an adviser (for example, a trade union official) or a friend; however, legal aid is not available to pay for this. Generally speaking, no costs are awarded; however, if a tribunal finds that you have acted 'frivolously, vexatiously or otherwise unreasonably' in bringing a claim, you may be ordered to pay your employer's costs (which could be high if he/she has employed a solicitor).

The majority of claims heard by industrial tribunals are concerned with

- unfair dismissal
- redundancy
- equal pay
- sex or racial discrimination
- trade union membership/non-membership
- maternity rights and pay
- unitemised pay statements
- suspension on medical grounds
- time off (for example, for ante-natal care, or to look for a job if you're being made redundant)
- failure to provide written particulars.

Claims that cannot be heard by an industrial tribunal, and for which you must therefore start civil proceedings in the county court to obtain compensation, are

- if you are owed wages
- if you were wrongfully dismissed (that is, sacked without the proper notice but on lawful grounds)
- if you have been injured as a result of negligence by the employer (this includes injuries caused by equipment, premises or a method of working, or by another employee's negligence – but such a claim can be difficult to prove because the onus is on you to show that the employer was negligent).

Applying to an industrial tribunal

There are strict time limits for making an application to an industrial tribunal; in most cases, the application must be received within three months of the events concerned, though in cases relating to redundancy or expulsion or exclusion from a union you have six months, and claims for equal pay can be considered at any time during your employment or up to six months after you have left the job. Only if you are able to convince the tribunal that the delay was unavoidable will a late application be considered (if you've missed the date through the failure of an adviser such as a solicitor to warn you of the deadline, you may be able to sue him/her for negligence).

Details of how to apply to an industrial tribunal and a description of what will happen are given in a free booklet, *Industrial tribunals procedure*, which also includes a table showing the matters that can be considered by a tribunal, the relevant legislation and the titles of the (mostly) free booklets you can consult for more detailed guidance. Applications are usually made on a standard form (IT1), and you should complete two copies so that you can retain one for your records. Both the booklets and the forms are available from your local job centre, employment office or unemployment benefit office.

The completed form must be sent to the Central Office of the Industrial Tribunals (in London, Glasgow or Belfast, as appropriate). If you are claiming unfair dismissal and have sent it in within seven days of the date your employment was effectively ended, you can claim 'interim relief'; this means that the tribunal will make a preliminary assessment of your claim and, if it seems likely to succeed, ask your employer to re-employ you until the hearing has taken place or, if he/she refuses, pay you at the full rate in the interim. Otherwise, applicants will usually be contacted by a conciliation officer from ACAS, who will try to arrange a settlement before the hearing. A pre-hearing assessment may take place, if either party requests it or the tribunal feels it would be helpful (usually because there is doubt about the strength of the applicant's claim). A case cannot be dismissed or decided at this stage but, if you are advised to drop your claim, you should take this seriously; otherwise, if you press on and the tribunal dismisses your claim at the hearing, you risk having costs awarded against you for being unreasonable.

If conciliation has proved unsuccessful and a hearing takes place, you will usually be told of its decision at the time; and in any case, you will receive a letter giving its reasons, either in summary or in full (full reasons must be given in certain cases, or if the applicant requests them at the time of the hearing or within twenty-one days of receiving the summary reasons). The tribunal's decision is final unless you want to appeal against it on a point of law (only in cases involving expulsion or exclusion from a trade union can you appeal on a point of fact), in which case you will need expert legal advice. Appeals, which must be lodged no later than forty-two days after the tribunal has sent you the full reasons for its decision (a summary is insufficient), are heard by the Employment Appeal Tribunal (in Northern Ireland, by the Court of Appeal) and can prove expensive, though legal aid may be available.

If a tribunal upholds your complaint and awards compensation but the employer fails to pay up, you will have to apply to a county court for leave to enforce the tribunal's order. The methods of enforcement are those described in Part One (see 'Getting your money', p 37).

Poor working conditions

If you are injured at work, you may be able to sue your employer for negligence, but it's obviously far better to take preventative measures. All employers have a duty to ensure the health, safety and welfare of their employees while they are at work, though only 'so far as is reasonably practicable'. In addition to a general duty of care, the law sets out specific regulations for certain types of premises; for example, if you work in a shop or office, there are a number of rules including one that is designed to prevent overcrowding and others intended to ensure the provision of sufficient clean and suitable lavatory and washing facilities.

Under the Health and Safety Act 1974, all employers with more than five employees must draw up and display a written policy statement setting out the company's general health and safety policy, identifying those responsible for implementing it, and describing practical arrangements (which usually include steps the employee must take). Your first step, if you spot a safety hazard or think that any health and safety regulations are not being observed, is to bring the matter to the attention of your head of department. If there is a recognised trade union at your place of work, there will be a union safety representative whom you can consult, and who can support your complaint. If, despite this, nothing is done, you should contact either the local office of the Health and Safety Executive (listed as such in the telephone directory) or, if you work in an office, shop or other non-industrial workplace, the Environmental Health Department of your local authority. An inspector will usually visit your workplace and may, if an employer is not observing health and safety law, serve a notice on him/her to make any necessary improvements or end a dangerous practice. Failure to comply with such a notice can lead to prosecution.

Complaints about advertising and the media

Advertising

The steps you can take if you wish to complain about an advertisement depend partly on whether a law has been broken by the advertiser, and partly on where the advertisement appeared.

WHEN LEGAL ACTION IS APPROPRIATE

Under the Sale of Goods Act (see p 50), all goods sold by either a trader or a private individual must be 'as described', and this means that any advertisement for them must be accurate; otherwise, you may be able to sue the seller for any loss you have suffered. Traders (but not private advertisers) selling goods and services are also liable to prosecution, under the Trade Descriptions Act 1968, if an advertisement is found to be dishonest or misleading; if you suspect that this law has been broken, contact your local Trading Standards Department.

Other laws that may be broken by advertisers are the Race

Relations Act 1976 and the Sex Discrimination Act 1975. If you spot an advertisement which you think is discriminatory, contact either the Commission for Racial Equality or the Equal Opportunities Commission, as appropriate, which may decide to take action (you cannot start legal proceedings yourself over a discriminatory advertisement). Write giving details of where and when the advertisement appeared, and what it contained (include a copy of it, if possible), and why you think it is objectionable. (See also 'Complaints about discrimination', p 226.)

WHEN THE ADVERTISING STANDARDS AUTHORITY CAN HELP

The Advertising Standards Authority (ASA) is a body set up by the advertising industry but independently run which acts as a watchdog to ensure standards within the industry. These standards are set out in the British Code of Advertising Practice, which is supported voluntarily by the major trade associations involved in advertising and the media. The Code covers advertisements which appear in newspapers, magazines or posters, on leaflets distributed through the mail or door-to-door, and in the cinema; it does not apply to radio or television advertisements (these are covered by a similar code administered by the Independent Broadcasting Authority – see below). The ASA's aim is to ensure that all advertisements

- are legal, decent, honest and truthful
- are prepared with a sense of responsibility both to the consumer and to society
- conform to the principles of fair competition as generally accepted in business.

The Code, which has nearly 500 rules, includes special regulations relating to advertisements aimed at children, and for certain goods and services such as cigarettes, alcoholic drinks and credit. A free leaflet giving an abridged version of the Code is available from the ASA, and you can consult a full copy at your local reference library or Citizens' Advice Bureau.

The ASA actively encourages members of the public to report any advertisement which appears to infringe either the letter or the spirit of the Code. If you have a complaint, write to the ASA giving details of where and when the advertisement appeared, what it contained (enclose a copy if possible) and why you feel it is objectionable. If there appears to have been a breach of the Code, the ASA will ask the advertiser to comment and may even insist that the advertisement is withdrawn while the investigation takes place. If the Code has been broken, the ASA has various sanctions:

- it can make the breach public by giving details in its monthly report

- it can arrange for advertising space or time to be withheld from the advertiser, by informing media companies which support the Code

- it can penalise the advertising agency which handled the advertisement

- it can inform other consumer protection agencies.

It cannot, however, order any compensation to be paid or start legal proceedings.

WHEN THE INDEPENDENT BROADCASTING AUTHORITY CAN HELP

The Independent Broadcasting Authority (IBA) will investigate any complaints about advertisements broadcast on television or radio. Its Code of Advertising Standards and Practice is similar to the ASA's Code, and in some ways is even stricter; for example, certain types of advertisement are completely banned (these include advertisements for cigarettes, moneylending and betting, or of a religious or political nature). If you have a complaint, write to the Advertising Control Department at the IBA, giving details of where and when the advertisement was broadcast and why you found it objectionable.

The press

If you have a complaint about a newspaper or magazine article (radio and television programmes are considered separately – see below), or about the behaviour of a journalist or other member of the press, there are various steps you can take, depending on the circumstances.

WHEN LEGAL ACTION IS APPROPRIATE

The circumstances in which you could seek redress through the law are:

- if you have been libelled, which is to say that the publication has published details about you which are untrue, and so damaged your reputation; if this happens, get advice from a solicitor specialising in defamation, as the law in this area is complex and any legal action could be lengthy and expensive (legal aid is not available in such cases)

- if you are being hounded by members of the press and they enter your property, in which case you can sue them for trespass (a photograph of a trespasser is useful evidence); again, get legal advice

- if you think that a publication contravenes the Obscene Publications Act, in which case you can report it to the police or, if they decide not to prosecute, you may be able to start criminal proceedings yourself; as this can be expensive, particularly if you lose the case, get expert advice first.

A LETTER TO THE EDITOR

For most types of complaint about the press, however, you should start by complaining to the Editor of the newspaper or magazine concerned. He/she is responsible for both the content of the publication and the behaviour of its staff. If you have a personal complaint about the accuracy of an article – for example, you were interviewed by a reporter and some of your remarks have been quoted out of context so that your meaning has been distorted – you can ask the Editor to publish a correction and apology. There's little you can do about a paper's political bias or general approach other than to stop buying it, though you can submit a letter on the subject for publication in its letters page, if it has one (if you don't want any letter you write to the Editor to be published, state this clearly in the letter itself). Always keep a copy of any correspondence about your complaint.

WHEN THE PRESS COUNCIL CAN HELP

If you feel that a newspaper's or magazine's Editor or staff have behaved unprofessionally or unethically, you can complain to the Press Council. This is a body set up by the newspaper industry to encourage high professional standards; half its members belong to the press, half do not. Complaints must be made in writing, within two months of the article or event concerned, and you should enclose a copy of the item (if appropriate), together with copies of any correspondence with the publication, and a full statement of why you are complaining. The Council will investigate, and you may be asked to attend a hearing. It will notify you of its findings in writing, and may also issue a statement to the press criticising the publication for its behaviour; however, it can't take any other action.

Television and radio

If you have a complaint about a television or radio programme, or about the way in which you have been treated by someone involved in making a programme, there are various steps you can take, depending on the circumstances.

WHEN LEGAL ACTION IS APPROPRIATE

The circumstances in which you could seek redress through the law are the same that apply to complaints about the press (see above), except that the Obscene Publications Act does not apply to broadcasting.

COMPLAINTS ABOUT A BBC PROGRAMME

The British Broadcasting Corporation (BBC), though it operates under government licence, is allowed to set its own standards and impose its own controls to ensure that its programmes are accurate, decent and of high quality. If you find a programme offensive or biased, or simply think it is bad, and you want to make an immediate protest, you can telephone the information department (in London, the duty officer) and register your complaint. You can also write to the producer of the programme (whose name appears in the *Radio Times*). Radio and television programmes devoted

solely to listeners'/viewers' letters of praise and criticism are
another way of getting your views across, or you can submit a letter
for publication in the *Radio Times*.

If you have a more general or more serious complaint, you can write
to the Director-General of the BBC; and in some cases, you can
complain to the Broadcasting Complaints Commission (see below).

COMPLAINTS ABOUT A COMMERCIAL TELEVISION OR RADIO PROGRAMME

The independent television and radio companies, under the
supervision of the Independent Broadcasting Authority (IBA), are
legally obliged to follow certain rules ensuring the accuracy and
decency of their programmes. These include a 'Family Viewing
Policy' which says that all programmes shown before 9 pm must be
suitable for viewers of all ages, and a code of practice limiting the
portrayal of violence on the screen. If you have a complaint about
the standard of a particular programme, you can write to the
programme controller of your regional television company, or to the
manager of the radio station. You can also submit a letter for
publication in the *TV Times*. If your complaint concerns a possible
breach of the IBA rules – for example, you have found a
programme offensively violent, or think the time it was broadcast
was out of line with the Family Viewing Policy – write to the IBA.
In some cases, you can complain to the Broadcasting Complaints
Commission.

WHEN THE BROADCASTING COMPLAINTS COMMISSION CAN HELP

There are two circumstances in which you can complain to the BCC
about a television or radio broadcast:

- if you think a programme has been unjust or unfair
- if you think your privacy has been infringed, either by what
  was broadcast or by the way in which material for a broadcast
  programme was obtained.

The Commission will not intervene, however, in cases involving, or
likely to involve, legal action.

If the Commission upholds your complaint, it can require the broadcasting company to publish or broadcast details of the complaint and the Commission's decision, but it can't take any other action.

Films

All public cinemas and cinema clubs run to make a profit have to be licensed by the local authority, which can therefore control which films are shown, and impose other restrictions such as limiting admittance to people above a certain age. Usually, local authority committees responsible for vetting films follow the guidelines provided by the British Board of Film Censors, which gives films certificates depending on whether they are suitable for children, either unaccompanied (U) or with parental guidance (PG), or should not be seen by people under 15 (15) or 18 (18). However, a local authority can decide to ban a film passed by the Board, or disregard its certificates.

Members of the public have no right of appeal against a local authority's decision. If you wish to complain about the showing or banning of a particular film, all you can do is to write to the committee's chairman (ask your Town Hall for details) or enlist your councillor's support; and you can also write to the British Board of Film Censors if you feel its certificate is misleading or inappropriate.

If you feel a film is obscene, you can report it to the police who may decide to prosecute under the Obscene Publications Act.

Books

There are a number of circumstances in which you can complain about a book:

- if it is poorly printed or pages are missing, or bound in the wrong order, you should return it to the bookseller from whom you bought it; or, if this is difficult, to the publisher

- if you think it contains inaccurate information, you can write to the publisher, who may pass the letter on to the author for comment.

- if you think you have been libelled – which is to say that the book has published details about you which are untrue, and so damaged your reputation – you should seek advice from a solicitor specialising in defamation; the law in this area is complex and any legal action would be lengthy and expensive (legal aid is not available in such cases)

- if you think your copyright has been infringed, get advice from a solicitor specialising in copyright law (information about what is covered by this law is available from books in your local reference library)

- if you think a book in a public library should not be there, or should be lent subject to certain restrictions, you can write to the Chief Librarian at the library, or to the County Librarian (your library or Town Hall will have his/her name and address); and you can try to enlist the support of your local councillor

- if you think a book is obscene, you can report it to the police who may decide to prosecute under the Obscene Publications Act.

Complaints about the police, traffic wardens and the prison system

The police

The majority of complaints about the police concern what is felt by the complainant to be an abuse of their powers, and these are investigated by the police themselves. All members of the police force are subject to a strict code governing the way in which they carry out their duties. Examples of complaints that might lead to disciplinary action include allegations of racial prejudice, a failure to follow the rules governing the collection of evidence, or an abuse of the power to stop and search a suspect. More unusually, you may think that a member of the force has broken the law; if this is the case, you may be able to sue for damages or, if a criminal offence is involved, the officer may be prosecuted.

Specific advice about your rights in a particular case, and about the action you can take, can be obtained from a Citizens' Advice Bureau or law centre, either of which may refer you to a solicitor with suitable expertise (this is particularly necessary in Northern Ireland, where the legal situation is complicated by laws introduced as a result of the violent conflict in the region). You can also contact the National Council for Civil Liberties or its Scottish counterpart, which may be able to offer guidance. If you are in police custody, you have a right to see a solicitor (except in certain circumstances when you can be denied such access for up to thirty-six hours) who can advise you if you have a complaint about the way you've been treated.

HOW THE POLICE WILL HANDLE YOUR COMPLAINT

In most cases, your first step when you have a complaint about a member of the police force is to go to a police station (preferably with a witness), where you'll be asked to make a statement giving details of why you wish to complain. Alternatively, you can write to the chief officer for your area (the Chief Constable or, in London, the Commissioner of the Metropolitan or City of London Police, as appropriate); your local police station or Town Hall will have the name and address. If your complaint is a relatively minor one (for example, you are alleging rudeness), and you are simply seeking an explanation or an apology, you can agree to a conciliation procedure. Otherwise, your allegation will be formally investigated, in serious cases by a senior officer from a different police force. The investigating officer will arrange to interview you (this needn't take place at the police station – for example, it could be at your home, in front of a witness, or in a solicitor's office) and ask you to sign a statement (you should always ask for a copy of this).

What happens next depends on the nature of the allegation:

- if a criminal law may have been broken (for example, you allege that you have been assaulted), the investigation report is passed to the Director of Public Prosecutions (in Scotland, the Procurator Fiscal) who decides whether the officer(s) concerned should be prosecuted (you will be informed of the decision)

- if there appears to have been a breach of discipline, disciplinary charges will be brought against the officer; unless he/she admits them, you have a right to attend the hearing and will probably be asked to give evidence

- if the senior police officer responsible for assessing the investigator's report considers that no criminal law has been broken and no breach of discipline has occurred, the case will be considered by the Police Complaints Authority, an independent body which can, if it disagrees with the assessment, insist that disciplinary charges are brought

- if the complaint involves death or serious injury alleged to have been caused by the police, the Police Complaints Authority will supervise the police inquiry; and it can choose whether to do so in any case where it feels that the public interest is involved.

A free leaflet, outlining the procedure for making a complaint about the police, is available from your local police station.

WHEN LEGAL ACTION IS APPROPRIATE

In certain circumstances, civil law may provide a means of redress and of obtaining compensation for any loss or injury you have suffered – for example, if you have been wrongfully arrested or detained (you may be able to sue for false imprisonment), or your property has been unlawfully searched (you may be able to sue for trespass), or you have been assaulted. You don't have to identify the individual officers concerned, as you can sue the chief officer. Ask your Citizens' Advice Bureau or law centre to suggest a solicitor, as you'll need specialist advice.

COMPLAINTS ABOUT THE GENERAL QUALITY OF POLICING

If you have a more general complaint about the policing of your area, for example that there are not enough police on patrol or that the needs and wishes of the community are not being sufficiently taken into account, there are various ways in which you may be able to make your views heard:

- by writing to the police authority for your area, which is responsible for maintaining an 'adequate and efficient police force': in England and Wales, these are committees made up of local councillors and magistrates (the exception is London, where the Metropolitan Police Force is directly answerable to the Home Secretary); in Scotland, the committees consist of regional councillors; and in Northern Ireland, they are appointed by the Secretary of State

- by seeking advice and support from an official local police–community consultative group, if one exists in your area (for details, contact the clerk of the police authority or ask at your local reference library)

- by seeking the support of your MP.

Traffic wardens

Traffic wardens are appointed and supervised by the police, and given powers to enforce parking regulations and direct the traffic (though only when in uniform). If you wish to complain about the behaviour of a traffic warden – for example, that he/she was rude or exceeded his/her powers – you should write to the chief officer of the area's police force; a police officer will then investigate your complaint. If you have been given a parking ticket but think you had a good excuse for breaking the regulations on that occasion, or that you have been treated unfairly, you can write to the Prosecution Officer at the ticket office (the address is on the ticket).

The prison system

Convicted prisoners have very few rights. Although the Home Office is responsible for administering the prison system, the treatment of prisoners, including the granting of privileges, is largely controlled by each prison's governor in consultation with its Board of Visitors (a group of people, including magistrates, who represent the public interest in the way the prison is run). Prison Rules drawn up by the Home Office are recommendations rather than enforceable regulations, and it is not possible for a prisoner to take legal action against the prison authorities if the Rules are disregarded.

Any prisoner who wishes to make a complaint about prison

conditions or a member of prison staff has to apply for an internal investigation before involving anyone outside the prison. The complaint should be made to the prison governor (or the medical officer or chaplain, if this is more appropriate); or, alternatively, to a member of the Board of Visitors. However, if dissatisfied with the response, the prisoner can take matters further by writing to his/her MP or solicitor for advice and support, and by complaining formally to the Home Secretary (a prison officer will be able to supply the official petition form). A friend or relative can write on the prisoner's behalf. Help can also be sought from any of the organisations concerned with prisoners' rights and welfare such as the Howard League for Penal Reform, Preservation of the Rights of Prisoners (PROP) and the National Council for Civil Liberties.

If the prisoner feels that there has been maladministration on the part of the prison authorities, a complaint can be made, via an MP, to the Parliamentary Commissioner for Administration (see p 199). If the allegation concerns an infringement of basic human rights, and the complaint has been rejected by the Home Secretary, it may be possible to appeal to the European Commission on Human Rights in Strasbourg.

APPEALS TO THE EUROPEAN COMMISSION ON HUMAN RIGHTS

Britain has no written constitution setting out the rights of its citizens. Instead, it has agreed, as a member of the Council of Europe, to abide by the standards set out in the European Convention for the Protection of Human Rights and Fundamental Freedoms. This confers various rights on all citizens of signatory states, regardless of their race, colour, sex or beliefs, such as the right to education, privacy and a fair administration of justice, and freedom from torture or inhuman or degrading treatment or punishment. However, the Convention is not part of British law, and so any British citizen wishing to assert his/her rights under the Convention has to apply to the European Commission on Human Rights at Strasbourg.

The basis of an appeal to the Commission is that your government has failed to abide by its agreement to accord you a particular right or freedom established by the Convention. To prove this, you must have exhausted all the legal remedies available under British law; for example, if a court decision is at issue, the case must first have been taken through the court hierarchy according to the usual appeals procedure (in the case of a complaint about prison conditions or regulations, an appeal could follow the decision of the Home Secretary).

If you think your basic human rights under the Convention may have been denied, you should seek legal advice from a solicitor, an organisation concerned with civil liberties in general (such as the National Council for Civil Liberties or its Scottish counterpart) or an organisation with a relevant special interest (for example, if you're complaining about prison treatment, the Howard League for Penal Reform). Applications to the Commission on Human Rights, which can be made by an individual, group or organisation, must be made within six months of the decision being appealed against, and a special form can be obtained from the Secretary of the Commission (see 'Addresses', p 231), to whom the completed application should be sent. There is no fee, and you will not have to pay any costs if your application is rejected or your appeal proves unsuccessful.

If the application is considered admissable, a report will be prepared (you may be asked to provide further information), and the government will be invited to comment, as will you. You may be asked to attend a hearing at Strasbourg (you can get legal aid to help with costs). The Commission will then reach a decision, and attempt to arrange an amicable settlement between the applicant and the government. If no settlement is reached, either of the following will happen:

- the Commission or the government concerned will refer the case to the Court of Human Rights (you as applicant cannot do so); you may be asked to attend the hearing as a witness, or your lawyer may be asked to assist with the proceedings, but you have no right to appear. The Court's decision is final, and it may include an award of damages or costs to the applicant, or lead to a change in the law

- if the case is not referred to the Court of Human Rights within three months of the Commission's decision, it will be considered by the Council of Europe's Committee of Ministers, who may themselves refer it to the Court, or alternatively reach their own binding decision.

Complaints about invasion of privacy

The European Convention for the Protection of Human Rights and Fundamental Freedoms (see p 222) gives everyone the right to respect for their private and family life, their home and correspondence, though it allows a public authority to interfere with this right in certain circumstances, 'in accordance with the law' of that country. British law, on the other hand, includes no general right to privacy. Instead, specific laws give the citizen limited rights in certain areas. For example, you can generally sue for trespass anyone who enters your property without your permission (unless he/she is an official authorised to gain entry). You can also sue a professional adviser (such as your doctor or bank manager) for breach of confidence if he/she discloses any personal information about you (although, again, the law allows exceptions). However, you have no right to stop a publication or broadcasting programme from giving details about your private life, however sordid, as long as they are true (if they are false you may be able to sue for libel – see p 214) and as long as they do not reproduce without your permission any material in which you have copyright (see p 218), such as letters you have written or photographs you own. Telephone tapping carried out by or on behalf of government security forces must, in law, be authorised by the Home Secretary; but private telephone tappers are not committing an offence unless they damage your telephone equipment or divert or waste electricity.

For most people, though, invasion of privacy is not a common cause for complaint. Yet information about our personal lives is often collected without our knowledge, let alone our permission, and stored in ways that make access to that information easy. We have no automatic rights to see all files kept on us, whether by government bodies or private organisations and individuals; for example, as a patient you cannot demand to see your GP's notes on your medical history, and as an employee you cannot demand to see your personnel file. However, in two areas, the law does give the citizen the right to check the accuracy of personal information held by others and to correct any mistakes.

Information held by a credit reference agency

Under the Consumer Credit Act 1974, you have a right to examine and, if necessary, correct any file held on you by a credit reference agency. This is to safeguard you against being refused credit because of inaccurate information, for example about your salary or financial commitments. You can exercise this right if you have been refused credit (and if you were applying for no more than £5,000), or at any time if you know of an agency and want to make a spot-check. There is a standard procedure for making the check, as follows:

- ask the person who has refused you credit to give you the name and address of any agency that has been consulted; you must make your request in writing, within twenty-eight days of the refusal, and the information must be supplied within seven days

- write to the agency enclosing the non-returnable search fee (at the time of writing, £1); give your full name and address, and your previous address(es), if any, for the past six years

- if the agency has any information on you, it must send you a copy, together with a statement of your right to correct it, within seven working days of receiving your request

- if you spot any mistake, write asking the agency to correct it

- if you are refused, or you disagree with the alteration proposed by the agency, or if you receive no reply within twenty-eight days, you can compose your own correction note (maximum 200 words) and send this to the agency, asking for it to be added to your file (you have twenty-eight days in which to do this, and the agency has a further twenty-eight days to confirm it has added the note)

- the agency is then obliged to send details of any correction to anyone who requested information about you in the previous six months.

If you follow the correct procedure but an agency fails to meet its legal obligations, you can write to the Director-General of the Office of Fair Trading, or seek help from your local Trading Standards Department or Citizens' Advice Bureau.

Information held on computer

Under the Data Protection Act 1984, new regulations have been introduced to control automatically processed data – in effect, information held on computer. Computers can greatly facilitate the collection and transfer of personal information, making it more widely and easily available. The new law recognises the potential for injustice that this technological development involves, and from 1987 individuals will have the right to see and, if necessary, correct information held on them by many computers. However, not all computerised files will be open to inspection and there are circumstances in which access normally allowed can be denied (for example, your demand to examine information held on a police computer can be refused if access is likely to prejudice 'the prevention or detection of crime or the apprehension or prosecution of offenders').

Complaints about discrimination

When discrimination is illegal

Discrimination can be based on many grounds, but only four types are covered by law, and then only in certain circumstances. These are acts of discrimination based on

- your race (which includes your colour, race, nationality or ethnic origin – for example, you are treated unfavourably because you are black, or Jewish, or Japanese, or the great-grandson of a West Indian)
- your sex (but not your sexual preferences – for example, discrimination against homosexuals is not illegal)

- your marital status (though only in matters of employment, and then only if you are married and as a consequence treated less favourably than a single person)

- your membership (or not) of a trade union, or your involvement (or not) in trade union activities (this applies only to victimisation at work and dismissal from your job).

Furthermore, you can seek redress through the law only if you have suffered personally as a result of the discrimination, and you cannot make a claim for any discrimination you have encountered in private, social relationships (for example, if a neighbour or fellow-worker ostracises you because he/she is prejudiced).

The laws setting out the circumstances in which discrimination is illegal are the Race Relations Act 1976 (which doesn't apply in Northern Ireland, where instead discrimination on the grounds of religious belief or political opinion is unlawful), the Sex Discrimination Act 1975 (which also covers complaints relating to marital status), the Equal Pay Act 1970 and later regulations bringing British law on equal pay more into line with EEC law, and various Employment Acts (for discrimination relating to trade union activities). Discrimination is a breach of civil law (though incitement to racial hatred is a criminal offence and should be reported to the police); consequently, it is up to the person who has suffered to get the law enforced, by either an industrial tribunal or a court.

Before starting legal proceedings

The law does not make all racial and sexual discrimination illegal; for example, certain types of job are exempted from the Sex Discrimination Act, and racial discrimination other than on the grounds of colour is allowed in the selection of sports teams, or to restrict club membership (see 'Clubs', p 126). It is therefore essential to check whether the law provides a remedy in your case before you become involved in any proceedings. You can get initial guidance from your local Citizens' Advice Bureau or law centre, or, in cases of racial discrimination, a community relations council if there's one in your area. You should also contact, as appropriate, either the Commission for Racial Equality or (for sex and marital status discrimination, including disputes over equal pay) the Equal Opportunities Commission, which are two watchdog bodies set up by government to combat illegal discrimination. In employment matters, the Advisory Conciliation and Arbitration Service (see p 207) should be able to help; if you belong to a trade union, ask your union representative to advise you. You can also consult a solicitor.

If your adviser feels you have a justified complaint, he/she may be able to resolve the problem by negotiation (the Commissions and ACAS provide a free conciliation service). However, if a swift and satisfactory settlement seems unlikely, you must not delay in pursuing your complaint further, as you may otherwise forfeit your right to take legal action.

Unless you are complaining about dismissal or victimisation in the context of trade union activity (in which case seek advice from your union or ACAS), start by getting information from the person whom you consider has discriminated against you, by sending him/her a copy of the standard questionnaire provided by either of the Commissions or a Citizens' Advice Bureau. Although you are not always obliged to do this, it is helpful to get the other person's explanation or defence of what has taken place, because the information will help your adviser to gauge your chances of success. Also, a refusal or failure to complete the questionnaire or to give reasonable answers can be useful evidence if you decide to take your case to tribunal or court.

Taking your case to an industrial tribunal

If you are complaining that your employer has discriminated against you, or that you have been refused a job because of your race, sex or the fact that you are married, you must make your complaint to an industrial tribunal within three months of the discriminatory act (if the dispute concerns the right to equal pay, you can apply at any time during your employment or up to six months after you have left the job). The application form you should use, and free information sheets and booklets about discrimination law and industrial tribunals, are available from unemployment benefit offices, job centres and Citizens' Advice Bureaux (for more details about industrial tribunals, see p 207–210).

If the tribunal upholds your complaint, it may do all or any of the following:

- award you compensation for loss of earnings and/or injured feelings

- order the other party to do something to put matters right (this cannot be enforced but failure to carry out the order will usually result in your being awarded further compensation)

- make a declaration of both parties' rights.

Compensation is not available, however, if the tribunal accepts that the discrimination was unintentional.

If the tribunal dismisses your complaint, you can appeal to the Employment Appeal Tribunal (see p 210), but only on a point of law.

Taking your case to court

In all cases of illegal discrimination not relating to employment, you will have to start civil proceedings in the county court if you want to claim compensation. However, damages will not be awarded if the judge accepts that the discrimination was unintentional. You will almost certainly need to be represented in court by a solicitor or barrister, which can be expensive; but either of the Commissions or a law centre may be willing to take your case on at no charge, or to provide financial assistance, or you may be eligible for legal aid (see 'How to get help with legal expenses', p 20). Court proceedings must be started within six months of the act about which you are complaining (though if you have applied to either of the Commissions for legal help, this is extended to eight months).

If you are complaining about discrimination against your child by a school or other state educational establishment, you should first give the head teacher and then the school governors a chance to alter the discriminatory decision or policy (see 'Complaints about education services', p 155). If this is unsuccessful, you cannot start civil proceedings until you have given the Department of Education and Science an opportunity to investigate and put matters right. In such cases, write giving details of where, when and how the discrimination occurred to the Permanent Under-Secretary of State for Education at the Department, and allow two months for appropriate action to be taken. If nothing happens or you are dissatisfied with the response, you then have up to eight months after the event in question to start civil proceedings.

Addresses

Action for the Victims of
Medical Accidents
135 Stockwell Road
London SW9 9TN
(01) 737 2434

Advertising Standards
Authority (ASA)
Brook House
2–16 Torrington Place
London WC1E 7HN
(01) 580 5555

Advisory Centre for
Education (ACE)
18 Victoria Park Square
London E2 9PB
(01) 980 4596

Advisory Committee on
Telecommunications
(England)
Atlantic House
Holborn Viaduct
London EC1N 2HQ
(01) 353 4020

(Wales)
Caradog House (1st floor)
St Andrews Place
Cardiff CF1 3PW
(0222) 374028

(Scotland)
Alhambra House
45 Waterloo Street
Glasgow G2 6AT
(041) 248 2855

(Northern Ireland)
Chamber of Commerce
and Industry
22 Great Victoria Street
Belfast BT2 7PU
(0232) 244113

Advisory Conciliation and
Arbitration Service
(ACAS)
(Head Office)
Almack House
26 King Street
London SW1Y 4LA
(01) 214 6000

Air Transport Users
Committee
129 Kingsway
London WC2B 6NN
(01) 242 3882

Approved Coal Merchants
Scheme
(Head Office)
2 Turnpin Lane
Greenwich
London SE10 9JA
(01) 853 0787

Architects Registration
Council of the United
Kingdom (ARCUK)
73 Hallam Street
London W1N 6EE
(01) 580 5861

Association of British
Insurers

Aldermary House
Queen Street
London EC4N 1TT
(01) 623 9043

Association of British
Laundry, Cleaning and
Rental Services
Lancaster Gate House
319 Pinner Road
Harrow
Middlesex HA1 4HX
(01) 863 7755

Association of British
Travel Agents (ABTA)
55–57 Newman Street
London W1P 4AH
(01) 637 2444

Association of Mail Order
Publishers
1 New Burlington Street
London W1X 1FD
(01) 437 0706

Association of
Manufacturers of
Domestic Electrical
Appliances (AMDEA)
593 Hitchin Road
Stopsley
Luton LU2 7UN
(0582) 412444

Association of Optical
Practitioners
233–234 Blackfriars Road
London SE1 8NW
(01) 261 9661

Association of
Photographic
Laboratories
9 Warwick Court
Gray's Inn
London WC1R 5DJ
(01) 405 2762/4253

Banking Ombudsman
5/11 Fetter Lane
London EC4A 1BR
(01) 583 1395

Bar Council
11 South Square
Gray's Inn
London WC1R 5EL
(01) 242 0082

British Airports Authority
(Head Office)
Gatwick Airport
Gatwick
West Sussex RH6 0HZ
(0293) 517755

British Association of
Occupational Therapists
20 Rede Place
London W2 4TU
(01) 229 9738

British Board of Film
Censors
3 Soho Square
London W1V 5DE
(01) 439 7961

British Broadcasting
Corporation (BBC)
Broadcasting House
Portland Place
London W1A 4WW
(01) 580 4468

British Chemical
Dampcourse Association
16a Whitchurch Road
Pangbourne
Reading
Berkshire RG8 7BP
(07357) 3799

British College of
Ophthalmic Opticians
10 Knaresborough Place
London SW5 0TG
(01) 373 7765

British Decorators
Association
6 Haywra Street
Harrogate
North Yorkshire HG1
5BL
(0423) 67292/3

British Homoeopathic
Association
271 Devonshire Street
London W1N 1RJ
(01) 935 2163

British Insurance Brokers
Association
BIBA House
14 Bevis Marks
London EC3A 7NT
(01) 623 9043

British Photographic
Association
7–15 Lansdowne Road
Croydon
Surrey CR9 2PL
(01) 688 4422

British Photographic
Importers Association
7–15 Lansdowne Road
Croydon
Surrey CR9 2PL
(01) 688 4422

British Wood Preserving
Association
150 Southampton Row
London WC1B 5AL
(01) 837 8217

Broadcasting Complaints
Commission
20 Albert Embankment
London SE1 7TL
(01) 211 8465

Building Employers
Confederation
82 New Cavendish Street
London W1M 8AD
(01) 580 5588

(for list of members and
details of guarantee
scheme)
BEC Building Trust Ltd

Invicta House
London Road
Maidstone
Kent ME16 8JH
(0622) 683791

Building Societies
Association
3 Savile Row
London W1X 1AF
(01) 437 0655

Bus and Coach Council
Sardinia House
52 Lincoln's Inn Fields
London WC2A 3LZ
(01) 831 7546

Central Office of the
Industrial Tribunals
(England and Wales)
93 Ebury Bridge Road
London SW1 8RE
(01) 730 9161

(Scotland)
St Andrew House
141 West Nile Street
Glasgow G1 2RU
(041) 331 1601

(Northern Ireland)
2nd Floor
Bedford House
16–22 Bedford Street
Belfast BT2 7NR
(0232) 227666

Central Transport
Consultative Committee
Golden Cross House
Duncannon Street
London WC2N 4JF
(01) 839 7338

Chartered Association of
Certified Accountants
29 Lincoln's Inn Fields
London WC2A 3EE
(01) 242 6855

Chartered Institute of
Arbitrators
75 Cannon Street
London EC4N 5BH
(01) 236 8761

Chartered Institute of
Public Finance and
Accountancy
3 Robert Street
London WC2N 6BH
(01) 930 3456

Chartered Society of
Physiotherapy
14 Bedford Row
London WC1R 4ED
(01) 242 1941

Child Poverty Action
Group
1 Macklin Street
Drury Lane
London WC2B 5NH
(01) 242 9149

Children's Legal Centre
20 Compton Terrace
London N1 2UN
(01) 359 6251

Civil Aviation Authority
CAA House
45 Kingsway
London WC2B 6TE
(01) 379 7311

College of Health
18 Victoria Park Square
London E2 9PF
(01) 980 6263

Commission for Racial
Equality
(Head Office)
Elliot House
10–12 Allington Street
London SW1E 5EH
(01) 828 7022

Commissioner for
Complaints
33 Wellington Place
Belfast BT1 6HN
(0232) 33821

Commissioner for Local
Administration
(England)
21 Queen Anne's Gate
London SW1H 9BU
(01) 222 5622

(Wales)
Derwen House
Court Road
Bridgend
Mid Glamorgan CF31 1BN
(0656) 61325/6

(Scotland)
5 Shandwick Place
Edinburgh EH2 4RG
(031) 229 4472

Confederation for the
Registration of Gas
Installers (CORGI)
St Martins House
140 Tottenham Court
Road
London W1P 9LN
(01) 387 9185

Consumers' Association
14 Buckingham Street
London WC2N 6DS
(01) 839 1222

Council for
Environmental
Conservation
Zoological Gardens
Regent's Park
London NW1 4RY
(01) 722 7111

Council for Professions
Supplementary to
Medicine
Park House
184 Kennington Park
Road
London SE11 4BU
(01) 582 0866

Credit Licensing Office
Government Building
Bromyard Avenue
London W3 7BB
(01) 743 5566

Department of Education
and Science
Elizabeth House
39 York Road
London SE1 7PH
(01) 928 9222

Department of the
Environment
2 Marsham Street
London SW1P 3EB
(01) 212 3434

Department of the
Environment for
Northern Ireland
Parliament Building
Stormont
Belfast BT4 3SY
(0232) 63210

Department of Health and
Social Security
Alexander Fleming House
Elephant & Castle
London SE1 6BY
(01) 407 5522

Department of Trade and
Industry
1 Victoria Street
London SW1H 0ET
(01) 215 7877

Direct Selling Association
44 Russell Square
London WC1B 4JP
(01) 580 8433

Disabled Living
Foundation
346 Kensington High
Street
London W14 8NS
(01) 602 2491

Domestic Coal Consumers
Council
Gavrelle House
2 Bunhill Row
London EC1Y 8LL
(01) 638 8914/8929

Electrical Contractors
Association
ESCA House
34 Palace Court
London W2 4HY
(01) 229 1266

Electrical Contractors
Association of Scotland
23 Heriot Row
Edinburgh EH3 6EW
(031) 225 7221

Employment Appeal
Tribunal
4 St James's Square
London SW1Y 4JU
(01) 214 3367

Equal Opportunities
Commission
(England)
Overseas House
Quay Street
Manchester M3 3HN
(061) 833 9244

(Wales)
Caerwys House
Windsor Place
Cardiff CF1 1LB
(0222) 43552

(Scotland)
249 West George Street
Glasgow G2 4QE
(041) 226 4591

(Northern Ireland)
Lindsay House
Callendar Street
Belfast BT1 5DT
(0232) 240020

European Commission on
Human Rights
Council of Europe
67006 Strasbourg Cedex
France
(010 33) 88 614 961

Federation of Master
Builders
Gordon Fisher House
33 John Street
London WC1N 2BB
(01) 242 7583

Federation of Ophthalmic
and Dispensing Opticians
40 Portland Place
London W1N 4BA
(01) 637 2507

Footwear Distributors
Federation
Commonwealth House
1–19 New Oxford Street
London WC1 1PA
(01) 404 0955

General Council and
Register of Osteopaths
1 Suffolk Street
London SW1Y 4HG
(01) 839 2060

General Dental Council
37 Wimpole Street
London W1M 8DQ
(01) 486 2171

General Medical Council
44 Hallam Street
London W1N 6AE
(01) 580 7642

General Optical Council
41 Harley Street
London W1N 2DJ
(01) 580 3898

Glass and Glazing
Federation
6 Mount Row
London W1Y 6DY
(01) 409 0345

Guaranteed Treatments
Protection Trust
PO Box 77
27 London Road
High Wycombe
Bucks HP11 1BW
(0494) 447049

Health Service
Commissioner
(England)
Church House
Great Smith Street
London SW1P 3BW
(01) 212 7676

(Wales)
Pearl Assurance House
Greyfriars Road
Cardiff CF1 3AG
(0222) 394621

(Scotland)
11 Melville Crescent
Edinburgh EH3 7LU
(031) 225 7465

Heating and Ventilating
Contractors Association
ESCA House

34 Palace Court
London W2 4JG
(01) 229 2488

Help the Aged
1 Sekforde Street
London EC1R 0BE
(01) 253 0253

Home Office
50 Queen Anne's Gate
London SW1H 9AT
(01) 213 3000

Housing Corporation
Maple House
149 Tottenham Court
Road
London W1P 0BN
(01) 387 9466

Howard League for Penal
Reform
320 Kennington Park
Road
London SE11 0PP
(01) 735 3317

Incorporated Association
of Architects and
Surveyors
Jubilee House
Billing Brook Road
Weston Favell
Northampton NN3 4NW
(0604) 404121

Incorporated Society of
Valuers and Auctioneers
3 Cadogan Gate
London SW1X 0AS
(01) 235 2282

Independent Broadcasting
Authority (IBA)
70 Brompton Road
London SW3 1EY
(01) 584 7011

Industrial Assurance
Commissioner
15 Great Marlborough
Street
London W1V 2AX
(01) 437 9992

Institute of Chartered
Accountants in England

and Wales
Chartered Accountants
Hall
Moorgate Place
London EC2P 2BJ
(01) 628 7060

Institute of Chartered
Accountants in Ireland
(Northern Ireland branch)
11 Donegal Square South
Belfast BT1 5JE
(0232) 221600

Institute of Chartered
Accountants in Scotland
27 Queen Street
Edinburgh EH2 1LA
(031) 225 5673

Institute of Chartered
Secretaries and
Administrators
16 Park Crescent
London W1N 4AH
(01) 580 4741

Institute for
Complementary Medicine
21 Portland Place
London W1N 3HF
(01) 636 9543

Institute of Cost and
Management Accountants
63 Portland Place
London W1N 4AB
(01) 637 4716

Institute of Photographic
Apparatus Repair
Technicians
228 Regent's Park Road
Finchley
London N3 3HP
(01) 346 8302

Institute of Plumbing
64 Station Lane
Hornchurch
Essex RM12 6NB
(040 24) 72791

Institute of Professional
Photography
Amwell End

Ware
Herts SG12 9HN
(0920) 4011

Insurance Brokers
Registration Council
15 St Helens Place
London EC3A 6DS
(01) 588 4387

Insurance Ombudsman
Bureau
31 Southampton Row
London WC1B 5HJ
(01) 242 8613

Labour Relations Agency
Windsor House
9–15 Bedford Street
Belfast BT2 7NU
(0232) 221442

Law Centres Federation
Duchess House
18–19 Warren Street
London W1P 5DB
(01) 387 8570

Law Society
(England and Wales)
8 Bream's Buildings
London EC4A 1HP
(01) 242 1222

(Scotland)
26–27 Drumsheugh
Gardens
Edinburgh EH3 7YR
(031) 226 7411

(Northern Ireland)
Royal Courts of Justice
Chichester Street
Belfast BT1 3JZ
(0232) 231614

Lay Observer
(England and Wales)
Royal Courts of Justice
Strand
London WC2A 2LL
(01) 405 7641

(Scotland)
22 Melville Street
Edinburgh EH3 7NS
(031) 225 3236

(Northern Ireland)
IDB House
64 Chichester Street
Belfast BT1 4LE
(0232) 233233

Lloyd's Consumer
Inquiries Department
London House
6 London Street
London EC3R 7AB
(01) 623 7100

London Regional
Passengers Committee
Golden Cross House
2 Duncannon Street
London WC2N 4JF
(01) 839 1898

London Regional
Transport
55 Broadway
London SW1H 0BD
(01) 222 1234

Mail Order Traders
Association (MOTA)
25 Castle Street
Liverpool L2 4TD
(051) 236 7581

Master Photographers
Association
1 West Ruislip Station
West Ruislip
Middlesex HA4 7DW
(08956) 30876

Mental Health Act
Commission
Hepburn House
Marsham Street
London SW1 4HW
(01) 211 8061

Mental Welfare
Commission for Scotland
22 Melville Street
Edinburgh EH3 7NS
(031) 225 7034

Motor Agents Association
75 Park Street
Bristol BS1 5PS
(0272) 293232

Motor Cycle Association
GB Ltd
Starley House
Eaton Road
Coventry CV1 2FH
(0203) 27427

Motorcycle Retailers
Association
31a High Street
Tunbridge Wells
Kent TB1 1XN
(0892) 26081

National Association for
Mental Health (MIND)
22 Harley Street
London W1N 2ED
(01) 637 0741

National Association of
Estate Agents
Arbon House
21 Jury Street
Warwick CV34 4EH
(0926) 496800

National Association of
Multiple Shoe Repairers
60 Wickham Hill
Hurstpierpoint
Hassocks
Sussex BN6 9NP
07918 3488

National Association of
Plumbing, Heating and
Mechanical Services
Contractors
Barnard Close
107–113 Powis Street
Woolwich
London SE18 6JB
(01) 855 4715/7438

National Association of
Retail Furnishers
17–21 George Street
Croydon
Surrey CR9 1TQ
(01) 680 8444

National Association of
Security Dealers and
Investment Managers
28 Lovat Lane

London EC3R 8EB
(01) 283 4814

National Board for
Nursing, Midwifery and
Health Visiting
(England)
Victory House
170 Tottenham Court
Road
London W1P 0HA
(01) 388 3131

(Wales)
Pearl Assurance House
Greyfriars Road
Cardiff CF1 3AG
(0222) 395535

(Scotland)
22 Queen Street
Edinburgh EH2 1JX
(031) 226 7371

(Northern Ireland)
126 Belmont Road
Belfast BT4 2AT
(0232) 652713

National Bus Company
172 Buckingham Palace
Road
London SW1W 9TN
(01) 730 3453

National Children's
Bureau
8 Wakley Street
London EC1V 7QE
(01) 278 9441

National Council for Civil
Liberties (NCCL)
21 Tabard Street
London SE1 4LA
(01) 403 3888

National Council for One-
parent Families
255 Kentish Town Road
London NW5 2LX
(01) 267 1361

National Council for
Voluntary Organisations
26 Bedford Square
London WC1B 3HU
(01) 636 4066

National Express
Midland House
1 Vernon Road
Edgbaston
Birmingham BN16 9SJ
(021) 455 7767

National Gas Consumers
Council
162 Regent Street
London W1R 5TB
(01) 439 0012

National House Building
Council
58 Portland Place
London W1N 4BU
(01) 637 1248

National Inspection
Council for Electrical
Installation Contractors
237 Kennington Lane
London SE11 5QJ
(01) 582 7746/735 1322

National Pharmaceutical
Association
Mallinson House
40–42 St Peters Street
St Albans Herts
AL1 3NP
(0727) 32161

Northern Ireland
Association for Mental
Health
Beacon House
84 University Street
Belfast BT7 1HE
(0232) 228474

Office of Fair Trading
Field House
15–25 Bream's Buildings
London EC4A 1PR
(01) 242 2858
Free leaflets published by
the OFT can be obtained
from Trading Standards
Departments, Citizens'
Advice Bureaux and many
libraries, or direct from
the OFT (Room 310c)

Office of
Telecommunications
(Oftel)
Atlantic House
Holborn Viaduct
London EC1N 2HQ
(01) 353 4020

Parliamentary
Commissioner for
Administration
(England, Wales and
Scotland)
Church House
Great Smith Street
London SW1P 3BW
(01) 212 6271/7676

(Northern Ireland)
33 Wellington Place
Belfast BT1 6HN
(0232) 33821

Patients Association
Room 33
18 Charing Cross Road
London WC2H 0HR
(01) 240 0671

Pharmaceutical Society of
Great Britain
1 Lambeth High Street
London SE1 7JN
(01) 735 9141

Police Complaints
Authority
10 Great George Street
London SW1P 3AB
(01) 213 5392

Post Office Users National
Council
(England)
Waterloo Bridge House
Waterloo Road
London SE1 8UA
(01) 928 9458

(Wales)
2 Park Grove
Cardiff CF1 3BN
(0222) 374028

(Scotland)
Alhambra House
45 Waterloo Street

Glasgow G2 6AT
(041) 248 2855

(Northern Ireland)
Chamber of Commerce
22 Great Victoria Street
Belfast BT2 7PU
(0232) 244113

Preservation of the Rights
of Prisoners (PROP)
BM PROP
London WC1 3XX
(01) 542 3744

Press Council
1 Salisbury Square
London EC4Y 8AE
(01) 353 1248

Public Carriage Office
15 Penton Street
London N1 9PU
(01) 278 1744

Radio, Electrical and
Television Retailers
Association (RETRA)
RETRA House
57–61 Newington
Causeway
London SE1 6BE
(01) 403 1463

Registrar of Companies
(England and Wales)
Companies House
Crown Way
Maindy
Cardiff CF4 3UZ
(0222) 388588

(Northern Ireland)
43–47 Chichester Street
Belfast BT1 4RJ
(0232) 234121

Registry of Friendly
Societies
15 Great Marlborough
Street
London W1V 2AX
(01) 437 9992

Royal Incorporation of
Architects in Scotland
15 Rutland Square

Edinburgh EH1 2BE
(031) 229 7205

Royal Institute of British
Architects
66 Portland Place
London W1N 4AD
(01) 580 5533

Royal Institution of
Chartered Surveyors
12 Great George Street
London SW1P 3AD
(01) 222 7000

Royal Society for
Mentally Handicapped
Children and Adults
(MENCAP)
123 Golden Lane
London EC1Y 0RF
(01) 253 9433

Royal Society for the
Prevention of Cruelty to
Animals (RSPCA)
Causeway
Horsham
West Sussex RH12 1HG
(0403) 64181

Royal Society of Ulster
Architects
2 Mount Charles
Belfast BT7 1NZ
(0232) 223760

St Crispin's Boot Trades
Association
St Crispin's House
Station Road
Desborough, nr Kettering
Northants
0536 760374

Scottish and Northern
Ireland Plumbing
Employers Federation
2 Walker Street
Edinburgh EH3 7BL
(031) 225 2255

Scottish Association for
Mental Health
67 York Place
Edinburgh EH1 3JB
(031) 556 3062

Scottish Bus Group
Carron House
114–116 George Street
Edinburgh EH2 4LX
(031) 226 7491

Scottish Development
Department
New St Andrews House
St James Centre
Edinburgh EH1 3SZ
(031) 556 8400

Scottish Glass Merchants
and Glaziers Association
13 Woodside Crescent
Glasgow G3 7UP
(041) 332 7144

Scottish House Furnishers
Association
203 Pitt Street
Glasgow G2 4DB
(041) 332 6381

Scottish Motor Trade
Association
3 Palmerston Place
Edinburgh EH12 5AQ
(031) 225 3643

Scottish Society for the
Prevention of Cruelty to
Animals (SSPCA)
19 Melville Street
Edinburgh EH3 7PL
(031) 225 6418/6419

Secretary of State for
Education (England)
Department of Education
and Science
Elizabeth House
York Road
London SE1 7PH
(01) 928 9222

(Wales)
Crown Buildings
Cathays Park
Cardiff CF1 3NQ
(0222) 825111

(Scotland)
New St Andrews House
St James Centre
Edinburgh EH1 3TV
(031) 556 8400

Secretary of State for
Energy
Thames House South
Millbank
London SW1P 4QJ
(01) 211 3000

SHAC (London Housing
Aid Centre)
189a Old Brompton Road
London SW5 0AR
(01) 373 7841

Shelter
157 Waterloo Road

London SE1 8UU
(01) 633 9377

Society of Chiropodists
8 Wimpole Street
London W1M 8BX
(01) 580 3228

Society of Motor
Manufacturers and
Traders
Forbes House
Halkin Street
London SW1X 7DS
(01) 235 7000

Stock Exchange
Old Broad Street
London EC2N 1HP
(01) 588 2355

Vehicle Builders and
Repairers Association
Belmont House
102 Finkle Lane
Gildersome
Leeds LS27 7TW
0532 538333

Welsh Office
Crown Buildings
Cathays Park
Cardiff CF1 3NQ
(0222) 825111

Index

abandoned vehicles 188
accountants 169
Action for the Victims of Medical
Accidents 144
acupuncture 152
advance payments 99
advertisements 211, 212
Advertising Standards Authority
(ASA) 75, 212
advice agencies 13
Advisory Centre for Education
(ACE) 159
Advisory Committee on
Telecommunications 118
Advisory Conciliation and
Arbitration Service (ACAS) 207, 228
advocates 160
Age Concern 205
air traffic 195
Air Transport Users Committee 135
Air Travel Organisers Licence
(ATOL) 131
airline strikes 128
airlines 134
airports 134
alternative medical treatment 152
Approved Coal Merchants Scheme
122
arbitration 8, 25, 36, 37, 90, 105,
118, 120, 130, 167
architects 108, 113
Architects Registration Council of
the United Kingdom (ARCUK) 113
Area Electricity Consultative
Council 120, 121
Area Health Boards 139, 141
Association of British Insurers 166,
167
Association of British Laundry,
Cleaning and Rental Services 107
Association of British Travel Agents
(ABTA) 130

Association of Mail Order
Publishers 76
Association of Manufacturers of
Domestic Electrical
Appliances (AMDEA) 106
Association of Optical Practitioners
47
Association of Photographic
Laboratories 107
attachment of earnings 38
auctions 52, 86

bank loans 69, 101
banking ombudsman 171
Bar Council 165
bargain offers 66
barristers 19, 164
bed-and-breakfast 124
boarding houses 124
bonding schemes 100
book-keeping services 169
books 76, 217
boundaries 178
breach of confidence 224
British Airports Authority 135
British Association of Occupational
Therapists 149
British Board of Film Censors 217
British Broadcasting Corporation
(BBC) 215
British Chemical Dampcourse
Association 111
British Chiropractors Association
152
British Code of Advertising Practice
75, 212
British College of Ophthalmic
Opticians 147
British Decorators Association 111
British Homoeopathic Association 152
British Insurance Brokers
Association 168

239